The Ballycastle Railway

Second edition

With additional material by Norman Johnston

Dr EM Patterson

Colourpoint

Dr EM Patterson, BSc, MSc, DSc, MPhil, MRIA, FRSE was born at Bangor, Co Down, in 1920 and educated at Bangor Grammar School and The Queen's University, Belfast. He was trained as a geologist but in 1941 he moved to Scotland to take up employment as a research chemist at ICI (Explosives) at Ardeer, Ayrshire. His interest in geology continued to flourish and in 1947 he moved to St Andrews University where he lectured in the Department of Geology and Mineralogy. In 1953 he married Violet Kirk (neé Adams), a Queen's graduate, and returned to ICI at Ardeer the following year, working there until his retirement in 1981. In Ireland his focus of interest was the railways in the north of the island. He wrote nine books, covering seven of the narrow gauge lines (two in his book *The Ballymena Lines*), as well as *The Great Northern Railway of Ireland* and *The Belfast and County Down Railway* (two books). An updated edition of *The Clogher Valley Railway*, with additional text, was published by Colourpoint Books in 2004. His last book was *The Castlederg and Victoria Bridge Tramway* (Colourpoint 1998), published just after his death. The posthumous award of MPhil in 1997 by The Queen's University was for his work on the industrial archaeology of gunpowder manufacture.

Dr EM Patterson, at Tiriach, Pitlochry, Scotland in October 1995.

6 5 4 3 2 1

Designed by Colourpoint Books, Newtownards
Printed by ColourBooks Ltd

ISBN 1 904242 49 9

Colourpoint Books
Colourpoint House
Jubilee Business Park
21 Jubilee Road
NEWTOWNARDS
County Down
Northern Ireland
BT23 4YH
Tel: 028 9182 0505
Fax: 028 9182 1900
E-mail: info@colourpoint.co.uk
Web site: www.colourpoint.co.uk

Colourpoint Books gratefully acknowledges the generous assistance given by Mr Wallace McNaul, of Ballymoney, in the preparation of this book. He is seen here (on left) with Norman Johnston, publisher of Colourpoint Books.

Cover pictures

Front: *Ballycastle Railway No 1* Dalriada *approaching the River Bush bridge.*
From a painting by Vic Jaycock, reproduced by kind permission of The Lord O'Neill.

Rear: *The view from the end of the Tow Viaduct towards Ballycastle station and yard on 15 August 1953, three years after the closure of the line and before the removal of the remaining rolling stock. The carriages to the right are believed to be Nos 350 and 353, Nos 318, 351 and 352 having been sold to the County Donegal Railways Joint Committee by that date. Nos 350 and 353 were withdrawn from UTA stock in 1954.* R Tourret

Contents

It is perhaps appropriate that we begin our photographic coverage of the Ballycastle Railway with this 1931 view of No 106 at Ballycastle station, as the young man chatting with Driver McKissick is none other than Edward M Patterson! On this occasion he had his first footplate visit but he didn't get a run for another seventeen years. JW Patterson, courtesy Anna D Singer

Prices and measurements

Prices are quoted in pre-1971 £sd without decimal equivalents (eg £4 8s 9d). There were 20 shillings (s) to the £, thus 1s 0d equals 5p. There were 12 old pence (d) to the shilling, 2d being roughly 1p. Even shillings are rendered 3s 0d, etc, and shillings and pence 3s 10d, etc. (In quotations shillings are sometimes rendered 3/-, etc, and shillings and pence 16/3, etc.)

Chapter 1

The Setting of the Railway

On the edge of the Atlantic

Geographers have compared northeast Ireland to a flat saucer which slopes gently inwards to Lough Neagh. Down a crack in this saucer the River Bann flows northwards to the sea and for most of its course separates County Antrim on the east from County Londonderry on the west.

Around the northern rim of the saucer, the high ground drops steeply down towards a coastline whose chief characteristic is a deficiency in good harbours. In the hundred miles between Lough Foyle and Belfast Lough, there is scarcely anywhere a ship may run to in a storm. Indeed, in January 1758, the Rev John Gage, proprietor of Rathlin Island, presented a petition to the Irish Parliament which, among other things, stated that there was virtually no place of safe anchorage from Lough Foyle to Lough Larne. Around this corner of Ireland, even bays are few, but on the shore of one of them lies the little town of Ballycastle, hemmed between Kenbane Head to the west and Fair Head to the east.

Behind the town of Ballycastle, Glenshesk and Glentow, two of the nine Glens of Antrim, reach into the swelling moorlands with the massive rounded hill of Knocklayd rising between them to a height of nearly 1700 feet. Offshore lies Rathlin Island, whence in 1306 King Robert the Bruce fled from his defeat in Scotland, and where he is reputed to have watched the spider. Far beyond Rathlin, the Hebridean hills of Islay and Jura lie blue on the horizon on a clear day.

Coal on the coast

Ballycastle is now a picturesquely-placed provincial town, with a winter population of around 2000. It combines, in a somewhat unusual way, seaside resort with weekly market facilities, and a Tuesday market has been held since 1606. The town which was constituted an urban district about half a century ago, is unique among Irish coast towns in owing its early development to coal, a commodity peculiarly scarce in Ireland. To the east of the town, the rocky cliffs contain seams of coal; the thickest of these was probably mined as early as the 13th century, since it was both obvious and easily accessible. The coal seams are associated with beds of ironstone, freestone and fireclay, and cover an area of about eight square miles. In consequence, a small mining industry grew up, centred on Ballycastle. Nowadays, traces of the mines are inconspicuous, and the rugged coast is colourful and unspoiled.

The first dependable allusion to the working of coal along the coast here dates from the middle of the 17th century, when Dr William Petty mentioned the existence of salt works at the Pans Rocks, and these must have been supported by locally-won coal.

In 1720 an application for financial assistance in developing the coalfield was placed before the Irish House of Commons, in the names of the Hon R Stewart, Thomas Burgh and others. Three years later a company was promoted which worked six mines in the vicinity of Ballycastle over a period of years, and received various Parliamentary grants towards driving adits and other works. Although a Parliamentary Committee reported in 1730 that the money had been judiciously spent, the company never paid any dividend. This was blamed, probably quite justifiably, on the lack of a proper harbour, which inhibited the ready export of the coal to its principal Irish market, the city of Dublin. Eventually, the working of the mines passed for a few years to Messrs Richard and William Maguire, merchants, of Dublin.

Hugh Boyd of Ballycastle

The Maguires were followed in their mining by one Hugh Boyd, a descendant of the noble family of Boyd, Earls of Kilmarnock. He was born in 1690, the eldest son of the Rev William Boyd, vicar of Ramoan, by Rose MacNeile, the only daughter and heiress of Daniel MacNeile, constable of Dunanainie Castle near Ballycastle. On 10 March 1736, Hugh Boyd was granted a mining lease by Alexander MacDonnell, 5th Earl of Antrim, at a yearly rent of £5 15s 0d. The lease required that Boyd was to give the Earl one ton of coal for every twelve tons mined, and that six able workmen were to be employed in the collieries for 150 days in any one year for the effectual working of the mines.

Boyd ably supplemented his improvement of the mines by obtaining a Parliamentary grant of £23,000 to build a harbour and quay, and by erecting glass furnaces, a brewery, a tanyard and an inn. He was a pious man and, in 1756, built a church in the Graeco-Italian style in the Diamond, or market square, of what was then a mere hamlet. Arthur Young, in his *Tour of Ireland*, includes Boyd's name in a list of excellent Irish landlords. Boyd was also responsible for the construction of what was probably the first tramway in Ireland. It was built in connection with the harbour at Ballycastle, and was used to convey stone to it from a quarry in the cliffs west of the town. It was of 3'0" gauge and 310 yards long. The rails were of oak or fir scantling, and there were four wagons, but it is uncertain whether they were moved by hand, or by donkeys or other suitable animals.

So long as Boyd was alive, the industries flourished around the shores of Ballycastle Bay. He had several hundred miners at work and the output of coal was between 10,000 and 15,000 tons a year. Horse-drawn carts took some of the coal inland, but the bulk was transported by sea to Dublin, in spite of an exposed coast and a harbour that was prone to silting. "I was pleased", wrote Boyd to a friend in 1750, "to see sixty ships lying in the harbour at Ballycastle, many of them loading coal for Dublin." With Boyd's death in 1756, the industries which he had founded began to decline for want of his guiding hand.

The Rev John Dubordieu, in his *Statistical Survey of the County of Antrim,* 1812, states that it was then considered that the most accessible coal had been worked out, and that only four collieries were functioning, compared with a maximum of 12 in Boyd's day. Though the prosperity of the middle 18th century was never to return to Ballycastle through coal mining, the winning of coal has, nevertheless, continued up to the present time, though production has now fallen to a few hundred tons a year.

Market Square rather than mines

In an area with a tradition of coal mining extending back for more than two centuries, it may seem surprising that the Ballycastle Railway did not owe its origin to the local coal seams, but it is understandable when the comparatively diminished activity of the collieries by the middle of the 19th century is considered. When the Ballycastle Railway Company came to submit its bill to Parliament, a map was attached showing that the Company proposed to place its northern terminus over half a mile from the shore and the harbour, and something like three times that distance from the nearest mine adit. The railhead, therefore, owed allegiance neither to the small harbour nor to the near-derelict coal mines. As indicated in the Parliamentary plans, the terminus was eventually built within a stone's throw of the market place, to which the railway turned for its trade in the years that followed.

The promoters of the railway must have visualised their line as a profitable concern, which would revifify the little coast town by connecting it to the major railway in the hinterland. They had apparently no expectations about its developing as a mineral line. In this, it differed radically from the little Campbeltown & Macrihanish Railway which, some years later, was built on the Kintyre peninsula of southwest Scotland to tap a coalfield comparable in size and position to that at Ballycastle.

At the inland end of the Ballycastle line was the little town of Ballymoney, with a population of around 3000. Its hinterland participated in the Plantation of Ulster by Scots settlers in the early part of the 17th century, and the growth of Ballymoney dated from that period. The local merchants, drawn from the countryside, developed such industries as hand-loom weaving, tanning, soap and candle making, woollen manufacture, rope making and flour milling. A public crane was set up in 1811, and a grain market in 1820. Through the 19th century Ballymoney grew in importance as a market town and a distributing centre for consumer goods. It lay on the course of the railway between Ballymena and Coleraine and, once the latter was completed, Ballymoney was the obvious site for the inland terminus of a rail connection with Ballycastle.

The schemes multiply

In 1855, twenty-five years before the Ballycastle Railway commenced operations, the ponderously-titled Ballymena, Ballymoney, Coleraine and Portrush Junction Railway had opened its line. As the crow flies, it passed 12 miles from Ballycastle, and connected the Belfast & Ballymena Railway to the south with the Londonderry & Coleraine Railway to the north. The BBCPJR lasted only six years before amalgamating with its neighbours, producing in the process the Belfast and Northern Counties Railway. In the middle 1860s the BNCR considered building a branch to Ballycastle from its main line; a bill was presented to Parliament towards this end but it failed to pass the House of Lords.

More or less concurrently, there emerged in 1876 two schemes which were designed to give rail access to Ballycastle. The first was promoted by William A Traill, a member of a well-known North Antrim family and a graduate civil engineer, who proposed that a railway should be built from Ballymena to Ballycastle, by way of Cloughmills, Loughguile and Armoy. Traill had been on the staff of HM Geological Survey of Ireland and was an authority on the mineral resources of his home area. In support of the line, it was cited that it would enable coal to be sent from Ballycastle to England more easily than shipping it from the inadequate harbour. At the time the mines were nearly inactive but, fired by his local patriotism and backed by his geological knowledge, Traill envisaged a revival of coal working on the lines of a century before. His proposed railway never progressed beyond the preliminary stages, and did not survive to see the drafting of a Parliamentary bill.

The next scheme was more modest in conception and was eventually successfully completed. A line was to be built between Ballycastle and Ballymoney, which was the nearest town of any importance on the main Northern Counties railway. Traill was not among the promoters, who were mainly businessmen and landowners from the north of County Antrim.

Public transport services in the Ballycastle district at that time were extremely primitive by modern standards. In 1880 the *Coleraine Chronicle* commented:

> . . . the only mode of conveyance that could be relied upon, and which existed for many years between Coleraine and Ballycastle, was a dilapidated 'long car', with a more dilapidated-looking pair of horses attached to it, which 'made a run' once a week. Ballymoney was favoured somewhat more, as a one-horse car plied daily between that town and Ballycastle.

The more independent merchants of Ballycastle were in the habit of carting their own supplies from Bellaghy station (later renamed Killagan) on the Northern Counties line; Killagan was not many miles further than Ballymoney, the road was at least as good as that between Ballycastle and Ballymoney and, as it was ten miles nearer Belfast by rail, there was a saving in cost.

A view towards Ballycastle, from above the bridge at Fairhill Street about 1947, with No 44 heading a train for Ballymoney. The carriage directly behind the locomotive is No 352; the other is No 353. These 1928-built carriages had corridor connections and electric lighting and had been transferred from the NCC's Ballymena and Larne section in 1933. KA Benington

Chapter 2

The Making of the Railway

Promotion and Incorporation

The promoters of the Ballycastle–Ballymoney railway formed a provisional committee; a survey was made of the course of the line and a bill was prepared for submission to Parliament. Leaving Ballycastle, the line was to head inland in a southwesterly direction to the village of Armoy, half that distance representing a stiffish climb up the valley of the River Tow. From Armoy, through Stranocum and Dervock, the line was planned to run along a low watershed between a stream variously named Stracam River, Doughery Water and Inver Burn, and to the south the much larger River Bush. A short way beyond Dervock, the River Bush was to be crossed and the line was then to skirt the east side of the great Garry Bog – said to be the second most extensive bog in Ireland – to within sight of Ballymoney.

From the beginning, it was planned to construct the line on the Irish narrow gauge of 3'0", thereby following the neighbouring Ballymena, Cushendall and Red Bay Railway which was opened in 1875–76, and the Ballymena and Larne Railway, then in course of construction. At Ballymoney a normal junction with the Belfast and Northern Counties Railway was therefore not possible, since the BNCR was built to the Irish standard gauge of 5'3".

The plan prepared by Lanyon and McKinnon shows the line entering Ballymoney by crossing *above* the Northern Counties line, to reach its south side some way to the east of the town, after which it was shown as running parallel to the main line to a terminus alongside the BNCR station. This awkward entry into Ballymoney would have avoided any interference with the Northern Counties yard and with the cattle or Fair Hill of the town, but it would have sited the Ballycastle company's premises on the far side of the main line from the town, and in a cramped site between the broad gauge railway and a stream. Apparently, some amicable arrangement was reached, for the Ballycastle Railway eventually did not fly over the main line, but kept decorously on its north side and shared the station and the goods yard.

The promoters' formal 'Estimate of Expense', dated Christmas Eve 1877, accompanied the bill and was signed by the surveyors, John Lanyon CE and James F McKinnon CE*:

Earthworks:		**Cubic yards**	**Price per yard**	**£ s. d.**	**£ s. d.**
Cuttings –	rock	25,912	2s 9d	3,562 14 0	
	soft soil	518,735	1s 1d	28,098 0 0	
	roads	1,376	1s 1d	74 16 0	
	Total	546,023		31,735 10 0	31,736 0 0
Embankments, including roads		406,230			
Bridges – public roads (16)					3,090 0 0
Accommodation bridges and works					3,710 0 0
Viaducts					1,800 0 0
Culverts and drains					1,870 0 0
Metalling of roads and level crossings					1,022 0 0
Permanent way, including fencing					
16 miles 1 furlong 8 chains.			Cost per mile: £1.040		16,874 0 0
Permanent way for sidings, and cost of junctions					963 0 0
Stations					5,850 0 0
Contingencies on £66,914 at 10 per cent				6,692 0 0	
Land and buildings		107 acres			8,090 0 0
				TOTAL	**81,697 0 0**

This is Ballymoney in August 1930, looking in the Coleraine direction. Note the covered footbridge and the station canopy. The canopy was removed in 1973 and the footbridge in 2005. The building on the extreme right was the goods office. It closed in 1962.
HC Casserley

The Act of Incorporation of the Ballycastle Railway Company+ was given the Royal Assent on 22 July 1875. Six County Antrim gentlemen were named as its first directors. The first was the Rev Sir Frederick Boyd, Bart, BA, JP, of the Manor House, Ballycastle, rector of Holwell, Bedfordshire, from 1865 to 1875, and great-great-great-grandson of Hugh Boyd of Ballycastle of 18th century fame. The others were John McGildowny, JP, DL, of Clare Park, Ballycastle; John Casement, MA, JP, of Magherintemple, Ballycastle; James Moore Knox, of Armoy; Richard M Douglas, JP, of Portballintrae; and Leopold G Filgate of Killagan.

The Act authorised the Company to make their line to the desired gauge of 3'0", and to raise £90,000 of share capital and £45,000 in loans. In view of the entry into Ballymoney, the Belfast and Northern Counties Railway Company was permitted, significantly enough, to subscribe £18,000 towards the share capital and to nominate two directors to the Board of the Ballycastle Railway. The names of the BNCR directors submitted to the Ballycastle Company on 29 July 1878 were Edmund McNeill, JP, of Craigdun, Cullybackey, near Ballymena, and John Young, DL, MA, of Galgorm Castle, near Ballymena.

A supplementary scheme

With the Ballycastle Railway Company firmly established, WA Traill, who conceived the abortive Ballymena–Ballycastle scheme in 1876, continued to take an active interest in local railway development. Supported by his brother, Dr Anthony Traill, of Trinity College, Dublin, he convened a public meeting in Bushmills Courthouse on 27 October 1879 to consider the best way of connecting Bushmills with the outside world. At the time, the course of the Ballycastle Railway would have been made public, though it had not received Parliamentary sanction. Acting on this knowledge, the Traills proposed to construct a

* *It is interesting to note that his father, Alexander McKinnon, of Cloughcorr House, Ballycastle, had the unusual distinction of living in three centuries. He was born in 1799 and died in 1903 aged 104, and is buried in Ballintoy churchyard, near Ballycastle.*

\+ *41-2 Vict cap 195*

narrow gauge railway, nine miles in length, from Dervock, on the Ballycastle Railway, along the valley of the River Bush to the small town of Bushmills, and thence to a terminus at the Giant's Causeway, an extensive natural formation of polygonally-jointed, basaltic rock on the northern coast. At Bushmills, a roadside tramway was to diverge from this railway and run to the BNCR station at Portrush.

A modified revival of Traill's previous scheme was a line, diverging from the Ballycastle Railway between Dervock and Stranocum and going by Lissanoure and Cloughmills to Rathkenny, which was a station on the Ballymena, Cushendall and Red Bay Railway. Considering the sparsely-populated country through which this contemplated line would pass, it was a grandiose scheme and it is not surprising that much of it perished for lack of financial support. Only the Portrush–Bushmills and the Bushmills–Giant's Causeway portions were constructed. Its story, as the Giant's Causeway, Portrush & Bush Valley Electric Railway and Tramway, has recently been told by Mr JH McGuigan.

Construction

In the Antrim Arms Hotel, facing the Diamond, as the market square of Ballycastle is called, the newly-constituted Board of Directors of the Ballycastle Railway Company took a private room for their first meeting on 3 August 1878. The Rev Sir Frederick Boyd was in the chair; Silas Evans, an Englishman who had looked after the affairs of the provisional committee, was formally appointed secretary; and Messrs L'Estrange & Brett, of Belfast, the Company's solicitors. Two civil engineers were present at the meeting, VG Bell in a consultative capacity (and apparently replacing Lanyon) and James F McKinnon, who had assisted in the original survey. Bell had re-examined the course of the railway and was able to suggest minor deviations from McKinnon's line in order to reduce the cost.

During the following weeks McKinnon was busily engaged in completing the details of the survey and preparing specifications. The directors at this stage apparently decided to economise by laying their permanent way with as light rails as possible. They studied two revised cost estimates for the track, £9125 if laid with 30 lb rails and £10,508 if laid with 40 lb rails. These suggested rail weights are surprisingly low, even allowing for the narrow gauge and the lighter rolling stock; the Ballymena and Larne Railway was laid in 44 lb rails, and 65 lb to the yard was the lightest rail commonly in use on the standard gauge in Ireland.

The Ballycastle directors lost no time in preparing for the next stages; at their meeting on 17 October 1878 tenders for the construction of the line were considered from the following contractors:

Kennedy & Co, Glasgow	£38,175	18	0
McCrea & McFarland, Belfast	£40,159	15	5
John Cunningham, Dalkey	£41,811	5	4
James Connor, Belfast	£41,926	13	0
Robert Worthington, Dublin	£44,076	6	0
Thomas Dixon, Carrickfergus	£44,157	11	11
John Edwards, Dublin	£45,369	18	9
William Dogherty, Dublin	£46,359	18	9
Charles King, Wigan	£46,022	0	0
Robert T Relf, Okehampton	£49,100	0	0

Although Kennedy's tender was the lowest, the firm was a new one, their sureties were judged unsatisfactory, and their offer was not further entertained. The next stage was to ascertain whether or not any of the next three would be prepared to reduce their offer. Connor who, as Messrs Connor & Manisty, had built the Dundalk, Newry and Greenore Railway and the Ballymena, Cushendall and Red Bay Railway, was persuaded to bring his price down to £39,200. On 13 December 1878 the contract was sealed.

Connor started construction in January 1879, but he lived only three months longer. News of his death was conveyed to the members of the Board on 26 March, when it was stated that his executors would attempt to carry on the work. The Board's reaction was to instruct their secretary, Evans, to complain to the executors that the work was making slow progress. One of the executors was a Mr Fry, of Messrs Butler & Fry, of Ballymena, and when James Connor's estate was wound up in February 1880, the contract was transferred to Butler & Fry, a firm which had not tendered in the first instance. Their work must, however, have been acceptable as, in January 1880, they had been asked to construct the station buildings.

The only noteworthy engineering works on the line were a stone viaduct of four arches a few yards from the Ballycastle terminus, a short tunnel at Capecastle, and the bridge across the River Bush, between Dervock and Ballymoney. The viaduct at Ballycastle carried the

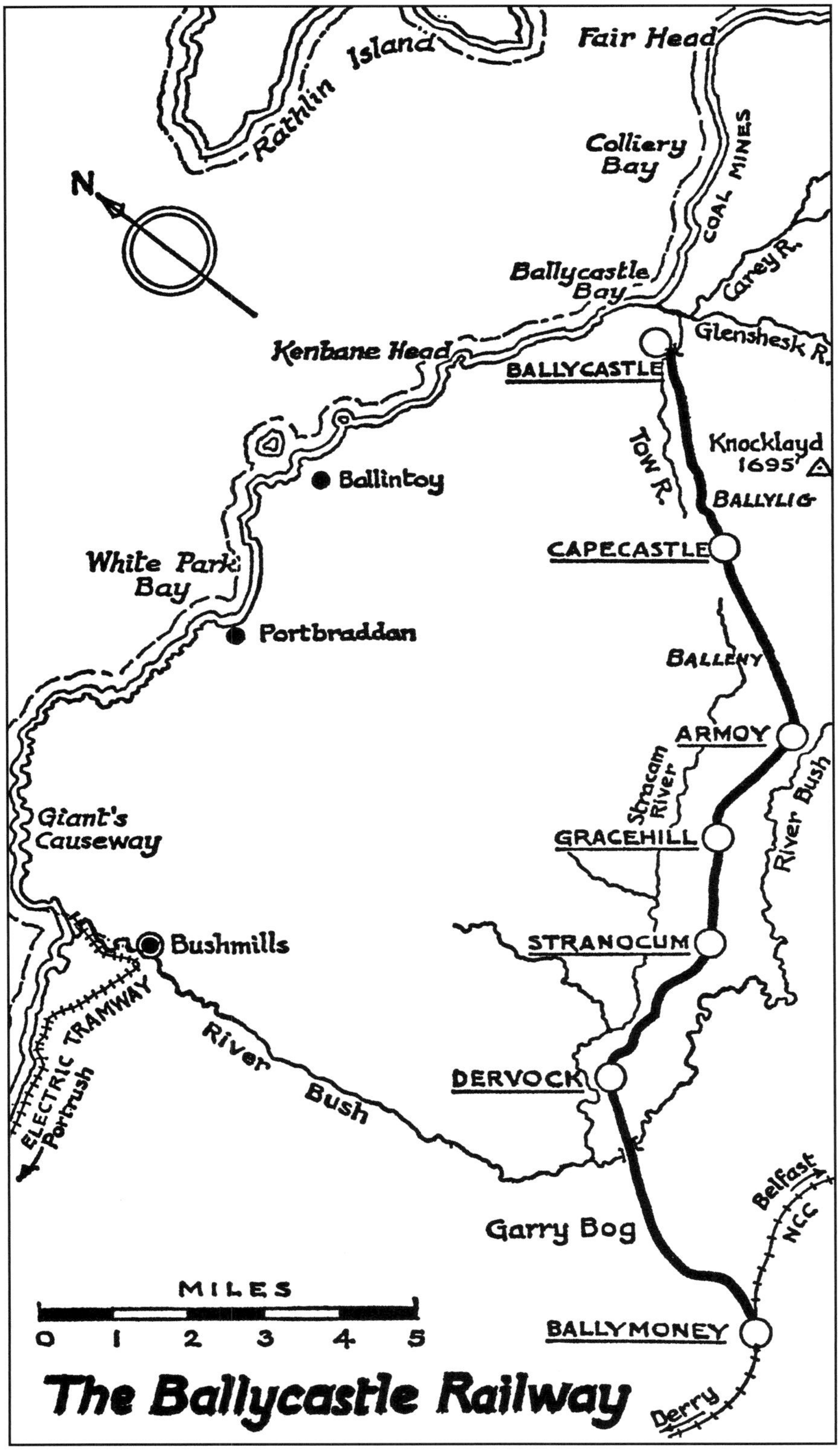
Rathlin Island
Fair Head
Colliery Bay
COAL MINES
N
Ballycastle Bay
Carey R.
Glenshesk R.
Kenbane Head
BALLYCASTLE
Tow R.
Knocklayd 1695'
BALLYLIG
Ballintoy
CAPECASTLE
White Park Bay
Portbraddan
BALLENY
ARMOY
Stracam River
River Bush
Giant's Causeway
GRACEHILL
STRANOCUM
Bushmills
ELECTRIC TRAMWAY
Portrush
River Bush
DERVOCK
Garry Bog
Belfast NCC
MILES
0 1 2 3 4 5
BALLYMONEY
Derry
The Ballycastle Railway

A Ballycastle train awaits departure from Ballymoney in 1936. It is formed of locomotive No 101, carriages 350 and 352, an open wagon and a brake van. Ian Allan Library/LGRP 7355

The Belfast end of Ballymoney with the narrow gauge on the right. This view shows the extension to the up main line/Ballycastle platform. The steps to the signal box were later moved to the Belfast end. Ian Allan Library/Real Photographs X303

railway over the Tow river and a minor road; it was badly constructed, but this was not discovered until March 1880, when McKinnon broke the alarming news to the members of the Board that " . . . a split longitudinally had taken place along the entire length of the bridge." He hastened to assure them that the defect could be remedied by strengthening the top part of the structure with a layer of concrete, and this was done during the summer.

At the same time as the repair of the Tow Viaduct, a wooden overbridge at Balleeny, 4½ miles from Ballycastle, where the county road between Armoy and Ballycastle crossed the railway, was found to be defective and was taken down and rebuilt. In the Minute Book this bridge is referred to as the 'Isle Bridge', since the adjacent townland of Magheramore is locally called 'The Isles of Magheramore'.

It was hoped to have the railway working by the summer of 1880, when tourist traffic was at its height. When this proved impossible, the directors had to content themselves with complaining about the delays to the contractors and to McKinnon, their complaint being transmitted by way of Silas Evans who, as a secretary, was distinctly versatile. During the spring of 1880 he made himself responsible for the purchase of the two locomotives and the rolling stock, eight passenger carriages, 60 wagons and a brake van being judged sufficient. A month after this order had been placed, the makers pointed out that the form of the arches of the overbridges was too low and that the distance from rail level would have to be increased by a further two inches. To fit the bridges which Butler & Fry were erecting, the carriage builders had already reduced the width of the vehicles by two inches and the height by four, but they still felt that the clearance was insufficient.

McKinnons scheme for laying the track with light-section rails went a stage further when, on 12 March 1879, the Board asked Evans to obtain prices for 30 lb and 40 lb rails. By early April, 14 companies had replied, but none could roll rails as light as 30 lb, and they offered either 40 lb or 45 lb rails at prices varying from £4 18s 0d to £6 11s 6d per ton. The West Cumberland Iron Company's tender was the lowest and the Ballycastle Company decided to take their 45 lb rails, a wise reversal of policy. The Company then tried unsuccessfully to get the price brought down to £4 12s 6d. Half the rails were to be delivered to Ballycastle and half to Portrush; those delivered to Portrush were to be railed over the Northern Counties line to Ballymoney and the track was to be laid from both ends. Sleepers were ordered in uncreosoted redwood at 1s 1½d each from WF Redmond of Newry. The Pheonix Nut & Bolt Co supplied spikes at £10 15s 0d a ton and fang bolts at £10 5s 0d a ton. Fish plates came from Ebbw Vale at £6 5s 0d and fish bolts from John Gault of Ballymena at £9 15s 0d. By the first week of July 1879 the SS *Kelburn* was discharging some of the rails at Portrush Harbour.

No details of McKinnon's specifications are known to survive, but as late as 7 January 1880 the Board decided that the roofs were to be slated and not covered with roofing-felt, as had been originally intended. At the Board Meeting on 28 January 1880, six tenders for the construction of the buildings were considered (the totals are as given in the minutes):

	1	2	3	4	5	6
	£	£	£	£	£	£
Ballymoney, carriage shed	240	202				
engine shed	190	157				
goods shed	650	514				
Dervock, station house	475	436				
Stranocum, station house	475	436				
Armoy, station house	475	436				
goods shed	165	156				
Ballycastle, station house	700	647				
engine shed	134	99				
goods shed	230	205				
carriage shed	285	247				
TOTAL	4154	3616	4365	3700	3400	3050

1, Dixon & Co, Belfast. 2, Henry Stewart & Co, Belfast (add if inter stations slated 3 at £26, included in total).
3, Robt Young, Ballymoney. 4, John Gault, Ballymena. 5, Butler & Fry, Ballymena. 6, Nolan, Belfast.

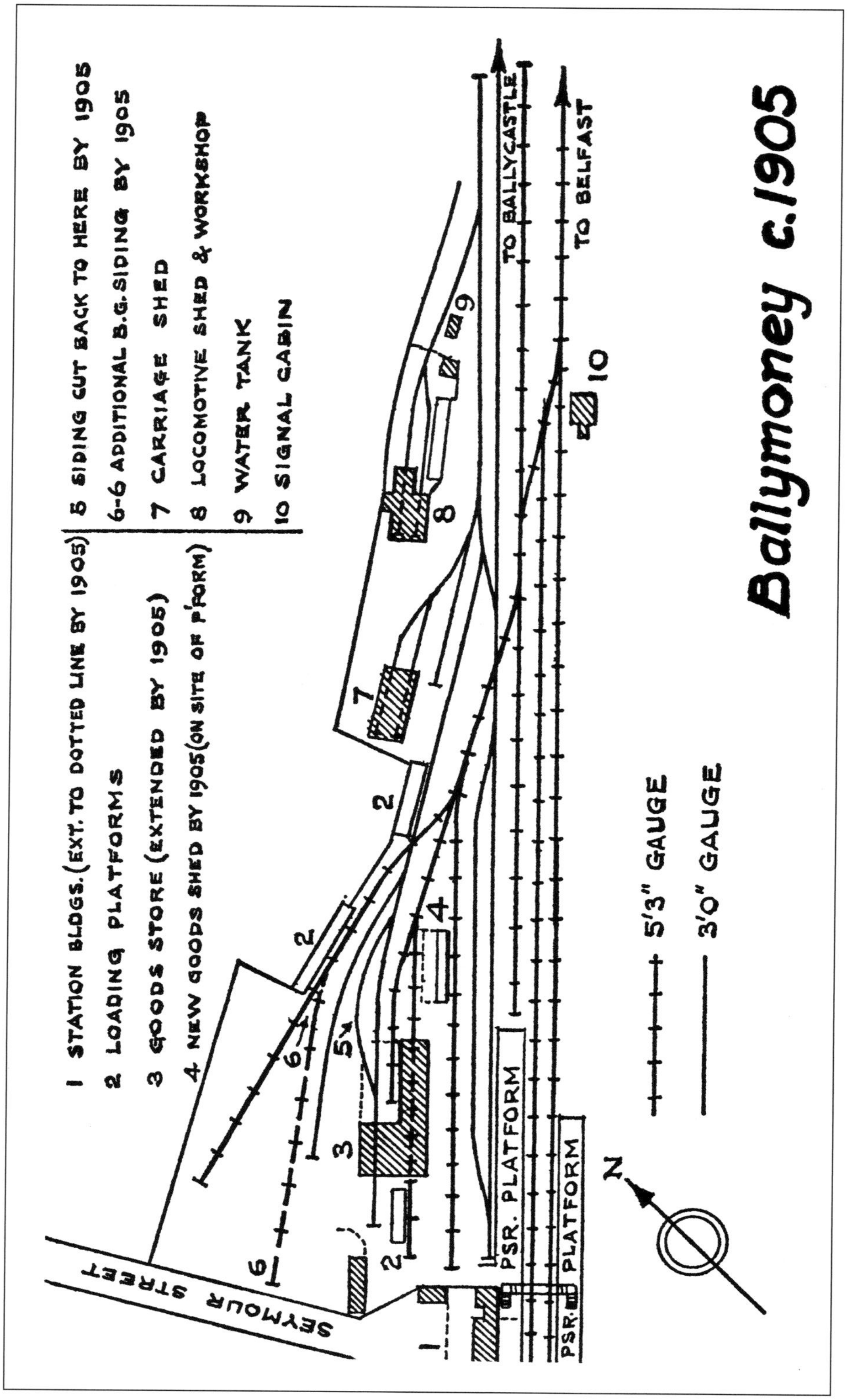
1 STATION BLDGS. (EXT. TO DOTTED LINE BY 1905)
2 LOADING PLATFORMS
3 GOODS STORE (EXTENDED BY 1905)
4 NEW GOODS SHED BY 1905 (ON SITE OF P'FORM)
5 SIDING CUT BACK TO HERE BY 1905
6-6 ADDITIONAL B.G. SIDING BY 1905
7 CARRIAGE SHED
8 LOCOMOTIVE SHED & WORKSHOP
9 WATER TANK
10 SIGNAL CABIN
5'3" GAUGE
3'0" GAUGE
Ballymoney c.1905
TO BALLYCASTLE
TO BELFAST
PSR. PLATFORM
PLATFORM
PSR.
SEYMOUR STREET
N

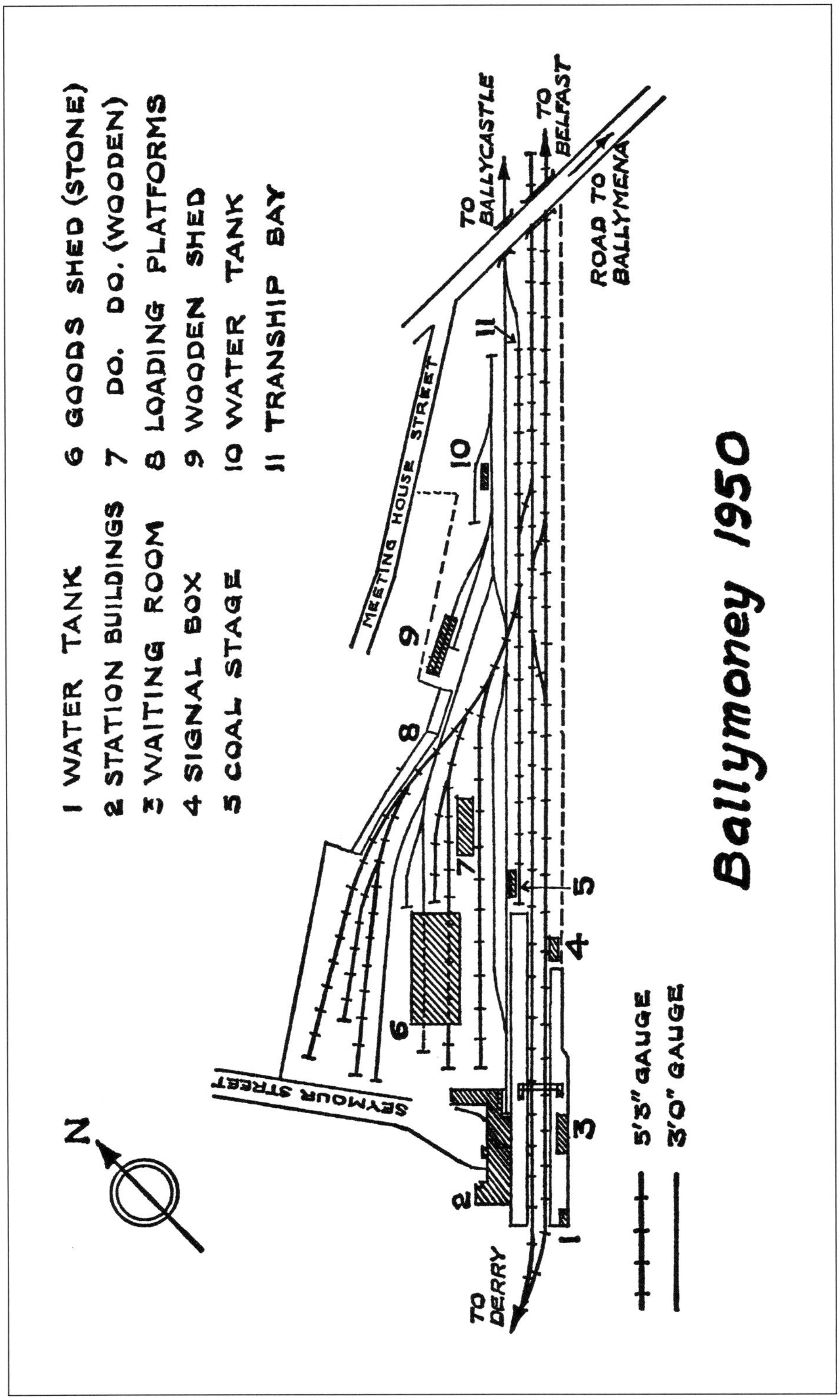
1 WATER TANK
2 STATION BUILDINGS
3 WAITING ROOM
4 SIGNAL BOX
5 COAL STAGE
6 GOODS SHED (STONE)
7 DO. DO. (WOODEN)
8 LOADING PLATFORMS
9 WOODEN SHED
10 WATER TANK
11 TRANSHIP BAY
TO BALLYCASTLE
TO BELFAST
ROAD TO BALLYMENA
MEETING HOUSE STREET
SEYMOUR STREET
TO DERRY
N
5'3" GAUGE
3'0" GAUGE
Ballymoney 1950

During March 1879, McKinnon estimated the costs of building the stations; the Minute Book lists these as:

Ballycastle, with approaches	£2603
Armoy, station only	£345
do. for goods	£235
Stranocum, station only	£285
Dervock, station only	£400

On 28 January 1880, the contract was awarded to Butler & Fry at their price of £3400, with the instruction that the roofs were to be covered in Bangor slates. Noteworthy in the tenders is the comparatively expensive goods store at Ballymoney which was substantially built in stone.

Minor complications arose about the termini. In February 1879 McKinnon estimated the cost of Ballymoney station in no less than three forms: first, as a joint establishment with the BNCR at £2900; then as a separate building at £3580, and finally as a joint station building, capable of being separated at a later date, at £3080. The station then began to be the subject of contention between the two companies and, in June 1879, financial discussions were held, concerning its joint character. While lower initial cost appealed to the Ballycastle Company, the prospect of endlessly paying an annual rent to the BNCR was less attractive. In July they resolved to have a separate station, but the BNCR would not agree and, as the largest shareholders, they got their way.

At the Ballycastle end of the line there was argument over a more trivial matter – the station approach – between two schools of thought. One wanted it to be from the Diamond, the other from Quay Road, as had been shown in the Parliamentary plans. The Quay Road approach seems to have been favoured, but the road was to be raised on an embankment and sliced across the foot of several gardens, the owners of which suddenly attached great value to their property. Finally, both approaches were built, as was proper in view of the geography of the town, and the matter was resolved in October 1880 when, unexpectedly selling 34 shares, the Company decided to use the proceeds to make the roadway and an approach to the station from the Diamond.

For ballasting the line, Butler & Fry obtained their own locomotive, a six-coupled saddle tank, built by Black, Hawthorn & Co of Newcastle. The date of its arrival on the site is uncertain but would seem to have been about June 1880, since the purchase of half an acre of land at Drummans for a ballast pit was not sanctioned until then. Moreover, a Board Minute of 7 June refers to ". . . the employment of John Nicholl's son as stoker or cleaner on one of the locomotives".* The engine was named *Lady Boyd* from the start, in honour of Lady Alice Emily Barbara Boyd, second wife of Rev Sir Frederick Boyd.

Inspection

By the middle of September 1880, the last of the tourists were packing their bags in the Ballycastle hotels and boarding houses, and the Company saw that its summer bonus had been lost for that year. However, it decided that it was ready for the verdict of the railway inspecting officer of the Board of Trade, and Colonel Rich duly came across from London and spent from 18 to 20 September on the line. The Company subsequently received this salutary letter from the Board of Trade:

> Col Rich has reported . . . that the fencing is incomplete; the engine is unsteady and that the Railway cannot be opened without danger to the public in consequence of the incomplete state of the works and engine. The Board of Trade therefore order the Ballycastle Railway to postpone opening of the Railway for one month.

The report also commented upon the unsatisfactory approach to Ballycastle station, and upon the lack of a platform awning at Ballymoney. The rawness of the works is reflected in a Board Minute seven months later, when McKinnon asked for permission to buy enough grass seed to plant 25 acres, and to buy 200,000 thorn quicks for hedging. He was allowed between 40 and 50 bushels of seeds, but was told to postpone the purchase of the thorn quicks for a year.

Colonel Rich returned to make a second inspection on 7 October 1880 and verbally passed the line as ready to be opened, though the ceremony did not take place until some time later.

* *'John Nicholl's son' (1857–1938) was the father of John Nicholl, timber and coal merchant, Ballycastle, and uncle of HA Boyd, Mowbray House, Ballycastle.*

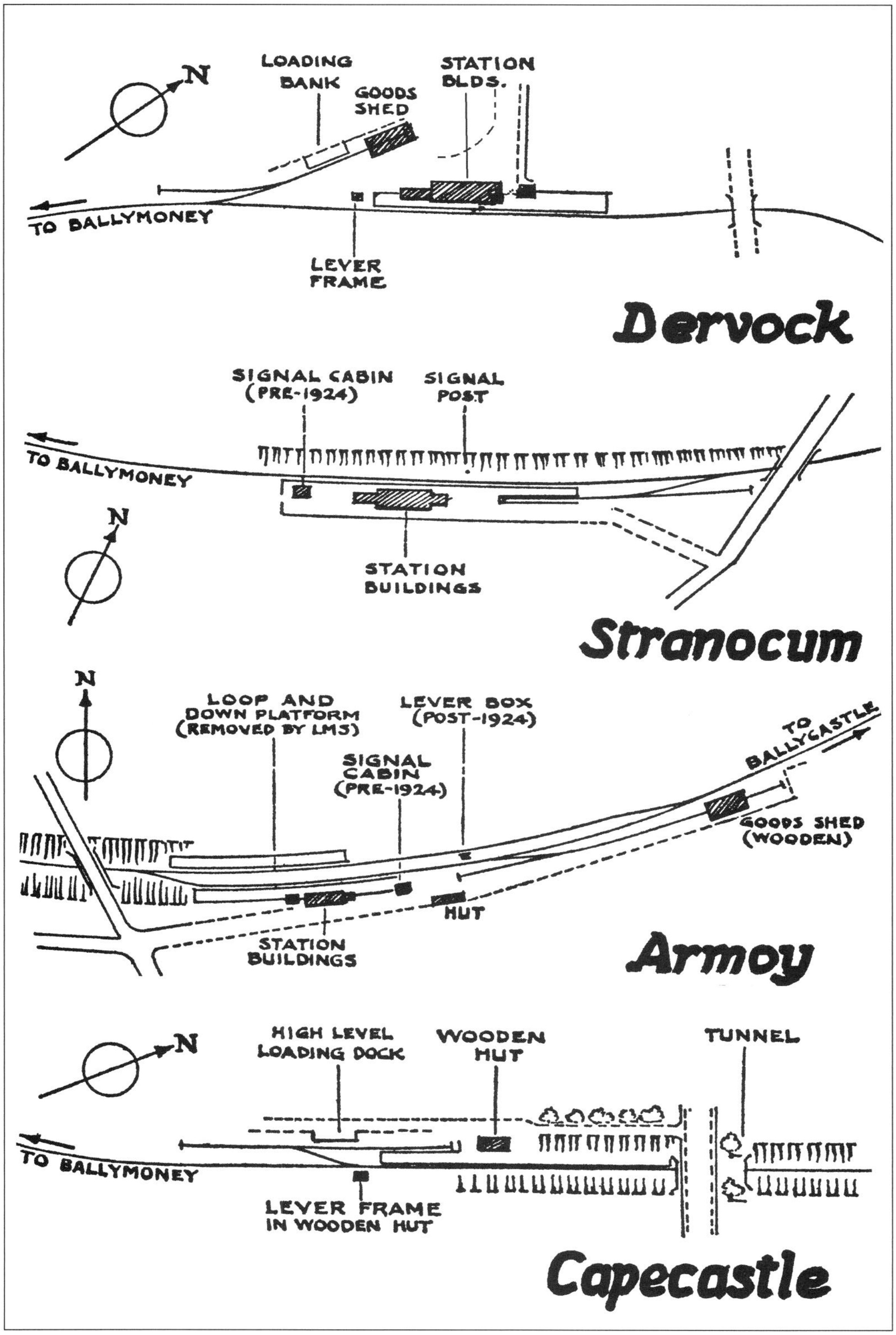
LOADING BANK
GOODS SHED
STATION BLDS.
TO BALLYMONEY
LEVER FRAME
Dervock
SIGNAL CABIN (PRE-1924)
SIGNAL POST
TO BALLYMONEY
STATION BUILDINGS
Stranocum
LOOP AND DOWN PLATFORM (REMOVED BY LMS)
LEVER BOX (POST-1924)
SIGNAL CABIN (PRE-1924)
TO BALLYCASTLE
GOODS SHED (WOODEN)
HUT
STATION BUILDINGS
Armoy
HIGH LEVEL LOADING DOCK
WOODEN HUT
TUNNEL
TO BALLYMONEY
LEVER FRAME IN WOODEN HUT
Capecastle

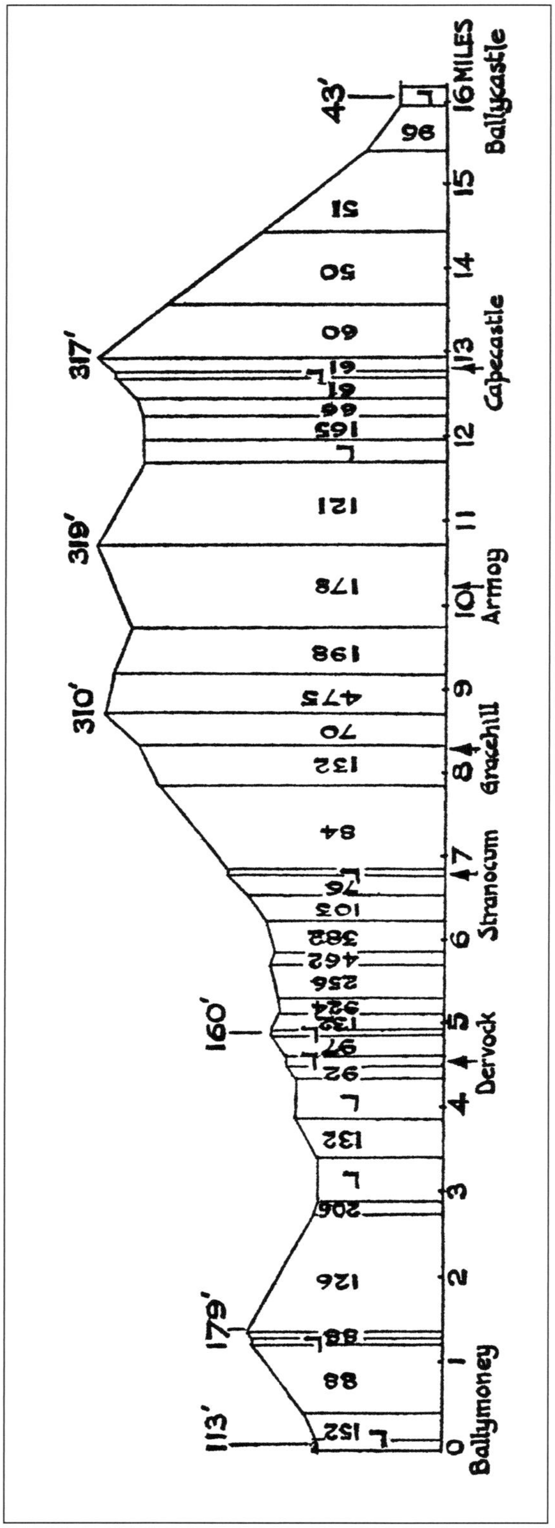
113'
179'
160'
310'
319'
317'
43'
Ballymoney
Dervock
Stranocum
Gracehill
Armoy
Capecastle
Ballycastle
16 MILES

Opening

Although the Board Minute Book does not mention the date upon which the railway began to carry traffic, both the next half-yearly report and the Board of Trade Railway Returns give it as 18 October 1880. In the course of a lengthy report in the *Coleraine Chronicle* of Saturday 30 October, it was stated that " . . . on Monday last, the new railway was formally opened". This indicates that the ceremony was held on 25 October, though, quite understandably, traffic was being run for a week before the formal opening.

The *Coleraine Chronicle* devoted five columns to a somewhat fulsome description of the activities of the day on which the formal opening took place:

> The opening ceremony was attended by a large number of gentlemen connected with the various railways in the North of Ireland. A special train started from Ballymoney shortly after 12 o'clock noon. The journey to Ballycastle was performed in three-quarters of an hour, and it appeared to be the prevalent opinion among the passengers that the train ran smoothly on the line and that altogether the railway was in every respect excellent. Shortly before two o'clock, Lady Boyd, who was attended by Mr John Casement, JP, and surrounded by a vast number of spectators, performed the ceremony of the opening the line by smashing a bottle of champagne against the engine, and declaring the line opened. The railway premises were decorated with flags in honour of the occasion, and at one o'clock, on the arrival of the train which conveyed those who were to assist at the ceremony, there was a display of pyrotechnics. Much interest seemed to be taken in the proceedings by the people of the town, and the railway station and its vicinity were crowded throughout the day . . . .

Preparations for the traditional celebrations had been made some days earlier, when a quotation had been obtained for a luncheon, at five shillings a head, plus a shilling corkage for the wines:

> At two o'clock a magnificent luncheon, supplied in splendid style by Mr Wegg, of the Antrim Arms Hotel, Ballycastle, was given in one of the goods sheds of the railway, which was suitably prepared for the occasion, and tastefully decorated. The champagne and other wines were of the very best and choicest quality from the cellars of Messrs Anderson & Stewart, Coleraine. Some 200 persons were invited.
>
> Mr John Casement, JP, presided. RM Douglas Esq, JP, William Woodside Esq, Thomas McElderry, Esq, and James M Knox, Esq, acted as croupiers . . . .

The report in the *Chronicle* records the wording of no less than eleven toasts, all of which were honoured in champagne. After this comprehensive coverage, ranging from the Queen to the carriage builders:

> . . . a cordial vote of thanks was passed to Mr Casement for the dignified manner in which he presided; after which the interesting proceedings terminated, and the majority of the guests left by special train for Ballymoney.

Even then the tumult and the shouting had not died away in what was still a comparatively small provincial town, but which could now proudly boast of its rail connection with the larger centres of population. The *Coleraine Chronicle*, in a final paragraph gives a brief description of what probably gave the townsfolk more to remember than those eleven toasts in the gaily decorated goods shed:

> In the evening a band of music paraded the streets, playing several popular tunes, and tar barrels were burned in the Diamond in honour of the auspicious occasion. Refreshments were liberally supplied to all who took part in the festivities.

The course of the line

At Ballymoney, the narrow gauge line of the Ballycastle Railway occupied a bay on the northwest, or town, side of the up main platform of the Belfast and Northern Counties Railway. The single buffer stop, rather attractively painted in white and red, was almost against the red-brick wall of the station offices. Part of the platform was protected by a wooden awning roof, but for much of its length it was open. The elevation of the terminus was about 113 feet above Ordnance Datum.

Leaving the platform end, the line lifted at 1 in 152 for a quarter of a mile, keeping alongside a broad gauge siding and running parallel to the broad gauge main line. The goods yard, shared by both railways, lay on the north side of the passenger platform but, unlike its counterparts in Larne and in Ballymena, it had no mixed gauge track. The

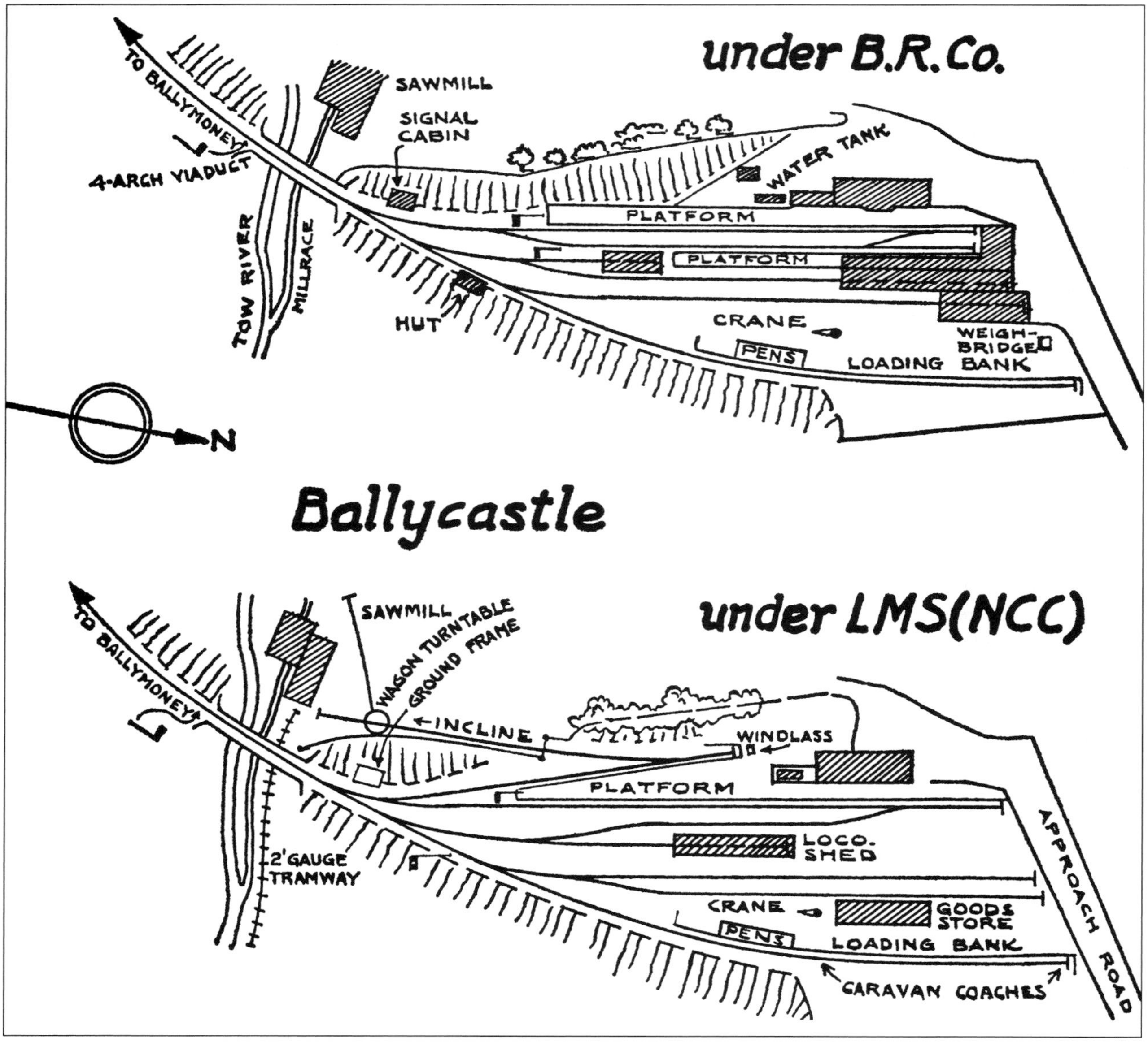

main goods shed, a substantial stone-built structure with interchange facilities, stood in the middle of the yard. A small cattle dock lay over at the north side of the yard, towards the Fair Hill, and was served by a siding which ran on to the goods shed. Going down the yard, the wooden carriage shed and the wooden locomotive shed and workshop were alongside the boundary wall against property in Meeting House Street. Beside the locomotive shed siding stood the water tank, a conspicuous, hemispherical-ended cylinder, supported horizontally on two high masonry piers. Coaling was also done here. The spires of two churches rose in the background. In later years a creamery was built beside the boundary wall.

Leaving the yard behind, the main road to Ballymena was carried on the skew across both narrow and broad gauge lines by the Roddenfoot Bridge, two-arched and built of dressed black basalt. The narrow gauge line passed through an arch which was distinctly larger than any others on the line, and was apparently made to take broad gauge vehicles, though it never had to do so. The larger arch across the BNCR was occupied by the single main line to Ballymena and by a siding.* Now on a 1 in 88 up-grade, the narrow gauge line soon climbed above the main Northern Counties metals as the latter turned away to the south. It then curved to the left around a low hill and, 1¼ miles out, had risen sixty-one feet above the level of the terminus and passed over a minor summit below the Ballymoney–Stranocum road.

Ahead of the train, now running easily with the regulator shut, an extensive view opened out across the brown and yellow expanse of the Garry Bog, a level area of some six square miles, dotted with the dark humps of turf stacks, and in summer with the white tufts of bog cotton. To the left, the train passed by Conagher and the farmstead of the ancestors of President McKinley of the United States of America, who was assassinated at Buffalo in 1901. Then, still on a down-grade of 1 in 126, the line descended towards the edge of the bogland and a half-mile of level running along its margin followed, bringing the rails up to the crossing of the River Bush, made on a metal girder bridge (No 679), resting on screw-piles.

The fourth mile-post was reached on a short rise of 1 in 132, and there followed a second half-mile of level running, close to the meandering Dervock River. Dervock village lay some way to the left of the railway; part of it built in the 18th century by the celebrated Lord Macartney, Great Britain's first ambassador to China, and landlord of the village. A rise of 1 in 92 brought the train past the facing points of a siding and into the station, 4½ miles from Ballymoney. Dervock once enjoyed, with places like Kilrea in Co Derry and Moy in Co Tyrone, great distinction as a centre for horse fairs, and its siding must have witnessed the comings and goings of many an equestrian celebrity.

Leaving Dervock station, the track swung sharply to the right and climbed at 1 in 97 on a 10-chain curve into the townland of Carnculliagh Lower, a place that gave the permanent way men continual trouble. The course of the line thus altered within a short distance from northeast to nearly southeast, and then to east, Keeping on a low ridge between the River Bush and the Stracam River.

On gently rising gradients of 1 in 132/256/382, milepost six came up, and then with a steepening climb to 1 in 103/76 Stranocum station was reached. This was 6¾ miles from Ballymoney, and had a single siding. The station was nearly

* *This bridge was numbered 667 by the LMS, who also assigned numbers to other bridges and culverts towards Ballycastle. These had no numbers prior to 1924.*

No 41 crossing bridge No 679 across the River Bush with Jack McDuff looking out.
KA Benington

a mile from the whitewashed houses of the village, and was sited where a secondary road ran towards the north coast.

Almost two miles of continuous climbing followed. Setting a course directly towards the massive curve of Knocklayd, the line rose for a mile at 1 in 84, passing on the way a standing stone at a place called Carnfeague. Slackening to 1 in 132, the short platform of Gracehill Halt was passed on the left, 1½ miles from Stranocum. This calling place was provided eleven years after the other stations in an attempt to serve a scattered agricultural community. It stood at about 280 feet above Ordnance Datum, and the line ran at right angles to a beautifully-wooded roadway leading to Gracehill House.

Rising at 1 in 70, and half a mile past Gracehill Halt, the track swerved sharply to the right in the townland of Chatham Hall, entering moundy country where a line of old moraines, left by the last Ice Age, swept down from the southwestern slope of Knocklayd. These gravel banks, in far-off times, diverted the original course of the River Bush, making it forsake its old seaward course directly towards where Ballycastle now stands, and turn through a right-angle towards Dervock.

Eight and three-quarter miles from Ballymoney, the line reached 310 feet OD and started on a gentle descent towards Armoy, losing only 21 feet of height in the process. There then followed exactly a mile of a climb at 1 in 178. Immediately before entering the station, and on the left side beside the overhead bridge, was a small creamery.

The little village of Armoy is attractively placed where the River Bush makes a semicircular sweep, and the surrounding country is more wooded than the bare boglands lying towards Ballymoney. A ruined round tower, said to contain the narrowest entrance door of any of its kind in Ireland, is situated in the parish churchyard a short way east of the houses. As at Stranocum, the station was placed some way from the village. In the days of the Ballycastle Railway Company, Armoy had two platforms and a passing loop, and though the loop and the platform were taken away after 1925, it remained the most important of the intermediate stations on the line. The station building was the same type as at Dervock and Stranocum, substantially built and containing the station agent's house and the office. Facing points beyond the platform led to a siding on the eastern side of the line, which ran through a goods shed, made of wood with an arched roof.

Once away from Armoy, the line curved towards the north under the swelling brown shoulder of Knocklayd. The summit of the line, at 319 feet OD, was reached at the end of the 1 in 178 rise, some 50 chains beyond Armoy station and 10¾ miles from Ballymoney; as a summit, it was not spectacular. A gentle decent at 1 in 121 followed, past the site of the Balleeny siding, used for the first twenty years of the line for lime traffic and for agricultural produce. Before the twelfth milepost came by, a short reach on the level had supervened, but there lay ahead ¾ mile on steepening grades, starting at 1 in 165 for 15 chains, then 1 in 66 for 22 chains, with a final lift at 1 in 61 through Capecastle station.

Capecastle was picturesquely placed just before the only tunnel on the line, a short straight bore with two refuge insets through a hill crowned by a plantation. The platform had no station building, and the affairs of the Ballycastle Railway Company were conducted in a small wooden hut, in one part of which was a waiting room and in the other the office. Entering the station from Ballymoney, a siding connection trailed in on the left, and led to a high-level loading bank used for the local lime traffic. The station was at a height of 310 feet OD.

Plunging into the tunnel, the line completed its climb, and as it passed the thirteenth milepost had reached a height of 317 feet OD, only two feet lower than the main summit near Armoy. There, at the apex of the only appreciable gable on the whole line, the scene changed with dramatic suddenness as the rails dipped towards the northern terminus. To the right, there appeared the slopes of Knocklayd, the second highest mountain in Antrim (1695 feet), where brown rushy land was succeeded by green turf, growing on the hidden limestone and scarred by the gleaming whiteness of the great lime quarry. Above it, brown grass and heather capped the rounded summit, which is crowned by the ruins of a prehistoric stone cairn, hidden from sight of the train windows by the sweeping curve of the mountain.

A quarter of a mile past Capecastle, running downhill at 1 in 60, the notorious reverse curves of Ballylig met the train and served to check its Gadarene descent seaward. A left, a right and a left in succession, the track ran partly through a shallow cutting whose width evidenced attempts by the engineer to ease the radius. Once around the serpentine, the view swiftly opened, the valley slope fell away to the left

No 44, driven by Barry Limerick, arrives at Ballymoney on the 1.05pm ex-Ballycastle on 28 June 1950, just a few days before closure.
EM Patterson, courtesy CP Friel

Ballymoney yard on 29 March 1950. The crane here, seen above the engine in the centre of the picture, came from Ballyclare.
EM Patterson, courtesy CP Friel

The approach to Ballymoney, viewed from the footplate of No 44 on 28 June 1950. Note the white-painted area on the bridge, to aid signal sighting. EM Patterson, courtesy CP Friel

Bridge No 677 at Conagher, built to avoid the need for a level crossing. KA Benington

No 44 at Dervock on 1.05pm ex Ballycastle on 28 June 1950. The bridge carrying the Carncullagh Road over the railway can be seen in the background. In 2006, the far parapet of this bridge remains in position. EM Patterson, courtesy CP Friel

No 44 at Stranocum on 16 June 1950. The signal cabin had been removed by 1924.
EM Patterson, courtesy CP Friel

No 41 at Armoy on 3.55pm ex-Ballycastle on 26 June 1950. The loop and down platform were removed in LMS days.
TJ Edgington

Opposite top: *This is the view of Capecastle station, looking towards Ballycastle. The wooden hut on the right was for the lever frame controlling access to the high level loading dock. The straight bore of the tunnel beyond is very obvious. There were two refuges in the tunnel.* Ian Allan Library/LGRP 9695

Opposite bottom: *In this picture we see Capecastle tunnel from the Ballycastle end. Part of the tunnel was cut through rock and it was this which contributed, ultimately, to the closure of the line, it being deemed too expensive to increase the size of the bore to accommodate broad gauge rolling stock.* EM Patterson, courtesy CP Friel

Having just run off the Tow Viaduct, an up train, with No 102 in charge, passes under the first overbridge out of Ballycastle, at Fairhill Street, in June 1934. A recent photo at this location can be seen on page 136. Parts of the fence seen at the far side of the bridge are still in situ in 2006! Wallace McNaul collection

towards the head streams of the little River Tow, a misfit in the valley that once held the River Bush. The downgrade steepened to 1 in 50, a road tumbled down from the hill face above, and at Drummans Bridge, beside the Hanging Wood, plunged below the rails. On a fine day, three miles off, and over the clustered chimneys of Ballycastle, Rathlin Island floated multicoloured on the blue of the northern sea, and the train passengers surely knew that they were nearing journey's end. One is tempted to wonder how the great inventor, Guglielmo Marconi, contemplated this scene when he arrived in Ballycastle on the 6.15pm train on Monday 29 August 1898. This visit was in the early days of his experiments in wireless, some of which were conducted in that year by Marconi's assistant, George Kemp, between Ballycastle and Rathlin.*

Now dropping sharply at 1 in 51, the ballast pit siding in the townland of Ballydurnian faced the train, to the right of the line and protected by a Pinkerton's Box. The riddled gravel workings left quantities of cobbles and boulders, and in later Easters these provided university students of geology with varied raw material for study. Crossing a swift mountain stream, and rattling downhill, the line then ran alongside Broombeg Wood, later replanted and known as Ballycastle Forest. The first houses of Ballycastle lay across the valley as, 15½ miles out from Ballymoney, the grade slackened to 1 in 96 and the line swerved to the left over the four-arched stone bridge which spanned the River Tow, and which had cracked and had been repaired before the line was opened. The terminus lay directly ahead, beyond the bridge, the yard and the platforms occupying a flat-

* *This was a memorable year in the history of Ballycastle for during it a motor car appeared in the town for the first time. This was an augury of things to come, for some half a century later the internal combustion engine sounded the death knell of the line.*

No 106 on the curves at Ballylig. HA Boyd

The track layout at the Ballycastle end of the Tow Viaduct can be clearly seen in this view. There was a sawmill on the right, below the viaduct. This was rail-connected by a incline from a siding by the station platform, wagons being moved up and down by a windlass. Ian Allan Library/LGRP 13982

Ballycastle station in 1948. The siding to the incline, for the sawmill, can be seen on the left. The engine shed is in the centre of the picture with the goods store to its right and the caravan coaches beyond the loading bank. Ian Allan Library/LGRP 13983

Ballycastle station on 18 April 1948 with No 43 taking water outside the engine shed. The water tank was situated on the platform and seen be seen to the left of the carriages. HC Casserley

topped, artificially embanked area built across the north slope of the valley.

The construction and levelling of this yard were not completed when the line was opened in mid-October 1880, and because of this state of unreadiness the yard contains buried treasure. The supplies of champagne on the day of the opening ceremony were so ample that a purloined crate was not missed or, if it was, there was no time to institute a hunt. The purloiner took it to the raw edge of the yard and hastily covered it with earth, meaning to recover it in darkness after the guests had gone. Unfortunately, he was transferred that day to Ballymoney, and kept so busy for the next two or three weeks that when he found time to go down again to Ballycastle the levelled ground extended yards beyond where he remembered it. There was nothing to identify the spot, and a systematic search was impossible. So a dozen of vintage champagne, 'of the very best and choicest quality', lie buried to this day, somewhere in the remains of Ballycastle station yard.

In its latter days, after 1925, Ballycastle had a single platform on the west side of the line and so returned to something like its original state, which lasted from the opening date until 1898. The alterations in that year provided a much more imposing two-road terminus, a new platform on the east of the old station being roofed for half its length. Sidings on the locomotive running shed, the carriage shed, the goods store and the cattle dock ran off to the east of the passenger station. Near the junction of the yard lines with the platform lines, a signal cabin stood to the left of the rails but after 1925 the wooden structure was demolished, and the once polished and painted levers in their frame were left exposed. To the right, there was once a brickfield, and to the left, behind and below the signal cabin, a sawmill. After 1925, a siding was laid in to the mill, facing points running off to the west close to the ground frame. Wagons were propelled to the end of this siding and lowered down an incline by a windlass to a wagon turntable at the sawmill. It was not used after 1940.

In latter years, and after the closure of the line, four caravan coaches were placed alongside the loading bank.

LMS (NCC) Caravan No 16, a former Ballymena and Larne Railway carriage, at Ballycastle in 1948. There were four caravan coaches at Ballycastle, and they remained there after the closure of the line. Ian Allan Library/LGRP 13979

Chapter 3

The Railway at Work

Tapping the hinterland

Once the excitement of the great opening day was past, the next public gathering the Ballycastle shareholders had to look forward to was the ensuing half-yearly meeting. This was held on 26 February 1881, the sixth of the series, and before it met they were presented with the usual printed half-yearly report. Little trace of Colonel Rich's astringent comments were to be read in it:

> The works being completed for the inspection of the Board of Trade in the early part of October last, Colonel Rich, one of the railway inspectors, examined the line and passed it as fit for public service. It gave at the time much satisfaction to the Directors to hear from Colonel Rich that he was much pleased with the substantial way in which the works were made, and the entire railway completed; this information will doubtless be pleasing to the Shareholders.
>
> The line was opened for Public Service on 18th October last, and from that date to the end of the year, about 2½ months, 9,298 passengers were carried over it . . . the quantity of goods in the same period being 882 tons.

The Company ran three trains a day in each direction when the line opened. While its Ballycastle railhead served that little town adequately, the country to the west and east remained largely untapped. There was a network of roads, but no network of public transport, radiating from Ballycastle and although the passenger potential was perhaps not large, something had to be done about providing feeder services.

East of Ballycastle, the population was largely confined to lower Glenshesk, the Carey River valley and the hamlet of Ballyvoy. Beyond that, the land rose to bleak moorlands south of Fair Head, with a few scattered farms, for the most part only fit for grazing sheep. West of the town, the road system towards Bushmills was more complex. The main road to Bushmills, constructed in 1833, led to myriad small farms scattered between areas of wet bogland and scarps of basaltic rock. Up to the Bush valley there was not a great deal of arable land, while beyond that river the folk naturally turned to Coleraine or to Portrush for rail transport. Small mines of bauxite and lignite were active near Ballintoy, but their output was very limited. The long-established coastal fisheries of Ballintoy, Carrickarade and Portbraddan, mainly taking salmon, seemed likely to contribute a seasonal traffic. To make the best use of the limited local passenger and goods potential, the Company soon began to organise feeders to their railhead.

ARMOY MARKETS.

THE ABOVE MARKETS WILL OPEN on WEDNESDAY, the 3rd NOVEMBER, instant, for the Sale of PORK, BUTTER, EGGS, and GRAIN.

Pork Market every alternate Wednesday, at 10 o'clock.

Butter, Eggs, and Grain Market every Wednesday, at 11 o'clock.

A number of Buyers, local and from a distance, have promised to attend the Markets.

Owing to the opening of the Ballycastle Railway, Goods of all kinds can now be carried quickly, and at low rates, either to Belfast or Portrush.

Farmers may depend upon obtaining good Prices for their produce.

Armoy, 18th October, 1880.

From the *Ballymoney Free Press*, 28 October 1880

During the winter months, when for much of the time high seas pounded the northern cliffs, tourists would have been conspicuous by their absence. Nevertheless, in December 1880 the Company made an offer of £10 a year to John Donnelly, of Ballintoy, if he would 'run a car' between Ballycastle and Ballintoy for six days of the week.

The Minutes do not record whether this service began as intended or whether it was maintained.

The summer tourists were next catered for. In May 1881, Messrs Wegg & McHenry wrote to Silas Evans, offering to operate a four-horse coach to the Giant's Causeway from Ballycastle, if the railway company would supply the necessary vehicle. The railway company, of course, had no parliamentary authority to run their own road service, and they had, therefore, to get someone to run it for them. So they welcomed the proposal and bought a 'Defiance' coach from Croall of Edinburgh for £20. The Giant's Causeway, already referred to in connection with the Traills' tramway scheme, was on the coast ten miles west of Ballycastle and six miles east of Portrush. By 1880, it had become one of the main focal points for tourists in the north of Ireland, a balance in its way to the softer beauties of Killarney in the south. People came from far and wide to view and wonder at the remarkable range of basaltic columns, ably demonstrated under a good veneer of local folklore by a squad of guides, who were usually retired Portballintrae fishermen.

The 'Defiance' coach was timed to leave Ballycastle at 10.30am. After a terrifyingly steep descent en route at Knocksoghy Hill into Ballintoy village it arrived at the Causeway Hotel in good time for lunch. Once fortified and replete, the tourists would emerge into the daylight, attach themselves to their bearded guides and start on their conducted geological excursion. The return journey began at 5.00pm with the tourists trudging up Knocksoghy to save the horses.

Details of the history of the coach service are not recorded in the Company's records, which is not surprising as, though they owned the coach, it was not a company concern. We do know, however, that the single fares, decided in collaboration, were 2s 6d outside and 3s 6d inside, with returns at 4s 0d and 5s 0d. The box-seat, with a magnificent view or exposure to the elements, depending on the prevalent weather, cost an extra half-crown. Single fares would have been taken by people continuing on towards Portrush by whatever horse-drawn vehicle they could command at the Causeway Hotel. Then, in February 1883, the Giant's Causeway Tramway opened from Portrush to Bushmills, and in July 1887 was extended to near the Causeway Hotel.

The 'Defiance' coach seems to have fallen into disuse by the summer of 1905, for it was then lying at the chairman's residence, Clare Park, and he and the secretary were authorised to sell it. By that time, jaunting cars could be hired and the Company had no need to organise, albeit indirectly, a transport service along the northern coast. The last one notes of the enterprise is a reference at a Board Meeting on 14 November 1908 to an ". . . old coach sold for £2".

General view of Ballycastle in Ballycastle Railway Company days.
AR Hogg & Co

Tramway plans

In the 1880s, much of the old part of Ballycastle was clustered around the Diamond, and even to this day those houses, many of them whitewashed, contrast with the newer residential villas that for the greater part of its length, string down one side of the tree-lined Quay Road towards the sea and the harbour. With the growing tourist industry, the Company had second thoughts about having sited their terminus nearer the Diamond than the shore, and on 28 September 1881 there was tabled at the Board Meeting a plan and estimate for ". . . a tramway from Ballycastle to the Shore Road". It was to have cost £1850. Though no details are given, it would undoubtedly have been horse-drawn, having regard to the suggested outlay. Perhaps the distant prospect of the horse-drawn Warrenpoint and Rostrevor Tramway in the south of County Down, three miles in length and opened in July 1877, initiated the scheme. In spite of its potential, no further action was taken, for the simple reason that no funds were on hand. As it was, the Company was finding it embarrassingly difficult to settle its account with its engine builders, and was in debt with its bankers to the tune of about £4000.

Free tickets

As an inducement for people from Ballymoney and further afield to come and live in Ballycastle, and travel to work, it was decided to follow a practice already adopted by some other railway companies, and issue from May 1883 'free building tickets'. These gave the owner of a newly-built house seven years of free first class travel, provided the valuation of his property for rating purposes was over £15. A third class ticket was offered if the valuation was between £10 and £15. The first 'free building ticket' was issued to a Mr Daniel Clarke on 4 July 1883, but the scheme was discontinued in November 1902.

An actuarial problem faced the Company in October 1885, when it received an offer of £20 from a certain reverend gentleman who wanted the Company to issue him with a first class ticket for life. As the Company was then known to be in financial straits, no doubt he reckoned that it would jump at his offer. The Company first ascertained the minister's age to be 51 and, either because he had too great an expectation of life, or because the Company was not keen to establish such a precedent, it refused his offer, but asked if he would be interested in a yearly ticket. The bargaining then went a stage further, and at the next Board Meeting the directors were faced with an offer of the odd sum of £1 11s 0d for a yearly ticket between Stranocum or Dervock and Ballymoney. This they also turned down, and there the matter rested.

Town improvements

One of the most important summer attractions in Ballycastle was the annual regatta and sports. The first such event ever held in the town took place on Thursday 27 August 1879, and by July 1882 the promoters thought the time had come to approach the local railway company for a subscription. The sports track was situated on the golf course, and may still be seen. It was banked and levelled free of professional charges by Mr BD Wise, engineer of the Belfast and Northern Counties Railway. In 1882 the financial position of the Ballycastle Railway Company was such that it had, with regret, to decline to assist the local regatta and sports fixture, though the secretary was asked to tell the organisers that " . . . the Company will do what it can for supplying trains on the next day of the regatta". By 1888 things had improved to such an extent as to allow the Company to subscribe £5 to the regatta organisers. Writing of Ballycastle regatta in that year, GH Bassett, author of *Bassett's County Antrim*, stated:

> Ballycastle is a good place to witness a coast regatta. It is generally held in August each year and occurs on the day following the fair for horse, cattle, sheep and pigs (the Lammas Fair). A great deal of originality is displayed in making up the programme and much innocent sport is very keenly enjoyed on the occasion by the assembled inhabitants of the surrounding country, including a large contingent from the neighbouring island of Rathlin.

In January 1888, the Rev Isaac Purcell Barnes, incumbent of Ballycastle Church, asked the Company for a subscription towards the erection of gas lamps on the Quay Road, and the sum of ten shillings was given towards that worthy object.

The Ballycastle Golf Club dates from 1891 and was then, and for many years afterwards, a nine-hole course. In December of that year the issue of combined railway and golf tickets was agreed upon with the Belfast and Northern Counties Railway. The fares were to be divided so that the

Ballycastle Railway received 2s 0d, the golf club 3s 0d, and the Northern Counties Company the rest. Local tickets were issued as single fares from Ballymoney, conditional upon return the same day, but only to members of the Ballycastle Golf Club and provided a membership card was shown.

There are occasional references in the Board Minutes to examples of assistance which the Company gave when they could afford it: £2 10s 0d was subscribed to the Route Hunt Ball in 1891, £5 to the Ballycastle Sports in 1897, £3 3s 0d to the Ballycastle Golf Club in 1898, and £5 towards the improvement of bathing accommodation at Bath Lodge in 1900.

Even by the turn of the century certain things in the little township were fairly primitive, but an improvement committee had taken matters in hand. On 7 June 1901, the directors considered an appeal from the committee for a subscription. They agreed to help by giving:

> . . . one fifth of the total amount subscribed by others, provided the manure heaps and other nuisances deposited on the Quay and North Street be immediately and permanently removed.

During 1902, floods washed away the footbridge erected about 1876 and spanning the Margie River, and in April 1903, £30 was subscribed towards the cost of a new one. The final record of tourist assistance occurs in May 1910, when £5 was given to a journalist, Edgar S Shrubsole, towards the production of a guide book to Ballycastle and a series of newspaper articles.

The stations and their staff

Though Ballycastle had at one time the most imposing station on the system, it became so by easy stages. From 1880 until 1898 it had only a single platform, and it had no engine shed until 1884. A letter from the Veterinary Department of the Privy Council, dated 17 August 1888, complained that the Ballycastle cattle-dock was unpaved and had no water supply, and went on to refer to overcrowding in a cattle wagon on 2 August. In September 1888, the backyard at the station house was roofed, making it into a scullery. Two years later, all was not well with the station sewage, and after a complaint had been received about "a nuisance", the engineer was told to lay a covered pipe.

In August 1892, the Ballycastle stationmaster was allowed to erect a stable and, in July 1894, he was granted £3 "as part cost of a kitchen range" – which the house had, presumably, lacked until then. The same stationmaster was in residence in December 1895 and was then suspended, only to be reinstated a month later. A minute of the board meeting on 22 January 1896 then shed daylight on the stationmaster's four-year-old stable and it appears that he was busily engaged in running some sort of hackney business as a sideline, for he had to pay:

> . . . all expenses incurred during his suspension and to be allowed to keep one horse only, one month being given to him to dispose of the others.

The restrictions proved too much; by April 1896 he had resigned, and reference is then made to the Armoy stationmaster, Baillie, who tried, unsuccessfully, to get partial repayment of the cost of a 'cow house' which he had erected, or in lieu of the erection of one for his use at Ballycastle, where the Company had transferred him, complete with cow, to fill the vacancy.

At the Board Meeting of April 1897, the term 'agent' is applied to the Ballycastle stationmaster, when he was given permission to erect and run a bookstall at the station, at a yearly rent of ten shillings. In the agreement, the company also allowed him ". . . to supply light refreshments of a good quality at the stall".

A special Board Meeting was held on 25 March 1898 to consider proposed improvements at Ballycastle station. The Minutes merely record that an engine shed and a second platform were to be built, and were to have a cost between £150 and £200. The proposals were submitted to the Board of Trade, and were provisionally approved in May 1898, though the company secretary noted that Colonel Marindin:

> . . . may have to ask for the switch for passing the engine from the incoming to the outgoing road to be connected with the cabin instead of being worked as at present.

According to Mr HA Boyd of Ballycastle, this 'cross-over road' switch was never connected with the cabin and was always hand-controlled. The improvement work was contracted for by John Harvey of Ballymoney at £105, and was to be completed by 1 July, in time for the heavy summer traffic. There was also an item for £40 7s 6d with Dutton & Company of Worcester for signal lines and other fittings.

By the close of the 19th century, the Ballycastle stationmaster and his family were finding that there was

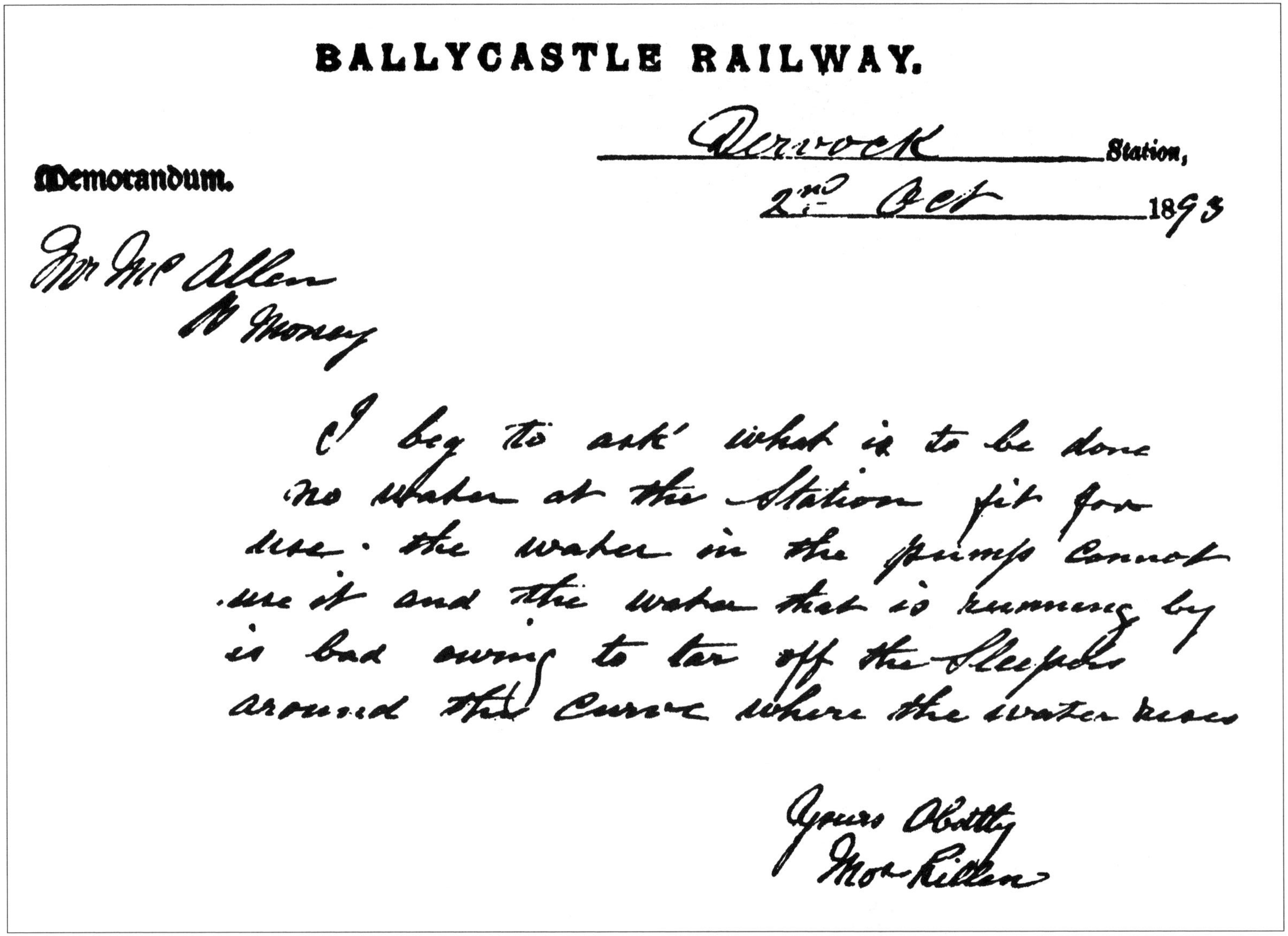

BALLYCASTLE RAILWAY.

Memorandum.

Dervock Station,

2nd Oct 1893

Mr McAllen
Ballymoney

I beg to ask what is to be done
no Water at the Station fit for
use. the water in the pumps Cannot
use it and the water that is running by
is bad owing to tar off the Sleepers
around the Curve where the water rises

Yours Obtly
Mo Killen

A copy of the letter dated 2 October 1893, from the stationmaster at Dervock to Company headquarters regarding the water supply at the station.

Ballycastle Railway Company No 3 at Ballycastle in 1911 with (left to right) John Baillie, stationmaster; Miss Baillie, clerk; James Conway, driver; Alex Dixon, guard; ?; Andrew Conway, postman; Ezekiel McLaughlin, fireman. IK McCollam

insufficient room in the station house. By May 1900 he had "... removed his family from the station house to a larger one in town". The Company approved of this transfer and used one of the vacated rooms as a left luggage office, allowing the stationmaster a proportion of receipts from the left luggage, a very fair arrangement. Then, in September 1900, he was given £6 a year "... in lieu of fire and light". What his income was at the time is not mentioned in the minutes, but in May 1907 it was raised to £60 a year.

Although trains did not stop at Capecastle until the line had been open for two years, it had the status of a station and nominally had a stationmaster. Unlike others of his ilk, he was not provided with a house by the Company, and as much of his activities originated from the products of the limestone quarry on the slope of Knocklayd, an arrangement was made whereby the quarry management carried some of the stationmaster's wages, and provided him with a free house. It is not clear when this sharing began, but a Board Minute of 15 August 1914 refers to the railway's payment as twelve shillings per week, to which the lime works company added 4s 0d.

Capecastle station was not near a village, but merely served a scattered community. Traffic was fairly light and the original station was simply a wooden shed, built by Young of Ballymoney for £11 5s 0d in the autumn of 1882. It was here that passengers to Ballycastle finally surrendered their tickets, issued (it might well be) at no less important place than Euston. After 1925, when the line was run by the LMS (NCC), the station was downgraded to a halt, and as the old wooden building had greatly deteriorated, it was demolished and its place taken by the body of a disused covered wagon.

Siding accommodation at Dervock was soon found to be needed, and a siding was laid there towards the end of 1881.

Thereafter, the station served its neighbourhood adequately for twenty years, when the local poultry society asked to be allowed to erect a store. There was some delay about this, and the building was not completed until July 1903.

The problem of large families at small stations forced the Ballycastle man to move into the town; at a later date his opposite number at Armoy became similarly affected and, in June 1912, he petitioned the directors to enlarge his house. To oblige him the Company spent £20 in incorporating a small waiting room, that was 'not being used', into the home. Word travelled fast in those parts and at the next Board Meeting a letter was read from the Stranocum stationmaster asking for similarly increased accommodation. His needs may not have been so acute, for the directors postponed action and, as nothing further was minuted, the matter probably solved itself.

The final addition to the intermediate stations came in December 1890, when the directors decided to make a platform in the townland of Gracehill, a country district about midway between Armoy and Stranocum. No permanent station buildings were erected there and the platform remained a conditional halt, where trains were scheduled to call on request or on Fair days.

A change of manager

Silas Evans, who had been the Company's secretary from the start, was elevated to the rank of manager and secretary from the beginning of July 1880. Relations with the directors were amicable enough for a time, but the differences in viewpoint subsequently became apparent, and it is significant that, though Evans never devoted his full time and energies to the Ballycastle Company, this must always have been known to his directors. Since 1872 he had been the secretary of the Ballymena, Cushendall and Red Bay Railway Company. Moreover, he was living in Belfast, and operating from an office at 9 Victoria Chambers in that city. After five years, the Ballycastle Railway was making a poor show of providing its shareholders with any profits, and in his capacity as manager the blame fell on Efans. The fact that he was living in Belfast afforded the directors an excuse. Already the Ballymena, Cushendall & Red Bay concern had been absorbed by Belfast & Northern Counties, the takeover having taken effect from November 1884.

On 28 October 1885, Evans received a letter from one of the directors, RM Douglas, requesting him to give notice, when calling the next Board Meeting, that he (Douglas) would move a motion:

> That the resolution of 30 June 1880 be so far rescinded that the Secretary and Manager be requested, for the better development of the traffic of the Railway, to reside either at Ballycastle or at Ballymoney.

Evans promptly answered Douglas in the following letter:

> Ballycastle Railway Company,
> Belfast, 29 Oct. 1885
>
> Dear Sir,
> I have your letter of 28th instant. I have been the Secretary for a very long period and I never knew of a Director sending the Secretary a notice for a motion to be brought forward at the next meeting of the Board. This I consider informal and I shall, therefore, decline to comply with your request. I shall bring your letter before the Directors on Thursday the 5 Novr.
>
> Yours truly,
> Silas Evans.
>
> RM Douglas,
> Knockanbuoy,
> Dervock.

Affairs now moved swiftly, and fireworks began at the Board Meeting on 5 November. Douglas handed in a motion for consideration at the following meeting; it read " . . . That Mr Evans' appointment terminate at the earliest possible date". Thirteen days later, while Evans sat by as secretary and manager, the Board met again. Douglas put his motion and Thomas McElderry of Ballymoney rose to second it. At the meeting, Evans had but one sympathiser, Hugh McGildowny of Clare Park, Ballycastle, who moved an amendment against Douglas's motion. But McGildowny got no seconder, and the first motion was carried. The chairman then told Evans that the Board was prepared to pay him whatever salary was due, plus £100 in lieu of six months' notice. He was then ordered ". . . to leave the Company's service in a few days and to hand over all the books, etc, in his possession belonging to the Company". Penned by the victim , the Minute Book then records that "Mr Evans then said in reply that he declined to do so". Disobedience and insubordination!

The feud continued during December, with the minuting now in the hands of a temporary secretary, TB Hamilton of Ballymoney. Evans began by claiming salary to the end of October 1885 and added a sundry account for the first half of the year amounting to £481. The Company first employed their solicitors to take steps to recover the books which Evans was refusing to give up, and then attempted to resist the claim. Evans' solicitor then served a writ for £1066 2s 8d, plus another £1000 for damages, a total that would have broken the Company financially. Inevitably, a compromise was reached, the members of the Board footed a bill of £714 19s 9d and retired to lick their wounds. Traffic was poor, receipts were down, and they could ill afford any added expense.

Control by Cotton

With Evans bought off, the directors wisely decided to place the management of their company in really sound hands. They approached the Board of the Belfast and Northern Counties Railway and an arrangement was made whereby the general manager of that Company acted in a similar capacity for the Ballycastle line. Thus the railway came under the jurisdiction of Edward John Cotton, already well established as an excellent manager, and surely one of the great characters of the Irish railway scene.

Joseph Tatlow's remarks on Edward John Cotton merit repetition:

> It is my belief that had our genial Cotton chosen the stage for a profession he would have found a place among the distinguished actors of his time, if not in tragedy, certainly in comedy. His face, voice, manner and style all proclaimed it. You had only to hear him read in public, which he loved to do, see how natural his dramatic action was, and feel the effect of a mere wave of his hand through his abundant hair, to be convinced of this. In railway circles throughout England, Scotland and Ireland he was widely known. He attended all railway conferences for he loved movement and travel. Shrewd and well informed, his knowledge was acquired not from books or study but from close observation of passing events and free and friendly intercourse with all whom he met . . . His coat may not have been cut by a West End tailor, his hat may not have been a Lincoln Bennett, or his necktie the latest production of Burlington Arcade, but who could wear a tall white hat with a black band, with the least little rakish tilt, and a light grey frock-coat with a rose in the buttonhole, with such an air and grace as he?

Cotton promptly made his arrival felt in the matter of fuel supplies and arranged for the railway to take delivery of the best Ebbw Vale steam coal for the locomotives at 15s 6d per ton. The Minutes triumphantly record that this resulted in saving 4s 0d a ton on what had been paid up to that time, and represented an annual saving of £75. Cotton followed this up by securing an improvement in the Post Office Mails contract from £125 to £300 per year, and later obtained very good contract prices for sleepers. In many ways he assisted the little company in making the best of their limited resources, and saw to it that their big neighbour at Ballymoney assisted them quietly: a Minute dated 9 June 1899 is an example:

> Mr Wise of Belfast and Northern Counties Railway offers to give 2000 feet of new rails in exchange for a like quantity of old rails and suggests the desirability of the Company purchasing an additional 2000 feet at a cost of about £120. Agreed to.

On 12 January 1898 a Special Board Meeting was called to consider the Company's finances – then in a healthy state – and to pay tribute to the man responsible. It was stated that Mr Cotton had completed twelve years as general manager *without any remuneration*. A formal resolution was moved by the veteran chairman, John Casement, and seconded by Thomas McElderry, conveying the Company's gratitude to Mr Cotton and asking him ". . . to accept a donation of £500 in recognition of his services to the Company".

Three days later, Cotton penned in reply:

> Belfast, 15th January 1898
>
> Dear Mr Casement,
>
> I find it difficult to express my thanks for the more than kind resolution passed by the Ballycastle Railway Board on Wednesday last. It is very gratifying to me to find that the Directors have taken the first opportunity afforded by their improved financial position to recognise in such a practical and generous manner the services which I have been able and pleased to render them during my connection with the Company, and I am especially gratified at the flattering term of their resolution.

> I take this opportunity of stating that during the period (12 years) in which I have had the general arrangement of your line, I have experienced nothing but kindness from the directors and other officers of the Company and any assistance which my long experience in railway matters has enabled me to offer the Company has at all times been as much a pleasure as a duty.
>
> I shall be glad if you will kindly read this letter at your next Board and oblige.
>
> Yours sincerely,
>
> Edw J Cotton

Following this striking tribute from the directors, Cotton remained as general manager of the Ballycastle Company. His tenure of office, however, lasted only another eighteen months, for he died, after an operation, on 14 June 1899. He was then seventy years of age.

Other officials

The temporary secretaryship which had followed the departure of Silas Evans was ended in April 1886 by the appointment of Hamilton McAllen as secretary and assistant general manager. Since 28 August 1880, McAllen had been the audit clerk, and he started in his new post with an increase in salary from £65 to £90 per annum. After a probationary year he received £100 a year, which after another four years rose by £30. In a small provincial town, men of McAllen's calibre and training are rare, and, as a result, in 1892 he was ". . . granted liberty to act as accountant and auditor to the Marine Hotel Company" in which some of the directors were interested. His work under the guidance of Cotton was sound and the directors recognised his worth. By March 1897 his salary had been increased to £230 per annum.

On Cotton's death in 1889, McAllen was the obvious successor and he then became both secretary and general manager, though his remuneration of £250 remained static for eighteen years, certainly a reflection on the Company's circumstances rather than on the man. It took the artificial conditions of wartime to bring him a long overdue rise of £30, granted "for the duration of the war" in January 1917, and another such increment came in the following year. Hamilton McAllen remained with the Company to the end of its independent life and then shouldered the melancholy task of acting as its liquidator, after forty-five years' service with the Company.

George Bradshaw was appointed locomotive and carriage superintendent on 25 August 1880 at a salary of £100 a year. He acquitted himself well on the new railway, and on 1 April 1885 was also given charge of the permanent way. This extension of responsibility, for which he received another £20 salary, came as a direct result of the Company's need to economise, and it coincided with the Board's decision on 25 March 1885 to dismiss their permanent way foreman, Thomas Butler, who was then getting £78 a year. In place of Butler it was decided to ". . . substitute two inspectors at lower wages . . . these men to work as other men." On Butler's dismissal, the permanent way gang consisted of three gangers, each drawing 14s 0d per week and seven men drawing 12s 0d. Economy was in the air, and the secretary minuted:

> . . . these men to be told that if they do not keep the line in order at their increased rate of payment, their wages would be again brought down to the present rate.

Bradshaw's salary received various increments which brought it to £156 by the end of 1891. In October of the following year there was an echo of Evans' day when, at a Board Meeting, a motion was put forward ". . . that Mr Bradshaw devote the whole of his time to the services of the Company"; this may well have been a minor grievance on the part of a director, for nothing more was heard about the matter and a few years later Bradshaw was earning £180 a year, Wartime brought its difficulties, and although the wages of the men were increasing, all that Bradshaw received was a bonus of £20, granted in January 1917 ". . . for extra work during the period when no fitter was employed", and in April 1918 a rise of £30 in salary.

After forty years' service, George Bradshaw was ageing, and in a Minute of a meeting of the Board on 28 February 1921 he is mentioned as being ". . . allowed to retain his temporary assistant", the first reference to such a person. On 6 June 1923 the Board was formally told of the death of George Bradshaw, and not long afterwards received an application for the position from James AQ Bradshaw, who had been his father's understudy for three and a half years. The younger Bradshaw was appointed on 18 July to follow his father, but he had joined a waning company, for within thirteen months, shortly after it had been decided to close the line, his services were terminated.

On the civil engineering side, James F McKinnon had been associated with John Lanyon in the original survey of 1877, and in November 1878 the pair were pressing the directors "for immediate payment" for services rendered. After the line opened, McKinnon remained with the Company, apparently in a consultative capacity, though no specific mention is made of his title in the Minute Books. He was not, seemingly, a salaried official when, in December 1882, he submitted his account for £118 and, preferring a bird in the hand, refused to accept the Company's alternative of £400 in shares. But he bargained, and proposed to take £600 in shares, provided that the Company made him their 'consulting engineer' at a retainer of £10 a year. The Company gave him the title he wanted but stuck to their offer of £400 in shares, and McKinnon appears to have continued as consulting engineer until his death in July 1905. He was not replaced, as by then George Bradshaw was no doubt judged to be fully competent. Nevertheless, in April 1906 an independent report was taken on the state of the permanent way from Mr Wakeman of the Great Northern Railway of Ireland.

Staff matters

On any small railway where there are only a limited number of competent men for any particular job, minor misdemeanours assume startling importance and may temporarily paralyse the system. To judge by what few written records remain, the Ballycastle men were a fairly well-behaved lot, but now and then someone broke out and came under the notice of the directors. One such occasion was in early February 1890 and disturbed the equanimity of a Sunday afternoon. The 3.15pm up train was delayed at Ballycastle ". . . due to drunkenness of the fireman and it was also stated that the driver was under the influence of liquor". Thirty-five minutes behind time, they took their train out, but continued to make it a memorable occasion for the passengers as they ". . . made use of party expressions at Dervock and Ballymoney station". It was as well for all concerned that the journey was in the up direction. Had the descent of the Capecastle bank been included in the itinerary, Ballycastle might well have witnessed an accident as spectacular and as serious as that which occurred at Donemana on the County Donegal line on another Sunday afternoon twenty-three years later.

In October 1891, EJ Cotton reported to the directors that he had placed the Stranocum stationmaster under notice of dismissal for being drunk and for neglect of duty ". . . during the last few days of August". What had happened must have been a well-kept secret, for nothing had been mentioned at the September Board Meeting. Once they heard that their stationmaster was under notice, the Stranocum people rallied round him and interceded so effectively on his behalf that it was decided he should ". . . have another chance".

The service of trains was such that the Ballycastle Company only needed two full-time drivers, both of whom became involved in differences with authority during the autumn of 1893. The trouble began in September, when Bradshaw dismissed Driver A for some misdemeanour not specifically mentioned in the Board Minute Book, though when the secretary reported ". . . that a wheel on one of the engines was broken and had been running in that condition for some time" there may well have been some connection. Driver A was aggrieved at what he considered unfair treatment, and petitioned the directors. Rather than be short of a driver, or so it would seem, he was reinstated pending an investigation by the Board.

By the following month the charges originally levelled at Driver A were extended to include Driver B, and matters became serious. Adjudicating, the directors told Bradshaw that either he must dismiss both men, or retain both with a caution. The conflict dragged on into the month of December; although Bradshaw had given them another chance, he wanted to fine them by a wage deduction of 1s per day for the odd period of thirteen months. Such a reduction in pay would have been a heavy imposition on those whose earnings were then only about 30s a week. The Board, when asked to approve the fine, considered it excessive, and instructed Bradshaw to withdraw the fine and let the matter drop. Peace reigned for less than a year. In August 1894, Bradshaw dismissed Driver A for drunkenness, and had the backing of his directors in his action.

In the early days of the Ballycastle line, the Welfare State of today was unknown, and the Company fulfilled a similar function, if in a more selective manner. At the same Board Meeting which approved a grant of £2 10s 0d to the Route Hunt Ball, 30s 0d were granted to Patrick McMullen, one of the men employed in the engine shed, "... to enable him to obtain a glass eye, he having lost an eye when on duty".

On 29 January 1892, Porter Martin was injured when his head was caught between two steps on the end of a guard's van and a carriage. Martin must have suffered quite serious injuries, for the Company eventually paid him £10 in compensation, and thereafter removed the two corner steps from the carriages.

There are various other instances of financial assistance given by the Company. In 1906, when one of the stationmasters died leaving a widow and family, the Company made them a grant of 5s 0d per week for eighteen months. Two years later, after Driver C had injured his hand, the Company paid him 20s towards his doctor's bill, and made up his insurance money to a total of 30s a week. Also in 1908, the Company saw their old ganger, who had been with them since the line opened, unable to work and paid him an "... annuity of 5s 0d (probably 5s 0d a week) during the pleasure of the Board".

Permanent way upkeep

It was fortunate that the early proposals to use 30lb or 40lb rails were not adopted as even the 45lb rails eventually used proved unduly troublesome. They were spiked to wooden sleepers, and much of the trouble undoubtedly arose from the waterlogged peat bog over which at least a third of the line passed. The difficulties were aggravated by an insufficiency of stone underlay and by bad ballast.

As early as September 1883, George Bradshaw told his directors that the permanent way was "... much out of order". When his permanent way inspector, Thomas Butler, was questioned, he did not fully agree with Bradshaw, and it was decided that two of the directors, Knox and McElderry, should walk the line in company with Bradshaw and Butler, and see whether the repairs called for were really justified.

At a Board Meeting held on 14 November 1883, Knox and McElderry admitted that the permanent way was "... not in good condition, that ballast was required in several places" and that "... they found some of the sleepers decayed". They advised increasing the strength of the permanent way staff by three men, and recommended that 500 sleepers should be bought, and the line ballasted where required. The fact that some of the sleepers were rotten after only three years on the ground was disturbing, and some were taken out and sent to a Belfast timber merchant for examination. It was then learnt that they were "... an inferior Baltic timber" and not the Riga redwood originally specified. After further expert confirmation of this finding, the suppliers were asked for an explanation. Meanwhile, Evans bought 500 redwood sleepers at 1s 6d each from Corry's, in Belfast, had them creosoted, and then hopefully presented the bill to the suppliers of the faulty material, who refused to pay it.

The repair work of 1883–84 was only moderately effective. A hard spell of frost in early 1886 made the waterlogged ballast heave badly and caused the directors to call for a report from McKinnon on the civil works. After referring to the permanent way as being "... in fair working condition", he asked the Company to purchase a quarter of an acre of land for a ballast pit and a quantity of wooden posts for fencing repairs. By July 1886 the rot had continued, and 400 sleepers were bought from J&J Knox, of Armoy, at 1s 1d each, though mention that "... a portion of them to be larch" suggests that they were locally grown softwood, which would need to be creosoted before use. In March 1897, a larger order went out under Cotton's aegis, this time for 1000 larch sleepers at 1s 4d, divided between Robert Hamilton of Cookstown and John Nicholl* of Ballycastle, As the original sleepers continued to decay, two large consignments were bought in – 3000 in November 1887 and another 3000 in February 1890. The best bargain was made in June 1899 when 500 were picked up at 9½d each.

For the first twenty years gravel ballast was used exclusively, as it was easily obtainable at the lineside from the gravel banks in the upper part of the Tow valley, between Ballycastle and Capecastle. Though it was cheap to dig and easy to spread, it tended to hold water more than did crushed stone, and this led both to decay of the sleepers and to frost damage. McKinnon made a special report to the directors in March 1902 and, as a result, Bradshaw was asked to pay special attention to wet places, of which there were probably many: then, for the first time, it was stated that only stone ballast was to be used in such places.

During the summer of 1902, Bradshaw put the permanent way gang on to the improvement of a hollow at

* *This is the same John Nicholl as mentioned in Chapter 2 above.*

Carnculliagh, and in the autumn made plans for improving the drainage of the line at Balleeny siding. In January 1903, the River Bush burst its banks in flood an inundated the line near the third milepost, so that the train service was suspended for one day. During the following summer a special effort was made to improve the standard of permanent way maintenance, and 16 men were employed until October, after which the extra hands were paid off.

During 1904, improvements to the ballasting continued. After a Board inspection in October a directive was issued for a bank in a boggy place to be raised *two feet* with new ballast, and the secretary was instructed to arrange the purchase of a piece of land from William McClarty beside their existing ballast pit, near the fifteenth milepost in the townland of Ballydurnian. In November 1904, a report on the quality of the ballast was made by Mr BD Wise of the BNCR, and it was minuted that ". . . the stuff at limestone quarries would not be suitable, but the ballast in the present pit is very good and would last ten years". More than likely the waste from the Capecastle limestone quarry had been tried as a cheap substitute for crushed whinstone.

Even though the Ballycastle Railway Company were very much under the guidance of the Northern Counties Railway, they were not averse to taking advice from the other large main line company in the north of Ireland – the Great Northern. On 14 April 1906, a report was submitted to the Ballycastle directors by Mr Wakeman of the GNR(I), following an exhaustive examination of the line. He recommended that no less than 4000 sleepers should be purchased, sufficient to relay two miles of the line. Wakeman also emphasised that stone ballast should be laid, ". . . taking the line in quarter mile portions, the worst parts first. A special gang (with ganger), say five in all, to be employed, as well as the ordinary four men". The Company was also asked to get prices for ". . . ten tons of fish plates and a few tons of heavier rails". It was probably as a sequel to this report that 500 second-hand sleepers were purchased from the North British Railway on October 1908.

Permanent way maintenance demanded continual attention, and it is evident from the directors' Minute Books that they found it hard to balance the need against their available funds. It was the practice to use the minimum labour force, and to engage additional unskilled labour as the need arose.

The acquisition of two new engines in 1908 was attended with further troubles. The engines were four-coupled, heavy and powerful, but had a low proportion of their weight available for adhesion. On 14 November 1908, the Board considered a report of a delay of fifty minutes which had occurred a few days before to the 10.30am up train, as a result of slipping at the Ballylig curves. It was decided to ease the curves ". . . as much as space will allow". More extensive work took place at Ballylig after the end of the First World War, and in February 1921 George Bradshaw was given authority to spend £1467 on repair work there. In May of the following year he suggested that the other curves on the system, those at Dervock, Chatham Hall and Ballycastle, should be relaid and the worn rails removed.

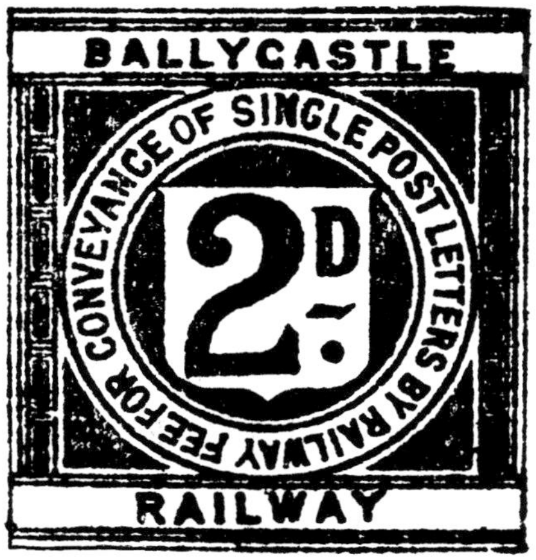

Railway letter stamp

The Dervock curve was the worst, and was relaid with 22 tons of 75 lb rails, while the others were relaid with worn rails taken from sidings. The work called for complete possession of the line by the engineering staff, and was done on Sundays as weather permitted.

For many years the Company suffered from a permanent way which had been laid too inexpensively and, as a result, failed to withstand the combined effects of weather and normal traffic. They cannot be blamed for this position, for available capital was insufficient to make the line as it should have been made. The legacy remained with the Company to the end, and burdened the balance sheet to a crippling extent. In 1922, when total expenditure amounted to 135% of traffic receipts, 'maintenance and renewal of way and works' accounted for 44.8% of that, and totalled £3769. That year they used 2520 cubic yards of ballast, 2550 sleepers and 21 tons of rails and, in addition, put up half a mile of fencing, the materials alone costing £1352. In 1923, the last complete year of independent operation, less materials were put into the line, but the total cost of maintenance was 35% of the traffic receipts.

Tow Viduct in 1948, looking northeast. The incline from the station to the sawmill ran down to the side of the whitewashed building, probably directly behind the tree. Ian Allan Library/LGRP 7361

Chapter 4

Economics

Traffic

A statement of the volume of traffic over the railway is given in most detail in the directors' reports to the shareholders, which were presented every six months up to 1913, and annually after that. The Railway Returns of the Board of Trade give a summarised version. In 1881, the first complete year, and for the next four years, the total number of passengers varied between 53,000 and 59,000.

In 1886 a marked upsurge took place in passenger traffic and the total for that year, over 85,000, showed an increase of 53% over the 1881–85 average. The closer integration with the Belfast & Northern Counties line, initiated by EJ Cotton, was undoubtedly responsible for this marked improvement, so it is perhaps unfair to couple this change with the dismissal of Silas Evans. It is noteworthy, however, that with the appointment of McAllen and Cotton to the management, the passenger traffic showed the striking increase mentioned, and moreover, maintained it for twenty-eight years, when normality was upset by the First World War.

Throughout the life of the Ballycastle Railway Company, third class passenger receipts amounted to between 91% and 94% of the total, as indicated by these results for a typical half-year (ending 31 December 1893):

	Number	*Receipts*	*Average Fare per passenger*
1st class	919	£87	1s 10d
2nd class	1337	£101	1s 6d
3rd class	32,669	£1331	9½d

When a comparison of this very high proportion of third class journeys on the Ballycastle Railway has been made for the same half-year, with other lines for which statistics are available, it is found that only the Cavan and Leitrim and the Derry Central lines were then carrying a higher percentage of third class fares. It is significant that all three lines had a purely agricultural hinterland, that there were no large industries in the towns or villages they served, so that the towns did not contribute any significant volume of what we now call commuter traffic. The connection between a lower third class component and suburban traffic is shown below:

Railway	*Percentage of passenger journeys*		
	3rd	2nd	1st
Cavan & Leitrim	96	-	4
Derry Central	94	4	2
Ballycastle	93	4	3
Donegal	89	9	2
Sligo, Leitrim & Northern Counties	87	8	5
Cork, Bandon & South Coast	85	11	4
Londonderry & Lough Swilly	84	12	4
Cork & Macroom Direct	83	12	5
Great Northern of Ireland	83	13	4
Midland Great Western	81	11	8
Great Southern & Western	81	12	7
Waterford & Central Ireland	75	21	4
Cork, Blackrock & Passage	70	-	30
Belfast & County Down	69	22	9
Waterford & Tramore	64	-	36
Dublin, Wicklow & Wexford	57	36	7

It is apparent that the bulk of the Ballycastle's clientele could only afford, and either was, or had to be, content with the standard of cushionless comfort offered by the third class. That the directors were aware of this is clear from a study of the Board Minute Books, for one cannot trace in them any specific references to attempts to popularise first or second class travel, other than the indirect concession offered by the Building Tickets, whereby the family of the house-owner might be expected to travel as fare-paying passengers in the same class. The Ballycastle Railway was firmly established from the beginning as a predominantly third class line. Indeed on many Ballycastle trains before 1896, accommodation in the superior classes must have been greatly under-utilised, though the purchase of the four bogie carriages in 1896–1900 increased the proportion of third class seats. In 1923 the coaching stock contained 83% of third class seats, 9% of seconds and 8% of firsts, while passenger journeys were 93%, 5% and 2% respectively. The chief problem for the management was the periodic one of finding enough accommodation for the heavy flood of passengers that descended upon the two termini on market or Fair days, and on the Twelfth of July. As mentioned in Chapter 7, the Company solved this problem for many years by using open wagons for the extra passengers.

Dissatisfied that there were only two classes of passenger accommodation at first, John Casement, the chairman, proposed at a Board Meeting on 6 April 1881 that second class accommodation should be provided by modifying some of the third class compartments. On this proposition being put to the meeting, the motion was defeated. Mr McElderry then moved that to encourage traffic, first class fares should be reduced and second class passengers from the Northern Counties Railway should be allowed to travel first class over the Ballycastle line. This proposal was adopted. Four years later, the decision to introduce second class travel went through smoothly at the Board Meeting on 22 April 1885.

Although second class travel only began in April 1885, it accounted for 4% of the journeys in that year. In the following year, and up to 1890, there were 6% of second class passengers, a decline then set in which brought the proportion down to 3% in 1896–99. After the turn of the century the percentage of second class journeys varied between 4 and 5. Although the introduction of second class travel coincided with the increase in total number of passengers carried, there is no casual connection between the two. Considered on the basis of total journeys, the start of second class travel was virtually without effect on the total of first class journeys. Considered on a percentage basis, the picture is different, the proportion of first class journeys fell, while third class was much less affected.

Season tickets issued by the Company show remarkable variations in number. Although only five were issued in 1880, the total became 71 in the following year and rose to a peak of 106 in 1883. From 1885 until 1901, the total averaged 46 and ranged from 26 to 72. In 1902, the total fell to 15. While the high rate of issues between 1883 and 1901 can be correlated with the house-free tickets valid during those years, it is difficult to account for the wide variations, and fluctuations in the limited commuter traffic are unlikely to have been the reason. Some of the total of season tickets are undoubtedly reciprocal free tickets issued to the managers of other railway companies, and a large proportion of the others must have been gratuitous issues made locally. The Minute Books refer to occasional issues of these; Lady Boyd, widow of the Company's first chairman, received one in April 1889; and another went to the farmer at the ballast pit in 1897.

Lack of support

The day-to-day working of the Ballycastle Railway went on against a background which was familiar to many of the smaller Irish companies, one of continual financial struggle. For forty-five years the fight to make profits went on, and for only one tenth of that period was any dividend paid to the shareholders. For the rest of the time it was a grim matter of remaining solvent.

The Act of Incorporation gave the Company powers to raise a total working capital of £135,000, two-thirds of which was to have been ordinary stock and one-third as debentures or loans. Of the expected total of £90,000 of ordinary stock, no more than £61,600 was ever taken up, and the balance of £28,400 remained unissued. This serious deficit faced the little Company squarely from the very beginning of its career, and determined the subsequent need to borrow heavily, so that the annual balance sheet was always loaded with a massive interest debt.

Even by April 1880, discussions were opened with the Irish Board of Works, and a Government Loan of £20,000 was obtained in July. This was subject to interest at 4%. Even with this loan the Company was in debt to its bankers to the tune of £4580 in August 1881. By that date it was only able to pay £100 to Messrs Butler & Fry, against a demand of £300.

Lack of ready money forced the Company to conclude an agreement for deferred payment with the suppliers of its carriage and wagon stock, through the Railway Rolling Stock Company. The stock had been estimated to cost £5280, and by March 1883 the agreement was made for a quarterly payment of £225. By April 1884, the Company had to ask the Railway Rolling Stock Company to allow the payments to lie over until the following year, and this was agreed to, but at 5% interest. The Board of Works was approached in May 1884 for a further loan of £20,000, but refused because the money was not required for new capital expenditure, but merely to pay off debts.

Matters had become so serious by July 1884 that a special Board Meeting was held on 7th to decide on future action. Three directors – Casement, Woodside and McElderry – attended, along with Silas Evans. It was decided to approach the Belfast and Northern Counties Company for a loan of £12,000 to discharge legal liabilities, or alternatively, to work the line for the Ballycastle Company. The BNCR, already holding £18,000 of ordinary stock, refused to assist.

The critical condition of the Company's finances continued into 1885 and legal advice was taken from a Mr Batten, BL, of London. He reported to the Ballycastle Board on 25 February that:

(1) The Company had no powers to issue shares at a discount.
(2) The Company could issue Lloyd's Bonds to its creditors in small amounts, to carry interest which could be recovered later by the issue of shares.
(3) Rolling stock could be sold to a company, and hired from it by an agreement to purchase it back in twenty-one years at 5% interest, plus 2½% of a redemption fund.
(4) A scheme could be obtained through the Court of Chancery to issue debentures for the amount of the debts of the Company. (This course of action was preferred by the consultant.)

To ease the situation, a loan of £350 was obtained from Messrs Casement and Thompson. A special meeting of shareholders followed upon the Board Meeting on 25 February 1885, and a committee was formed to consult with the directors as to the best methods of reducing expenses, meeting liabilities, and developing the traffic of the line. The last-mentioned crystallised into a certain Dr Kidd promising to lend the Company the limestone quarry at Capecastle rent-free for a year. A sub-committee was then formed to inquire into the lime traffic and the working of quarries in the district. Significantly, there was no mention of coal traffic making any contribution.

In mid-March 1885, the sub-committee recommended that the Company should buy in limestone, but should not attempt to quarry it, and that it should construct two limekilns at Ballymoney to burn the mineral to quicklime. Evans was asked to prepare plans for the kilns and sidings, but they were never built, and this plan to make an honest penny by going into the lime-burning trade was clearly a policy of desperation.

On 7 May 1885 the Company formally admitted that it was not able ". . . to discharge its liabilities" and that it was, to all intents and purposes, bankrupt. A week later it received a pressing request from the Board of Trade for the payment of £1650, which was overdue interest on the £20,000 loan.

The wretched state of the Company continued until 1886; on 20 October the secretary reported that the Sheriff had seized three of the carriages and was advertising them for sale. Unfortunately for the Sheriff, they did not belong to the Company: the secretary, McAllen, sent the following telegram to the Railway Rolling Stock Company: "Carriages seized by Sheriff advertised to be sold next Saturday. Shall our solicitor notice Sheriff on your account. Wire reply." As a result, the Sheriff did not proceed with the sale of the carriages, but seized instead a quantity of coal and 70 tons of rail, and advertised them in turn. It is not clear what happened next, for the Minute Book merely records that the sale was postponed at the Company's request. Another formal seizure was made in April 1890.

Messrs Casement, McElderry and Cotton met Mr Jackson, a financial secretary to the Treasury, on 20 November 1886 and extracted a promise that the matter of a loan would be laid before the Lords of the Treasury. A further sum of £23,000 was asked for, and the directors proposed to guarantee this considerable amount personally. Nothing came of the request, though it was renewed in May 1887.

Although the carriage and wagon stock had seen nearly seven years of use, more than half of their cost remained unpaid. A total of £3125 was still outstanding. The Board discussed the matter with the hire-purchase company, and it agreed to let it stand at interest and pay off a total of £5400 at the rate of £500 per annum – an unappealing prospect, but one from which there was no escape as long as the ordinary shares remained unsold. But the Company's history of zero dividend payments was now so firmly established that there was no incentive, other than local patriotism, for investors to risk their money in the hope of good times ahead. By way of compensation to the harassed directorate, there was an increase in every class of traffic during 1887, as the integration with the BNCR became evident. Henceforward, the Company began slowly to improve its financial position, thanks to the able guidance of Edward John Cotton.

A breathing space and a dividend

With a background of various Parliamentary Acts designed to assist railway development in Ireland, the Commissioners of Public Works in 1896 offered for sale their interest in the railway. The loan of £20,000, plus arrears of interest amounting to £4118, were thus acquired by the directors for £12,000, raised by the issue of debenture stocks.

At the half-yearly meeting of shareholders in August 1897, a balance of receipts over expenditure of £853 was reported. Of this total £534 went to pay off loan interest, and £319 was carried forward to credit. Six months later a dividend of 1% was declared on the Ordinary shares, and this modest rate of interest payment was continued until 1900. Over the second half of 1899 the improvement was well marked and, after meeting debenture interest, a net revenue balance of £1158 remained. The debt on the rolling stock was finally cleared off, as were some 5% mortgage bonds. Improvements had been made to the station layout at Ballycastle, and were also in progress in the matter of carriage stock. The Company was, however, balanced precariously, and the purchase of two new carriages further embarrassed it, so that on 21 December 1900 it was agreed to raise £500 in debentures ". . . to be paid to the Metropolitan Railway Carriage and Wagon Co, in part payment of their account for £902 5s 6d".

The acquisition of the new carriages left the ordinary shareholders without any reward from 1900 until 1906, when a dividend of 1% appeared again, and was raised to 2% the following year. At the half-yearly meeting in February 1907 the directors gave the shareholders encouraging news of a net balance of £615 on the previous six months' working, while they had £2768 at credit in the bank. That autumn, they felt sufficiently elated to order two new engines, costing £2380 apiece. A bank overdraft became necessary, and the slender dividend vanished for good.

War and its aftermath

War conditions from the autumn of 1914 imposed abnormal conditions on the Company. In common with all the other railways in Ireland, it came under Government control at the end of 1916 and was administered by the Irish Railways Executive Committee. Control continued until August 1921, nearly three years after the end of the war. During this period wages and costs – particularly the cost of coal – rose steeply, while fares lagged behind. Even by 1917, the Ballycastle Company was in difficulties, for at a Board Meeting on 28th it was stated that, pending arrangements with the IREC to supply funds to carry on the business of the Company, the MR(NCC) had lodged £300 to their credit as an interest-free loan. The annual meeting of the shareholders took place immediately after the board meeting, and they were told that while gross receipts were up on the previous year by £563, expenses had increased by £622, of which the bill for locomotive coal accounted for £517.

During the four and a half years of IREC direction no direct payment was received for the transport of military and naval personnel and stores, and the companies were guaranteed the same net earnings as in 1913. The receipts and expenditure alike soared high above the prewar figures, as the following abstracts show:

Year	*1914*	*1916*	*1918*	*1919*	*1922*	*1923*
Gross Receipts	£5944	£6043	£10572	£12514	£8416	£8213
Expenditure	£4208	£5042	£9455	£11326	£11398	£11266
Net Receipts	£1736	£1001	£1117	£1188	Dr£2982	Dr£3053

The matter of compensation turned out to be too complicated to be settled on the 1913 basis, and was cleared by the Irish Railways (Settlement of Claims) Act of 1921, under which a round sum of £3,000,000 was divided between the various companies and paid in several instalments. The Ballycastle Company received between £8000 and £9000, which had immediately to be set against losses in working.

The civil disorders of the troubled period from 1920 until 1921, during which Ireland was divided into two self-governing portions by the terms of the Irish Treaty, did not cause any significant damage to the Ballycastle Railway. Granted that this was only in the nature of a respite, for the Company's finances were in a parlous state and it was already apparent that, with the growth of motor traffic, there was no future for the line as an independent concern. On 17 October 1923, Messrs Casement and Woodside interviewed the Minister of Finance for Northern Ireland, the Rt Hon HM Pollock, and "... submitted to him a statement on the financial position and future of the Company".

By the end of 1923, the Company had expended £103,997 on capital account, while the total receipts from shares and so on was only £99,726. There was, therefore, a debit balance of £4271 and there had been a loss on the year's working of just over £3000. Events now moved swiftly towards the end of the Company's existence and the conclusion of the independent working of the railway. On 21 January 1924, a resolution was submitted to the Board to the effect:

> . . . that owing to the financial position of the Company it is impossible to carry on the working of the railway except at a loss, and that it is desirable to discontinue the working of the line.

On 8 February, an Extraordinary General Meeting was convened and the directors were given formal authority to close the line. Four days later the Board decided to terminate the workings on and from Monday 24 March 1924, and this news was conveyed to the shareholders at a meeting on 29 February, over which the chairman, RP Woodside, presided.

Since the Government of Northern Ireland, in spite of the recommendations of the 1922 Commission, was not prepared either to subsidise, or to nationalise, the line the only alternative was to sell it either as a 'going concern' or as scrap. The obvious purchaser was the owner of the neighbouring line – the Northern Counties Committee – which, since January 1923, had been a part of the London, Midland & Scottish Railway.

On 19 March 1924, a meeting was held in Belfast between a deputation of the Ballycastle directors and Mr F Tatlow, a member of the Northern Counties Committee. Terms of purchase were discussed and eventually Tatlow said that he was prepared to recommend that his Company give £10,000 for the whole undertaking, but free of all obligation. This figure was a disappointing one for the Ballycastle representatives, who had seen practically £104,000 go into equipping their line. But if not for scrap, it was certainly not 'a going concern'. They pressed for an increased offer but without success; Mr Tatlow stated that officials of his Company had reported that, in order to bring the railway up to the proper standard, it would be necessary to expend about £30,000 on the undertaking within the following three or four years. The unbraked rolling stock had caught up with its owners at last.

The outcome of the meeting was communicated to the shareholders who thereupon, on their own behalf, convened a meeting on 11 April, some three weeks after railway workings had ended. Dr Taggart, a solicitor in Ballymoney, attended as the representative of the majority of the debenture holders, who were on their own account negotiating with the LMS (NCC) with a view to increasing the offer of £10,000. It was pointed out that the debenture stock was amounted to £28,199 and, as considerable expenses in transfer must be incurred if the NCC's offer was accepted, the debenture holders would get about one-third of the par value of their stock, while the Ordinary shareholders would get nothing.

After further negotiations the LMS (NCC) increased their offer to £12,500. On 2 May 1924 another Extraordinary General Meeting was held, at which it was moved by Mr TM Greer, a Ballymoney solicitor, and seconded by Mr HA McAllister of Ballycastle, that:

> Having been informed that the London, Midland and Scottish Railway was prepared to offer the sum of £12,500 . . . (it) therefore hereby approves of a sale of the Company's property . . .

The summer of 1924 passed, with the rails gathering rust and the summer holiday visitors deprived of the sight and sound of their little train. The NCC reopened the railway on Monday 11 August, though they were not yet legally the owners of the line. A bill had to be passed by Parliament before that could be effected. On 13 February an Extraordinary General Meeting was held to give formal approval to the bill. Only four persons were present: Mr RP Woodside, Carnsampson, Ballycastle, in the chair; Roger Casement, Magherintemple, Ballycastle, and son of John Casement, one of the first directors; Hugh McC Hamilton, The Gables, Ballymoney; and Thomas Macafee, Currysheskin, Ballymoney. All of them were directors. Proxies were received from seven other people.

The last Board Meeting was held in Ballymoney on 8 June 1925. The secretary intimated that the bill, vesting the Company's undertaking in the LMS (NCC) was likely to receive the Royal Assent on 9 June. When that was passed, he would then take up the duties of liquidator. On the motion of Captain Lyle, seconded by Mr Casement, it was unanimously resolved that the secretary be paid his salary up to 7 July 1925. An Extraordinary Meeting was held on 3 July to decide the liquidator's remuneration, and this was fixed at 1½% of the monies received. Four days later the appointment of Hamilton McAllen as secretary and general manager ended. On 7 August 1925, the NCC was formally permitted "... to enter into possession of the line and work it".

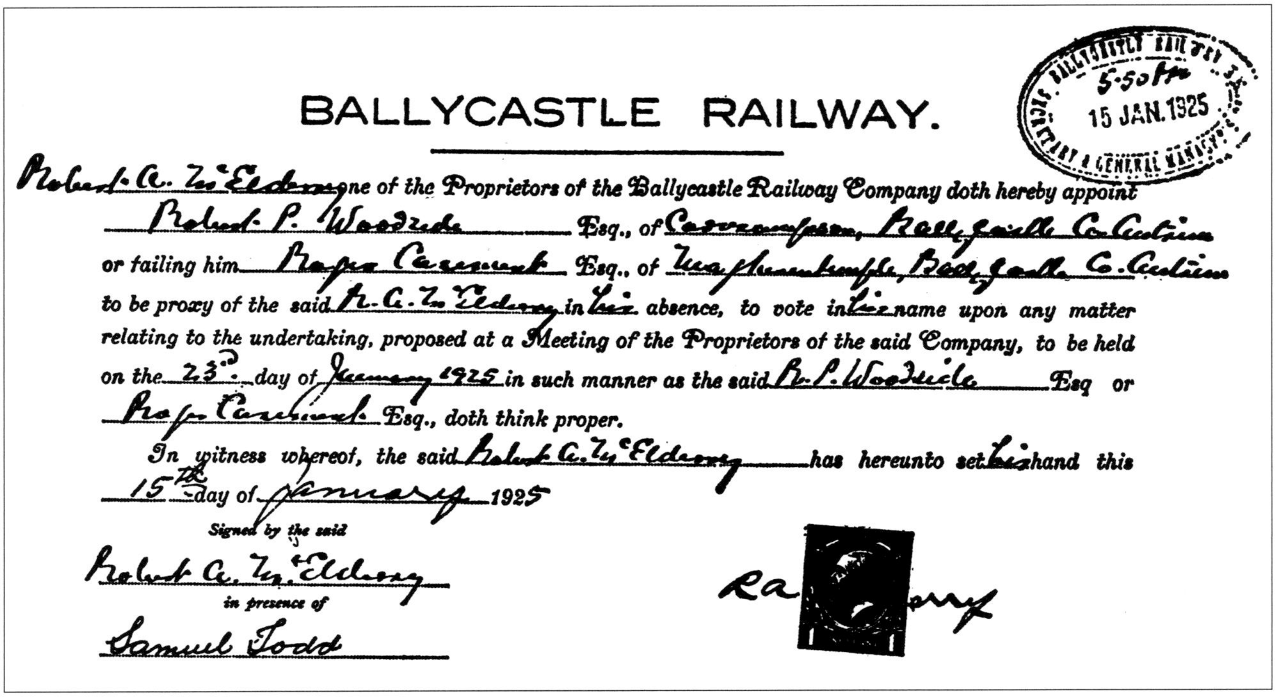

BALLYCASTLE RAILWAY.

Robert A. McElderry one of the Proprietors of the Ballycastle Railway Company doth hereby appoint Robert P. Woodside Esq., of Carnsampson, Ballycastle Co. Antrim or failing him Roger Casement Esq., of Magherintemple, Ballycastle Co. Antrim to be proxy of the said R. A. McElderry in his absence, to vote in his name upon any matter relating to the undertaking, proposed at a Meeting of the Proprietors of the said Company, to be held on the 23rd day of January 1925 in such manner as the said R. P. Woodside Esq or Roger Casement Esq., doth think proper.

In witness whereof, the said Robert A. McElderry has hereunto set his hand this 15th day of January 1925

Signed by the said Robert A. McElderry in presence of Samuel Todd

Ballycastle Railway Secretary & General Manager 5.50pm 15 JAN. 1925

The NCC reopened the line between Ballycastle and Ballymoney on Monday 11 August 1924, though they were not legally the owners of the line as a bill had to be passed by Parliament before that could be effected. An Extraordinary General Meeting of the Ballycastle Railway Company was held on 13 February 1925 to give formal approval to the bill. Only four persons, all directors, were present. They were Mr RP Woodside, Carnsampson, Ballycastle, in the chair; Roger Casement, Magherintemple, Ballycastle; Hugh McC Hamilton, The Gables, Ballymoney; and Thomas Macafee, Currysheskin, Ballymoney. Reproduced above is the form submitted by Mr Robert McElderry appointing Mr Robert Woodside to be his proxy.

Chapter 5

Life under the LMS and the UTA

Integration and simplification

While through the summer of 1924, the Ballycastle Railway Company went through the tortuous legal formalities connected with the winding-up of its affairs, the rails became red with rust. The four engines, the carriages and the wagons lay silent and unused in the sidings at Ballymoney and elsewhere. The public found their rail link gone, and on 29 March 1924 the *Coleraine Chronicle* commented:

> The Ballycastle Railway Company, pursuant to notice, have closed down their line, and there is no longer any railway service between Ballycastle and Ballymoney.
>
> The closing is due to the fact that for some time the line has been run at a loss. The services of all the staff have been dispensed with except a few patrol men and the stationmasters at Dervock, Stranocum, Armoy, Capecastle and Ballycastle, who for the time being are retained in order to take care of the various station premises. The rolling stock is housed partly at Ballymoney, and partly at Ballycastle.
>
> Very serious inconvenience has been occasioned by the closing down of the line and the withdrawal of railway facilities. Merchandise to Ballycastle and the intermediate towns has now to be conveyed by road, motor-lorries and horse-drawn vehicles being employed for the purpose. The plight of passengers who wish to reach Ballymoney or places further afield is very awkward, since there is no regular service for this special purpose.
>
> The difficulty is to some extent met by the fact that a motor service for the conveyance of mails to and from Ballycastle and Ballymoney and the intermediate towns was instituted on Monday morning. The motor vehicle leaves Ballycastle at 7am and catches the morning trains northward and southward at Ballymoney, returning with the mails to Ballycastle at 9.50am.*
>
> There is a similar service in the afternoon connecting with the usual afternoon trains at Ballymoney. As a result the old prewar delivery of letters at 6pm in Ballycastle has been revived, but there is no longer an early afternoon delivery of letters. There is but one outward and one inward mail service for the intermediate districts named above.
>
> There is much anxiety to have the service restored, and hopes are entertained that the LM&S (NCC) Company may do so.

Meanwhile, the new owners were taking stock of their assets and were making arrangements to re-start working. It would have been uneconomic merely to continue to operate the line as formerly, for the last few years' reports had shown a rapidly increasing debit balance. It was obvious that the railway was considerably over-provided, not only with engine power and rolling stock, but also in the matter of staff. Four engines were more than was necessary to maintain the proposed service, while for the entire life of the independent Company the presence of 59 wagons had been more of an embarrassment than a necessity. The carriage stock had been adequate, except on Fair days. The line was a potentially useful adjunct to the NCC system, but if it were to become economically viable, drastic simplification and streamlining were necessary.

The flitting

The actual movement into Ballycastle of the NCC rolling stock and personnel took place on either Friday 8 or Saturday 9 August 1924, when an engine, with a dead engine, carriages, two brake vans and a number of wagons were worked from Ballymoney to Ballycastle. On this train there travelled the staff who were to re-open the stations and run the line. In charge was Inspector W Getty, who remained over at Ballycastle for the opening, and with him there was Inspector J McDonald. At Dervock, Reliefman E Grant

**This was a taxi driven by Mr Hugh Simpson.*

was set down to open up and take charge, and at Armoy, Reliefman D O'Neill. Reliefman T Rainey and J Davidson were conveyed to Ballycastle where the former acted as stationmaster and the latter as signalman. The guard of the train was Billy Waterman, and he took over the duties of guard on the re-opened line on the following Monday, and stayed for six weeks. The train was driven by Bob Kirkpatrick, with Jack McDuff firing to him – a combination that knew the road well, for they were both ex-Ballycastle men. Also on the train were Driver James McKissick and Fireman R Kemp, who were being transferred from the broad gauge to form the second engine crew.

Some time later, when working had settled down, permanent staff were appointed. George Wilmot took over the guard's duties from Billy Waterman. At Dervock, the relief man's place was taken by Halt Attendant W Pollock, while at Armoy, W Laverty took over. The first permanent stationmaster at Ballycastle was Stewart Laverty; later occupants of the office were Charles McDaid, Wilson Madill and TM Hutchinson.

Rolling stock replacement

A critical survey had already been made of the Ballycastle Company's engines and rolling stock. The two saddle-tank engines, *Dalriada* and *Countess of Antrim*, were soon to need new boilers and rather than expend money on engines which had seen nearly half a century of use, and which moreover were non-standard in NCC terms, it was decided to scrap them. Although the two Kitson tanks were heavy and clumsy – they slipped notoriously – they had the merit, in spite of their poor reputation, of being still comparatively young, so that the cost of necessary heavy repairs could be justified. So they both went to the LMS (NCC) shops at York Road, and after modifications were used on the Ballymena and Larne section. Only one of them, the former No 3, renumbered 113, ever again returned to the Ballycastle line, and that was for a short period some twenty years later.

The Ballycastle carriages, six-wheelers and bogies alike, and the wagons, were all time-expired. Lacking continuous

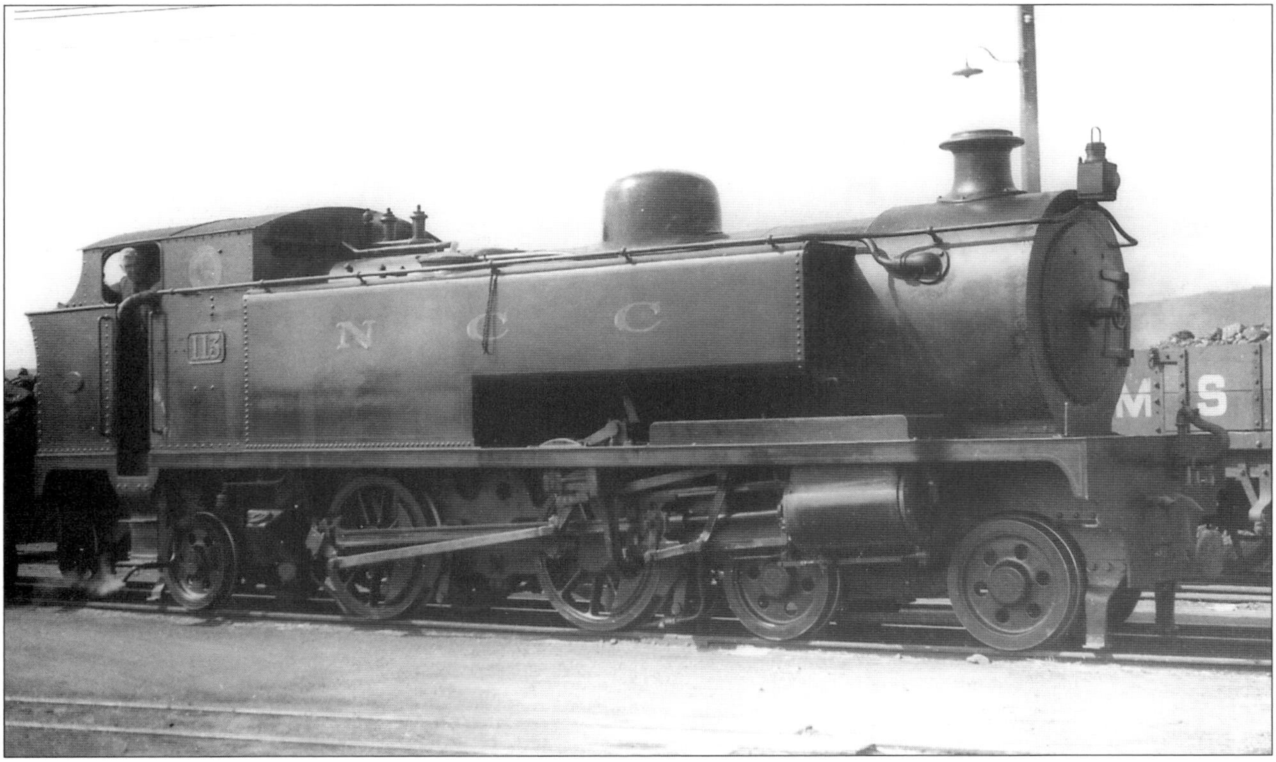

Above: *When rolling stock from the narrow gauge lines required attention at York Road works, it had to be moved to Belfast on a transporter wagon such as this, seen at Ballymena on 9 August 1930. A view of No 102 on a transporter wagon can be found on page 102.* HC Casserley

Right: *No 43 returns to the narrow gauge rails at Ballymoney having been moved from York Road works on the transporter wagon. This wagon was a six-wheeler, 35'6" in length and could carry a load of 35 tons. It was built in 1926 and numbered 3045.* KA Benington

Opposite: *No 113, possibly at Ballymoney.* CP Friel collection

brakes, they were out-dated by any standard. Replacement vehicles were easily made available from the Ballymena lines, but the different buffer height inhibited mixing the two breeds. Thus the entire Ballycastle carriage and wagon stock was declared redundant, and was auctioned locally. The carriages played their part in the new fashion of the 1920s – the desire to own a seaside cottage away from the week's work in Belfast. Caravan coaches were not yet in vogue, cartage was still fairly cheap, and the carriage bodies found ready buyers. They finished up in various fields around the North of Antrim, where their new owners modified them as they saw fit.

With excellent maintenance facilities now available at Belfast, the small workshops at Ballymoney were closed and dismantled. The Ballymoney engine shed shared in the demolition. At long last, a transfer siding was provided at Ballymoney to permit the easy loading of narrow gauge stock on and off the broad gauge transporter wagons.

Post-war conditions, and the decrease in the iron ore and bauxite traffic in the south of the county, had produced a surplus of motive power and rolling stock on the narrow gauge lines that ran out of Ballymena, to Parkmore and to Larne. The three saddle-tanks of the old Ballymena, Cushendall and Red Bay Railway had all been scrapped by 1924, but eleven narrow gauge engines were still at work. Five of these had begun work in the days of the Ballymena and Larne Railway, while two had been purchased new by the Belfast and Northern Counties Railway Company, and four had been built at Belfast by the Midland Railway (NCC). These engines were then of four different classes, and eventually representatives of three of these classes found their way to the Ballycastle line.

Operating changes

The changed conditions led to drastic simplification of certain aspects of the operating side. The headquarters offices at Ballymoney were closed, and overall control was centred on Belfast, while local administration was moved to Ballycastle. The wooden locomotive shed there was retained for some years, but was later replaced by a concrete building of unmistakably NCC parentage, capable of holding two engines which was all that was needed to work the line. Light repairs were done in a pit at the back of the shed, the fitter coming up from Ballymena shed when needed.

Throughout the Ballycastle Railway era, Armoy had been a passing place, but under the new regime the loop was removed, making the entire line single track, so that it was operated as one section. Only Ballycastle retained the status of a station, Dervock and Armoy being worked as attended halts. Stranocum, Gracehill and Capecastle were reduced to unattended halts without parcels or goods traffic facilities. Only Ballycastle handled the entire range of passenger, parcels, goods, mineral and livestock traffic.

Down at Ballycastle, the station buildings were judged to be unnecessarily elaborate, and under the supervision of SF Jones, one of the NCC's civil engineers, the station was largely demolished. The station house, with its bay window, was extensively remodelled so as to present a flat front to the platform on which it stood. The booking office with its pendant clock, the second platform, its wooden awning and the diagonally-slatted fence erected in 1898, were all swept away and the place reverted to the unilateral simplicity of its earliest days: a simplicity which the Ballycastle Railway Company had tried so hard to grow out of in its short-lived period of prosperity. Even the signal box that squatted on the verge of the embankment above Nicholl's sawmill was deemed unwanted, and was taken to pieces, leaving Pat Duffin's geraniums and the ten-lever ground frame alike exposed to the elements. The townspeople of Ballycastle were more than a little indignant and shocked at the transformation so rudely wrought by the new owners; their local pride was wounded, for undoubtedly the re-modelled station lacked much of the snug character of its predecessor.

At other places signalling was simplified now that single line working was in force over a single section stretching from Ballycastle to Ballymoney. Stranocum perhaps suffered the worst, for the six-lever signal cabin with its remarkable array of distant and home signals, points and points lock levers, was dismantled, and a Pinkerton's Box substituted to control the siding. The signal with arms on each side, that had stood in the centre of Stranocum station, was hewn down. Dervock and Armoy also had their signal cabins demolished and replaced by Pinkerton's Boxes.

Renewals

Apart from the curves, much of the track was still laid with the original 45lb rails. The NCC gradually replaced these with 60lb rails, with spike, soleplate and bolt fastenings, and 6-bolt, L-section fishplates. Extensive re-ballasting and re-sleepering was done on a long-term basis. To save the expense of running a special ballast train, the NCC adopted the rather unsatisfactory practice of combining ballasting jobs with normal working of down trains. For example, the mid-morning mixed from Ballymoney might stop along the line, between stations, while permanent way men threw off sleepers or shovelled off ballast from one or more wagons, and the passengers either watched, fascinated, from lowered windows, or grumbled at the delay. Such was the writer's introduction to the line in the early 1930s, and it seemed then an entirely appropriate way of beginning a holiday. The practice obviously saved much time and expense, but it did not endear itself to the regular passengers, particularly Ballycastle people who were frustrated on their return journey, and who saw in these stops for ballasting a clear indication of the NCC's disinterest in their welfare, rather than one of the ways by which their little railway's existence was being prolonged.

In connection with the provision of new centre-corridor rolling stock in 1928, a profile train was made, to check bridge clearances. It was worked over the two Ballymena narrow gauge lines, and then taken over the Ballycastle section before construction of the stock began. The train was worked from Ballymoney to Ballycastle through a snow-covered landscape on Sunday 23 January 1927, and was hauled by locomotive No 107.

Once established, the working of the Ballycastle section went on efficiently and uneventfully, and the ruffled feelings of the Ballycastle folk were somewhat smoothed by the eventual arrival of comfortable bogie carriages, a total of five being eventually assembled after the passenger traffic ceased between Ballymena and Larne in 1933. The day of the famous Lammas Fair continued to maintain its tradition of heavy passenger traffic, and the periodic sheep fairs at Ballycastle contributed their share to the income. For sheep transport, a rake of open wagons was assembled and kept for this purpose; termed the 'sheep cages', they had an awning of heavy netting wire stretched horizontally across to prevent the occupants from jumping to freedom while in transit.

Weathering the war

Unlike its effect on other parts of the NCC's system, the Second World War did not exercise much impact on the Ballycastle section. The heavy troop-trains to and from Larne Harbour passed by unnoticed, though many of the military personnel travelling through Ballymoney must have been intrigued by the glimpse of the narrow gauge train across the platform. Likewise, the German bombers, which created such havoc by fire and high explosive on the NCC's terminus at Belfast in April 1941, caused no damage in north Antrim. It is believed that only one special train conveying military personnel ran on the section. The normal quota of carriages was sufficient to carry the occasional military parties to the rest-camp which had been established at Ballycastle. For most of them, it must have been their first acquaintance with narrow gauge railway travel. On at least one occasion, while still in Ballymoney, the uniformed occupants of Carriage No 318, discovered its soft suspension, and how by united effort, properly timed and aided by song, the whole carriage body could be made to rock. And rock it they did, from side to side, until the entire train crew wondered how long it would be before it left the rails.

A more serious aspect of wartime concerned the Ministry of Food's policy for the decentralisation of foodstuffs, particularly from localities vulnerable to air attack. As part of this scheme, such essential commodities as flour, tea and sugar, which would normally have been concentrated in wholesale warehouses in Belfast, were stored in provincial towns such as Ballymena, Ballymoney, Ballycastle and Coleraine. A double traffic was thus created for the railways since, in addition to dispersing the foodstuffs to these centres, the stocks there were kept turning over and the same traffic would be hauled back to the city some months later. Because of the shortage of storage accommodation in Belfast, this policy of dispersal went on even after the risk of air raids had passed. One major item in this distribution of essential foodstuffs was the urgent conveyance on one occasion of 800 tons of flour from Belfast to Ballycastle within one week. The narrow gauge line coped well with this unexpected strain – it would have represented about three years' flour traffic in the days of the Ballycastle railway Company – and the traffic was delivered well within the allotted time. Several months later it was all worked in the reverse direction.

Trial by snow

In the north of Antrim, snowfall is often less severe than in inland parts of Ulster, and although the Ballycastle trains had been troubled by snow from time to time, it was never considered necessary to fix snowploughs to the engines.

In the memorable hard weather of early 1947 the line was paralysed by a particularly heavy fall of snow, which drifted in a severe northerly wind. It was 12 March, and it had been snowing all day. The afternoon down train, headed by No 41 with Barry Limerick driving, had encountered drifts between Armoy and Capecastle but struggled through them. For the last up train there were seventeen Belfast passengers and NCC's Ballymena engine fitter, McCrum, and his helper. It was uncertain whether the up run should be attempted; Limerick and the guard, Jimmy Irons, explained the condition of the road to the passengers, and were implored to try and get them to Ballymoney, as the first stage homeward. As Barry Limerick tells it:

> It was grand until we passed Capecastle. She went into the first drift and she shouldered herself out of it. The second drift was the same, and again she got through it. Then when we went into the third drift, she pushed and pushed and pushed till she stopped altogether. It was pitch blackness.

They were then close to milepost 11¾, on a level piece of line between Capecastle and Armoy, with ahead of them a rise at 1 in 121 through a cutting and below an overbridge. So struck they were:

> Then I couldn't get back, with that much snow around the brake van, or I'd have put the brake van off the road. We were lucky enough, for there was a farmhouse just beside us – Delargy they called him – and Jim Delargy came across to see how many passengers there were. He brought across a bag of bread and a great big buttermilk can of tea, and as many cups as he could carry. We stayed there all that night, with the passengers huddled in the van. There was a fire in the van at first, but it was briquette coal. Now briquettes burn all right in the engine with a draught, but there was no draught in the van. So we tried to burn the briquettes as best we could, and kept poking them, and the more we poked, the more they went out . . .

Driver Barry Limerick on the footplate of No 44 on 16 June 1950. In his spare time, Barry taught the violin.
EM Patterson, courtesy CP Friel

The next day a relief train got through to them from Ballycastle and took off the passengers, bringing them back to their starting point a day after they had left it. The engine crew and the guard stayed there all that day, with their engine still embedded in a six foot drift. The second night out they spent in Delargy's house, sitting in the farm kitchen around the turf fire, while draughts from the blizzard outside crept under the half doors. The next day about 100 men were dispatched from the labour exchanges and dug out the cuttings, freeing the engine and its train at 3.00pm, as dusk was gathering on the third night.

The runaway trains

It was rather remarkable that, during the forty-four years when the Ballycastle rolling stock had no continuous brakes, there was never a runaway on the Capecastle bank. It was equally remarkable that when the inevitable did occur, it was in LMS days, with modern, fully-fitted carriage stock in use.

The first such incident occurred on Saturday 9 January 1943, when No 41 was bringing down a heavy train of two carriages, ten 8 ton wagons and a brake van. The wagons were, of course, unbraked, and each contained about ten tons of artificial manure. James McKissick was driving, with Heffron firing to him. On the straight section below the Ballylig curves the train got away on them. Bob Devenny, in the van, once he felt the speed increasing, put on his van brake, but it failed to hold the train and the van probably skidded a good part of the way down the hill. The heavy wagons took control, and literally heaved the carriages and the engine ahead of them. Fortunately

No 41 got stuck in a snowdrift, between Capecastle and Armoy in March 1947. The location has now been identified as being about 250 metres on the Armoy side of the bridge under the A44. Delargy's farmhouse was to the rear of the train, at the far end of the narrow field bounded by the railway and the hedge. The photograph above was taken from a Miles Gemini Mark 1 aircraft, specially chartered from Londonderry Air Charter Ltd, Newtownards, with Wing Commander TWT McComb OBE as pilot.

Belfast Telegraph (above)/ TM Hutchinson (below)

nothing derailed at the dangerous left-hand bend over the Tow viaduct, though the relieving crew, Barry Limerick and Jack McDuff, who had been watching the rake's progress down the bank, were fully expecting the engine to leave the road there. What speed they reached on the 1 in 50 will never be known; it was popularly estimated at a mile a minute, but it was probably nearer 40 mph and certainly was much more than McKissick's usual creeping entry. John Heffron was standing on the lower step as they entered the station and as soon as they were clear of the points he jumped clear. McKissick stayed on the footplate, doing what he could to slow the train. But '41' went through the buffer stop, taking it with her "like a piece of paper", demolished the fence, crossed the roadway, went through another fence, and finally went down a bank into a small stream, but luckily stayed upright. The carriages straddled the roadway at a point where omnibuses usually waited. McKissick had some minor head and body injuries and suffered from shock, but nobody else was much hurt, and the train was almost undamaged. A gang of 60 men worked all Saturday night to get the carriages back on the line, and traffic was resumed on Sunday. It took nearly a week to raise the engine from the stream bed.

The second runaway was a milder affair, and occurred on Tuesday 4 January 1949 after a snowfall. It was really more in the nature of a grand skid on a frosty rail by the 11.05am ex-Ballymoney, a mixed train with four wagons, following a rather fast entry into Ballycastle station. It would have been Barry Limerick's train, but he had been off ill and Jack McDuff was handling No 44, with Anthony McKinnley, the cleaner, firing. When the brakes were applied to bring the engine to a stand by the stationmaster's window, she slid on, taking the stopper with her and finished on her side in the roadway. The carriages stayed on the line and, apart from a slight shaking, the passengers were none the worst for their experience.

Coal in hampers

One of the endearing features of the Ballycastle section during NCC days concerned the use of wicker baskets, or 'hampers', for storing and conveying coal. Steam coal was brought to Ballymoney in a broad gauge flat, which was run in on one side of the coal stage. On the stage were the hampers, perhaps a dozen or so of them, like huge wastepaper baskets, and these were filled from the broad

No 41 ended up in a stream at Ballycastle on Saturday 9 January 1943 when it ran away with a heavy train of two carriages, ten wagons and a brake van. No 41 remained here for almost a week.
IK McCollam

On Tuesday 4 January 1949, No 44, arriving at Ballycastle with the 11.05am from Ballymoney, slid on frosty rails and ploughed straight through the buffers. Fortunately, the carriages stayed on the line. IK McCollam

gauge wagon. To coal the Class S engines, the small bunker on the fireman's side was filled, and the contents of an extra couple of hampers piled against the boiler. Finally, four hampers were emptied on the footplate opposite the firebox doors, making enough in all for the double journey. On the down trip, the crew stood literally ankle-deep in coal. For lighting up the spare engine, a small stock of lump coal was occasionally brought down to Ballycastle in a couple of hampers, which made the journey perched conspicuously between the buffer beam and the smokebox door. In due course, the empty hampers were returned the same way. While the use of hampers might not have withstood modern work study techniques, it served its day well.

Grinding to a halt

The decline of traffic on the railways of Northern Ireland was neither an isolated nor a new phenomenon. It had started after the end of the First World War, the result of inflationary rises in the cost of materials and manpower, Governmental pegging of rates and fares, and the upsurge of road traffic. As the process gathered momentum in the 1930s, it was apparent to many that the existence of the railway was threatened. Many of the lines had ceased to be profit-making, and there was no evidence that action either by the owners or by the Government could reverse that process. The six counties as many separate railway or tramway concerns, which grouping might have rendered less vulnerable the prevailing circumstances. But a lethargic Government merely postponed the day when they would have statutorily to integrate the systems, and it was apparent that if railways were to exist at all they would have to do so with a subsidy from the taxpayer.

The Second World War forced the railway into an unnatural period of apparent health, when profits were again made, but as soon as hostilities ended the railways speedily reverted to their prewar plight. A decade before, the multitudinous omnibus companies and road

No 44 being coaled at Ballymoney on 28 June 1950 with Harry Mooney (above) and Jack McDuff (below). The coal stage was originally of timber construction but was later rebuilt in brick. EM Patterson, courtesy CP Friel

No 44 stands by the coaling platform at Ballymoney on 28 June 1950. The broad gauge line was to the right, the coal being transferred from wagon to engine in wicker baskets or 'hampers'. In this view Jack McDuff heaves a coal hamper on to the footplate. Note, too, the coal piled across the firebox. EM Patterson, courtesy CP Friel

haulage firms had been grouped into the nationalised Northern Ireland Road Transport Board, and the services which it provided competed with, rather than complimented, the existing railway services. Unified control of both road and rail was clearly necessary, and the first steps towards it came about when a Government White Paper, *Public Transport in Northern Ireland*, was issued in 1946. The next stage was the passing of the Transport Act (NI) which became law on 10 August 1948. From this Act there was constituted the Ulster Transport Authority, which commenced work on 1 October 1948.

At first the UTA consisted of the NIRTB and the Belfast and Co Down Railway. It did not include the NCC but, in fact, the incorporation of that concern had already begun. From 1 January 1948 the NCC had been transferred 'as a going concern' to the NIRTB, subject to the passing of the Transport Bill. Simultaneously, its cross-channel owners, the LMS, ceased to exist, for it was among the undertakings that passed with its assets to the British Transport Commission, and it went to form British Railways. The BTC was quick to shed the profitless anomaly of its Irish possessions, which included, as well as the NCC, the Dundalk, Newry & Greenore Railway. After valuation of the NCC at £2,668,000, its sale to the NIRTB was arranged, but the event did not legally take place until 1 April 1949. From that inauspicious date therefore, the old NCC system became a part of the nationalised UTA. Like its British counterpart, the UTA was charged with making its revenue cover its expenses.

The NCC was always extremely efficiently run, and its management had kept under constant review the position of its non-paying branch lines. Even before the Second World War, a considerable mileage had been closed to passenger traffic. There had been included in this the two narrow gauge lines out of Ballymena, as well as some broad gauge branches which experience had shown were hopelessly uneconomic. Post-war events had shown that certain other substantial portions of the system had become non-profit-making, and could no longer be carried along by the main lines. The Ballycastle section was among them.

So far as the Ballycastle line was concerned, part of its non-viability was due to the need to maintain non-standard stock for the narrow gauge. In 1948, serious official consideration was given to re-gauging the section, and making it a normal branch. Notwithstanding the need to strengthen and widen the underbridges, it is likely that the scheme would have been carried through, had it not been for the more serious obstacle of the Capecastle tunnel. The bore of this was not sufficient to take broad gauge trains, and it was evidently considered that the considerable expense of enlarging it could not be justified.

In the early part of 1950, the UTA gave notice to the public of its intention to withdraw certain services from 82 miles of broad gauge and 28 miles of narrow gauge track of the old NCC. Of the former, the goods workings to Draperstown, Dungiven and Ballyclare were to end, and much of the Derry Central road was to close. The long branch to Cookstown was to be retained for goods traffic only. On the narrow gauge, the 28 route miles were made up of the 16 miles between Ballymoney and Ballycastle, and the 12 miles that still remained of the old Ballymena and Larne Railway, on which the goods traffic had dwindled to an occasional goods train between Larne and the Ballyclare Paper Mill.

The public were empowered to lodge formal objections to the proposed railway closures and to ask to have their case examined. Though this had been done in connection with certain proposals affecting the County Down lines, no formal objection was raised against the Ballycastle proposal. The way was then open for the UTA to effect the closure. The withdrawal date was advertised on and as from Monday 3 July 1950, and since there was a Sunday service, the last train ran on 2 July.

On that evening, the last up train left Ballycastle at 6.30pm and was double headed, with McKissick and Heffron on No 41 piloting Limerick and McDuff on No 44. They had four carriages and two brake vans behind, and in an attempt to liven the sad occasion someone had brought out coloured paper-chains from a forgotten Christmas and draped them round the funnels smokeboxes, to cover the UTA's funereal livery. So, with paper decorations dancing in the breeze, they crossed the Garry Bog, breasted the last hill, and ran alongside the main line to Ballymoney platform. Only a handful of interested people greeted its arrival, or travelled on the little train. The two engines, uncoupled from the carriages, ran together up to the buffers and backed down to the tank for water. An hour later, and two carriages lighter, the last down train went away at 8.50pm, into the brightness of that northern summer evening with No 44 piloting now, bunker first down to the sea and to silence. For McKissick and McDuff, veterans of the line, that last run meant retirement; for Limerick and Heffron a return to broad gauge.

The line remained in a state of suspended animation for over three years, during which the track became progressively less serviceable, as the drainage choked, the ballast grew weeds and the sleepers rotted. In 1951/2, three carriages were sold to the County Donegal Railways Joint Committee, but that

Fireman Jack McDuff applying the long feeder to No 101 outside Ballycastle shed in June 1939. EM Patterson

concern had no need for engines. It was not until 31 August 1953 that the necessary Abandonment Order was made. On 21 January 1954, the Ballycastle–Stranocum section was sold, and on 1 July 1954, the Stranocum–Ballymoney portion followed. The engines were cut up were they stood, leaving only a line of camping coaches in the Ballycastle yard to bear mute witness to the railway that had brought them there, and to the lost case of champagne below the ballast.

ULSTER TRANSPORT

WITHDRAWAL OF RAILWAY SERVICES

BETWEEN BALLYMONEY AND BALLYCASTLE

On and from MONDAY, the 3rd of JULY, 1950, the Section of the Authority's Narrow Gauge Railway Line between Ballymoney and Ballycastle will be closed to all passenger and goods traffic, and Railway Services will no longer be available at the following Stations and Halts:

DERVOCK	ARMOY
STRANOCUM	CAPECASTLE
GRACEHILL	BALLYCASTLE

Time Tables of Augmented Road Passenger Services

Road Services will replace the Railway Services to be withdrawn.

Time Tables of the Road Passenger Services are shown on Pages 284-285 and 346-348 of the large combined Time Table, and on Pages 110-111, 140-142 of sectional Time Table No. 5, dated 19th June, 1950.

A Leaflet Time Table will also be available to the public on Friday, 23rd June, 1950, and may be obtained on application at local offices and depots of the Authority.

Issue of Railway Tickets

Rail fares between Ballymoney and Ballycastle and intermediate halts will be cancelled and bus fares will apply.

The issue of ordinary railway tickets from Ballycastle to stations beyond Ballymoney (including Cross-channel stations) will be continued. Passengers must obtain such tickets at Ballycastle station before boarding omnibuses.

Similarly, through ordinary railway tickets will continue to be issued to Ballycastle from the Northern Counties stations and Cross-channel stations.

These tickets will be valid by connecting omnibuses from Ballycastle to Ballymoney and vice versa. In addition, tickets issued to stations south of Ballymena will be available by connecting omnibuses from Ballycastle to Ballymena and vice versa.

Unexpired Railway Tickets

Passengers holding unexpired railway tickets may travel by bus without extra charge during the period of their validity. If the holders wish to surrender such tickets appropriate refunds will be made.

Parcels by Passenger Services

Parcels will be accepted for conveyance by the Authority's services at Ballycastle station as heretofore. Parcels not exceeding 56 lbs. will be accepted at Stranocum and Armoy by the Parcels Agents enumerated below for conveyance by omnibus services.

The Authority's representation in the area will be as follows:

Mr. J. M'Callion, District Traffic Manager, Ulster Transport Authority, The Railway Station, Coleraine. Phone, Coleraine 466.

BALLYMONEY STATION—Phone, Ballymoney 5.

STRANOCUM—Miss A. Cross, Grocer, Stranocum (Bus Parcels only).

ARMOY—Mr. C. Malloy, Grocer, Armoy (Bus Parcels only); F. & A. Cusick, Post Office, Armoy (Phone, Armoy 200): Freight.

BALLYCASTLE STATION—Phone, Ballycastle 365.

The Authority are confident that the Transport requirements of the Public will be fully met by the new arrangements, but if any further information is desired, the public are invited to communicate with the above, or with Mr. R. E. M. Hughes, Passenger Manager, or Mr. H. C. Botshi, Acting Freight Manager, Headquarters, 21 Linenhall Street, Belfast.

ULSTER TRANSPORT AUTHORITY

22nd June, 1950.

This notice, issued by the UTA on 22 June 1950, confirmed the withdrawal of rail services and gave details of the replacement bus services and arrangements regarding through ticketing, parcels, etc. It is interesting to note that through rail tickets could still be issued to and from stations in Great Britain.

Near the end of services, Nos 43 and 44 are seen outside the engine shed at Ballycastle. No 44 would pilot No 41 on the last train into Ballycastle. CP Friel collection

Shortly before 6.30pm on that first Sunday in July 1950, a young enthusiast poses by No 41 as it is made ready for the final departure from Ballycastle. CP Friel collection

Ballycastle station slumbers peacefully in 1953. It looks like the next arrival could be due any time, but the only rolling stock still visible at Ballycastle are a couple of vans, carriages Nos 350 and 353 and the line of caravan coaches. A replacement Ulster Transport Authority bus rests by the station building. Stations UK

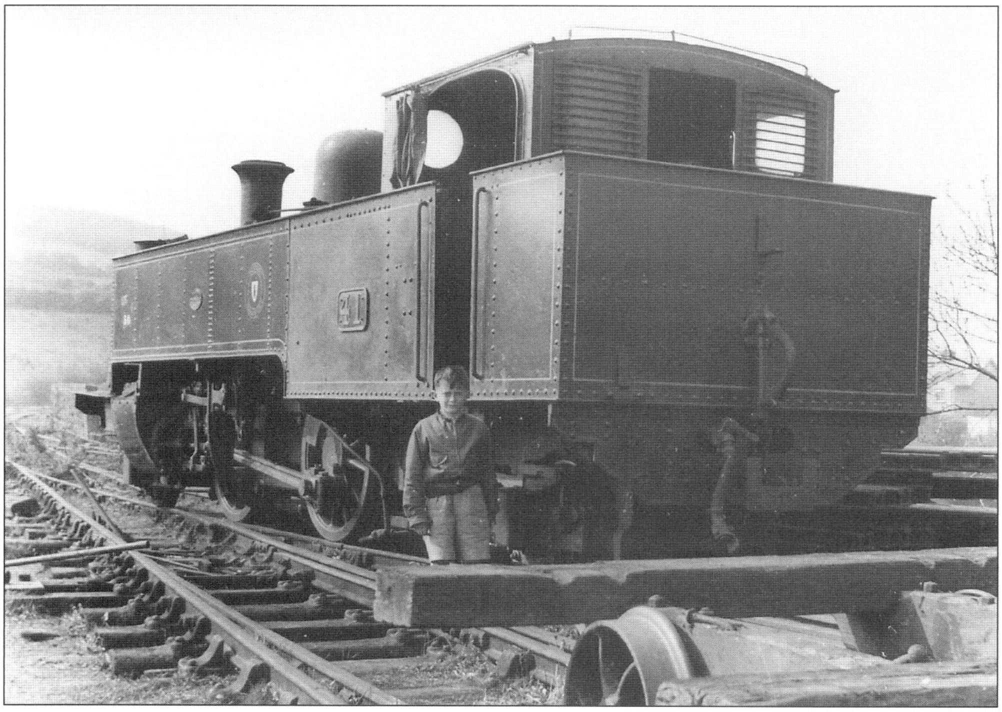

No 41 awaits the scrapman's torch at Ballycastle. That fate came in 1954. The auctioneer's lot number is stencilled at the front of the tank.
CP Friel collection

At 8.50pm on Sunday 2 July 1950, Nos 41 and 44 left Ballymoney for the last time. Three-quarters of an hour later they arrived at Ballycastle and the seaside town was left without a rail connection. Nos 44 and 41 are seen here at Ballycastle after closure, sitting close to where they were stabled that July night. Close examination will show that the UTA roundel was placed in a slightly different position on each engine, that on No 41 being nearer the cab and an even closer look will show that the roundels were also different, that on No 41 being nonstandard, with a smaller shield and condensed lettering. Also visible are the auctioneer's lot numbers stencilled on the tanks, No 44 showing Lot 50. Both locomotives were cut up for scrap in 1954 (see page 159).

MJG Collins collection

Chapter 6
Working the System

Train services under the Ballycastle Company

The Company opened their line with three trains in each direction on weekdays and one on Sundays. The timings in October 1880 were all listed as fifty minutes, but as goods traffic developed, some sixty minute timings began to be introduced. The timetable for the opening of the railway was advertised in the *Coleraine Chronicle* of 16 October 1880 as follows:

TRAINS FROM BALLYCASTLE

Stations		*Weekdays*			*Sundays*
		am	am	pm	am
Ballycastle	dep	7.10	10.55	3.20	3.20
Armoy	dep	7.28	11.13	3.38	3.38
Stranocum	dep	7.38	11.23	3.48	3.48
Dervock	dep	7.46	11.31	3.56	3.56
Ballymoney	arr	8.00	11.45	4.10	4.10

TRAINS TO BALLYCASTLE

Stations		*Weekdays*			*Sundays*
		am	am	pm	am
Ballymoney	dep	8.50	2.12	5.50	8.30
Dervock	dep	9.04	2.26	6.04	8.44
Stranocum	dep	9.12	2.34	6.12	8.52
Armoy	dep	9.22	2.44	6.22	9.02
Ballycastle	arr	9.40	3.02	6.40	9.20

The first up train, on the move at 7.10am, met the two 7.00am trains ex-Belfast and ex-Derry, at Ballymoney, where they crossed. Once the branch line traffic had been loaded, the first down train returned to Ballycastle at 8.50am.

The second up train connected at Ballymoney with the slow 9.50am Belfast–Derry, and also with the 10.30am Derry–Belfast Mail, which gave ample time for cross-Channel passengers to get the 4.00pm Belfast–Larne Harbour train. The second down train was run in connection with the midday Mail from Belfast, which was timed to leave Ballymoney for Derry at 2.02pm.

The last up train left Ballycastle at the early hour of 3.20pm, to catch the 2.45pm Mail ex-Derry, and passengers from it were into Belfast by 6.45pm.

Six months before the Company started their train services, the members of the Board had their first taste of Sunday observance versus train services. It is doubtful whether they ever had contemplated running an extended service on that day, but the Presbytery of the Route (the local name for the district) was determined to impress its views well in advance. On 27 May 1880, a deputation from that body addressed the Board Meeting. As Silas Evans wrote in the Minute Book afterwards:

> They said that they were desired to impress upon the Directors the wish of their Presbytery, that on the opening of the railway and afterwards that the train service on the Railway on the Sabbath should only be what was absolutely necessary to carry out the obligations of the Company in regard to the Post Office in carrying the Mails and such other things as the public necessarily required but they hoped that no excursion traffic would be permitted or any alteration of the fares made by the Sunday trains, from that charged on other days which would have the tendency of inducing the public to use the line for pleasure only. At the close of the conversation which followed, the Chairman said the Board would duly consider the wishes of the Presbytery when they made their arrangements for the train service of the Railway.

Thus solemnly warned, the management started their Sunday service with one up and one down train. The 6.10am Mail from Belfast left Ballymoney at 8.20am, and ten minutes later the narrow gauge train headed out on its way to the coast. The return working left Ballycastle at 3.20pm, met the 2.30pm Derry–Belfast Mail, and had

BALLYCASTLE RAILWAY.

For the information of the Public the Trains on Ballycastle Railway are given underneath, but General Notices, &c., in this Book apply only to the Northern Counties, Derry Central, and Carrickfergus and Larne Railways.

UP TRAINS FROM BALLYCASTLE. Miles	STATIONS.		WEEK DAYS. a. m.	a. m.	p.m.			SUNDAYS.	p. m.	
	Ballycastle	dep	7 0	10 45	3 20	..	...	..	3 20	..
3¼	Capecastle	,,	a7 11	10 56	3 29	..	..	..	..	..
6	Armoy	,,	7 22	11 7	3 38	..	..	..	3 38	..
9½	Stranocum	,,	7 34	11 19	3 48	..	..	..	3 48	..
11¾	Dervock	,,	7 48	11 28	3 56	..	..	..	3 56	..
16¼	Ballymoney	arr	8 0	11 45	4 10	..	..	..	4 10	..

DOWN TRAINS TO BALLYCASTLE. Miles	STATIONS.		WEEK DAYS a. m.	p.m.	p.m. b			SUNDAYS.	a. m.	
	Ballymoney	dep	8 50	2 12	5 50	..	..	..	8 30	..
4½	Dervock	,,	9 4	2 26	6 7	..	..	..	8 44	..
6¾	Stranocum	,,	9 12	2 34	6 16	..	..	..	8 52	..
10¼	Armoy	,,	9 22	2 44	6 28	..	..	..	9 2	..
13	Capecastle	,,	9 31	a2 55	6 39	..	..	..	..	..
16¼	Ballycastle	arr	9 40	3 2	6 50	..	..	..	9 20	..

a Stop only on Ballymoney and Ballycastle Market and Fair Days, and on Armoy and Dervock Fair Days
b On Saturdays this Train will not leave Ballymoney till 6.25 p.m.

BNCR timetable 1883

city passengers back by 6.45pm. The service was thus calculated to encourage travel into Ballycastle rather than out of it. After a year, the policy of running excursion trains on Sundays was debated by the Board, but the members decided against the practice, and the principal of a single Sunday train was adhered to throughout the years of independent working. They did, however, offer returns at single fares on Sundays from May 1881.

Market days at Ballycastle, Ballymoney, Armoy and Dervock were an important source of income, and the new railway undoubtedly did much to facilitate this long-established combination of business and social gathering. To encourage market-goers, the suggestion was soon made that cheap tickets should be offered, but after consideration in August 1881 the idea was dropped, as it was felt that any increase in ticket sales would not compensate for the reduction in fares. Later, the decision was reversed temporarily, and 'market and fair day' tickets were offered from 1 November 1883 until 1 November 1884. Passengers were, however, encouraged on Ballycastle market days by the provision of an extra train in spring and autumn, which left Ballymoney on Tuesdays at 12.20pm and returned from Ballycastle at 4.30pm, meeting the main line Mail that had left Belfast at 3.30pm. For the Ballymoney market, held on the first and third Thursdays of each month, trains were introduced in September 1885, one leaving Ballycastle at 9.00am and returning from Ballymoney at 3.00pm, and making a last run out of Ballycastle at 5.20pm.

The 1896 timetables show a winter service that was basically unaltered from the 1880s, save for a 3.10pm down and 5.50pm up on Thursdays only. The summer service had, however, expanded to four trains on every weekday, leaving Ballycastle at 7.30am, 10.35am, 3.00pm and 6.15pm, and Ballymoney at 8.55am, 10.25am, 12.50pm and 5.25pm. In addition, a Fridays-only train left Ballymoney at 7.25pm and Ballycastle at 8.25pm. By this time BNCR were running their 'Portrush Flyer', a midday express, on Saturdays only from Belfast to Portrush. This called at Greenisland, and thereafter ran non-stop to Ballymoney in 68 minutes. Departures of both the broad and narrow gauge trains from Ballymoney were tabled for 1.20pm and a non-stop run was made to Ballycastle in forty-five minutes. Off this train excursionists could spend nearly four and a quarter hours in Ballycastle before the departure of the last up train. Alternatively cheap weekend tickets from Belfast, available for return on the Monday, were offered by the BNCR at 10s, 8s and 6s 3d for the three classes. This Saturday express continued in vogue up to the outbreak of the First World War, and the Ballycastle Railway always provided a non-stop connection to the coast. By 1904, if not before, the time for the run was reduced to forty minutes.

Excursion parties were welcome on the Ballycastle Railway, and the BNCR timetables advertised special fares. The Belfast Naturalists' Field Club travelled twice over the line in its early days. In those spacious times the Field Club published its own journal, which gave lengthy descriptions of its activities. The first of these was on 19 July 1882, when:

> . . . changing at Ballymoney into the carriages of the narrow gauge line of the Ballycastle Railway, the party were in high anticipation of the pleasant day to be spent on the sunny heights of Benmore. Scarce, however, had the merits and demerits of the narrow gauge system of railway as branch lines for Ireland been discussed when the speed gradually declined, and a standstill was made near Stranocum. This, on a comparatively new line, was not considered remarkable, but on inquiry it was ascertained that something was wrong with the locomotive. Wiring for additional power was of no avail, and field naturalists and others alike were compelled to wait with such patience as they could command the arrival of the next train their way, thus losing about two hours of the best part of the day.

Two days later, ". . . seated in the comfortable carriages . . ." the party ". . . this time performed the return journey to Ballymoney with speed and pleasing smoothness".

From 8–10 July 1885, the Field Club held another Ballycastle sortie. Again, the visit gave them something out of the ordinary, for when they arrived at Ballycastle at 1.20pm they found ". . . the platform in an extraordinary bustle and vast quantities of luggage . . . piled about". They soon discovered that a Dominion Line ship, the SS *Sarnia*, had gone aground on Rathlin Island on the previous day, and the unfortunate passengers and their belongings were

BALLYCASTLE RAILWAY.

For the information of the Public the Trains on Ballycastle Railway re given underneath, but the Northern Counties Committee of the Midland Railway do not accept any responsibilitv for the observance of the Time Table.

Up Trains from Ballycastle

STATIONS	WEEK DAYS							SUNDAYS	
	a m	a m (M'ndays only.)	a m	p m	p m	p m (Fridays only)		p m	
BALLYCASTLE ..dep	6 35	8 40	11 0	3 20	6 20	8 45	..	6 25	..
Capecastle.......... ,,	6 45		11 10	3 30	6 30	8 55	..	6 35	..
Armoy.............. ,,	6 53		11 18	3 38	6 38	9 3	..	6 43	..
Stranocum.......... ,,	7 3		11 28	3 48	6 48	9 13	..	6 53	..
Dervock .... ,,	7 10		11 35	3 55	6 55	9 20	..	7 0	..
BALLYMONEY ..arr.	7 25	9 22	11 50	4 10	7 10	9 35	..	7 15	..

Down Trains to Ballycastle

STATIONS	a WEEK DAYS							SUNDAYS	
	a m	a m	p m	p m (Sats. only.)	p m	p m	p m (Fridays only)	a m	
BALLYMONEY ..dep	8 25	10 0	12 15	1 20	2 55	5 30	7 30	10 40	..
Dervock .... ,,	8 39	10 14	12 29		3 12	5 44	7 44	10 54	..
Stranocum.......... ,,	8 46	10 21	12 36		3 22	5 51	7 51	11 1	..
Armoy.............. ,,	8 57	10 32	12 47		3 38	6 2	8 2	11 12	..
Capecastle .... ,,	9 6	10 41	12 56		3 49	6 11	8 11	11 21	..
BALLYCASTLE ..arr.	9 15	10 50	1 5	2 0	4 0	6 20	8 20	11 30	..

The 6-35 a.m , 11-0 a.m., and 2-55 p.m. Trains stop at Gracehill on Thursdays.
a 12-15 p.m. does not run on Saturdays.

MR (NCC) timetable 1904

being transferred to Belfast. The Ballycastle was probably having its first taste of emergency.

By 1904, the summer weekday service amounted to four trains, leaving in the up direction at 6.35am, 11.00am, 3.20pm and 6.20pm, and five in the down direction at 8.25am, 10.00am, 12.15pm, 2.55pm and 5.30pm. In addition, there was an 8.40am up on Mondays only, which crossed at Armoy with the 8.25am down, and which did the run in forty-two minutes. It connected with the 8.00am ex-Derry, which reached Belfast at 11.00am, presumably early enough for weekending members of management to get into the office.

By the end of the First World War, shortages of coal and mounting costs combined to cut the service back to two trains a day. The June 1918 public timetable shows two up trains, leaving at 7.00am and 3.15pm each weekday, with balancing workings out of Ballymoney at 9.00am and 7.00pm. On Thursdays, when the Ballymoney market was held, there was an 11.00am out of Ballycastle with a return train ex-Ballymoney at 1.30pm. On Ballycastle market days, the Ballymoney folk could leave at 10.40am and come back from Ballycastle at 2.15pm. The Saturday express had vanished, and the Sunday train still made it possible for Ballycastle's inhabitants to see the outside world, but mercifully gave city folk nearly twelve hours away from home.

The early last train from Ballycastle seems to have remained in force after the end of the war, and in the winter of 1921–22 the service was back to 1880 standards, with the 7.00am, 10.45am and 3.40pm up, and 9.00am, 1.15pm and 5.00pm down. Timings were at fifty minutes, and thus by six o'clock of an evening, the last train had arrived in Ballycastle and the engine was heading for the shed. Those last years of independent working were a struggle, with no money to run extra trains.

Train services under the LMS and UTA

Under new management, the service of trains was increased, and in the summer it became the practice to run five trains each way on weekdays. In June 1929, these

BALLYCASTLE RAILWAY.

For the information of the Public the Trains on Ballycastle Railway are given underneath, but the Northern Counties Committee of the Midland Railway do not accept any responsibility for the observance of the Time Table.

STATIONS.		WEEK DAYS a m	a m (Thurs. only.)	p m (Runs Ballycastle Fair Days.)	p m					SUNDAYS p.m.	
BALLYCASTLE	dep	7 0	11 0	2 15	3 15	..	..	..	..	4 55	..
Capecastle ..	„	7 11	11 11	2 26	3 25	..	..	..	..	5 5	..
Armoy	„	7 22	11 22	2 37	3 33	..	..	..	..	5 13	..
Stranocum ..	„	7 34	11 34	2 49	3 43	..	..	..	..	5 23	..
Dervock	„	7 43	11 43	2 58	3 50	.	..	..	..	5 30	..
BALLYMONEY ..	arr	8 0	12 0	3 15	4 5	..	..	..	..	5 45	..

DOWN TRAINS TO BALLYCASTLE.

STATIONS.		WEEK DAYS am	a.m. (Runs Ballycastle Fair Days.)	p.m. (Thurs. only.)	p m				SUNDAYS a m	
BALLYMONEY ..	dep	9 0	10 40	1 30	7 0	..	..	..	10 45	..
Dervock	„	9 17	10 57	1 47	7 14	..	..	..	10 59	..
Stranocum ..	„	9 26	11 6	1 56	7 21	..	..	..	11 6	..
Armoy	„	9 38	11 18	2 8	7 32	..	..	..	11 17	..
Capecastle ..	„	9 49	11 29	2 19	7 41	..	..	..	11 26	..
BALLYCASTLE	arr	10 6	11 40	2 30	7 50	..	..	..	11 35	..

MR (NCC) timetable for 1918

BALLYCASTLE RAILWAY.

For the information of the Public the Trains on Ballycastle Railway are given underneath, but the Northern Counties Committee of the Midland Railway do not accept any responsibility for the observance of the Time Table.

STATIONS.		WEEK DAYS											
		a m	a m	p m									
BALLYCASTLE	dep	7 0	10 45	3 40	..	..	..	..	..	..	..	..	
Capecastle ..	"	7 11	10 56	3 50	..	..	..	..	..	..	..	..	
Armoy	"	7 22	11 8	3 58	..	..	..	..	..	..	..	..	
Stranocum ..	"	7 34	11 19	4 8	..	..	..	..	..	..	..	..	
Dervock	"	7 43	11 28	4 15	..	..	..	..	..	..	..	..	
BALLYMONEY ..	arr	8 0	11 45	4 30	..	—	..	..	..	..	..	..	

DOWN TRAINS TO BALLYCASTLE.

STATIONS.		WEEK DAYS										
		am	p.m.	p m								
BALLYMONEY ..	dep	9 0	1 15	5 0	—	..	..	..	—	—	..	—
Dervock	"	9 14	1 32	5 14	—	..	..	—	..	—	..	—
Stranocum ..	"	9 21	1 41	5 21	—	..	—	—	..	—	..	—
Armoy	"	9 32	1 53	5 32	—	..	..	—	..	..	..	..
Capecastle ..	"	9 41	2 4	5 41	—	—	..	..	..	—	..	—
BALLYCASTLE	arr	9 50	2 15	5 50	..	..	..	..	..	..	..	—

MR (NCC) timetable 1922

BALLYCASTLE LINE.

DOWN TRAINS.		MONS. TO FRIS.						SATURDAYS.							SUNS.			
		a.m.	a.m.		p.m.	p.m.	p.m.	a.m.	a.m.	a.m.	p.m.		p.m.	p.m.	a.m.	p.m.	p.m.	
BELFAST ....dep.	1	6 5	9 50	...	1 10	3 50	6 20	6 5	8 25	1030	2 15	...	5 45	9 25	1020	2 0	7 45	1
LONDONDERRY „	2	...	...	...	1 10	3 50	5 50	...	8 30	1050	1 55	...	5 20	8 30	1030	2 0	6 10	2
BALLYMONEY .dep.	3	7 40	1130	...	2 45	5 35	8 15	7 40	9 45	1220	3 50	...	7 25	1045	12 5	3 45	9 25	3
Dervock .... „	4	7 52	1142	...	2 57	5 47	8 27	7 52	9 57	1232	4 2	...	7 37	1057	1217	3 57	9 37	4
Stranocum .... „	5	7 59	1149	...	3 4	5 54	8 34	7 59	10 4	1239	4 9	...	7 44	11 4	1224	4 4	9 44	5
Gracehill............... „	6	8 3	1153	...	3 8	5 58	8 38	8 3	10 8	1243	4 13	...	7 48	11 8	1228	4 8	9 48	6
Armoy................... „	7	8 9	1159	...	3 14	6 4	8 46	8 9	1014	1249	4 19	...	7 54	1114	1234	4 14	9 54	7
Capecastle .... „	8	8 16	12 6	...	3 21	6 11	8 53	8 16	1021	1256	4 26	...	8 1	1121	1241	4 21	10 1	8
BALLYCASTLE...arr.	9	8 25	1215	...	3 30	6 20	9 5	8 25	1030	1 5	4 35	...	8 10	1130	1250	4 30	1010	9

UP TRAINS.			Thx	Tho														
		a.m.	a.m.	a.m.	p.m.	p.m.	p.m.	a.m.	a.m.	a.m.	p.m.		p.m.	p.m.	a.m.	p.m.	p.m.	
BALLYCASTLE...dep.	1	6 35	8 45	9 45	1 20	3 55	6 50	6 35	8 45	11 0	2 20	...	5 30	8 40	1045	2 30	8 5	1
Capecastle .... „	2	D	...	9 57	1 35	4 7	7 3	D	...	1112	2 32	...	5 42	8 52	1057	2 42	8 17	2
Armoy................... „	3	6 55	9 2	10 4	1 43	4 18	7 10	6 55	9 2	1119	2 40	...	5 49	9 0	11 4	2 49	8 24	3
Gracehill............... „	4	D	...	10 9	1 49	4 23	7 16	D	...	1124	2 45	...	5 54	9 5	11 9	2 54	8 29	4
Stranocum .... „	5	7 6	...	1014	1 54	4 28	7 21	7 6	...	1128	2 50	...	5 58	9 10	1113	2 58	8 33	5
Dervock .... „	6	7 14	9 16	1024	2 3	4 36	7 29	7 14	9 16	1135	2 58	...	6 5	9 18	1120	3 5	8 40	6
BALLYMONEY .arr.	7	7 25	9 26	1035	2 15	4 50	7 40	7 25	9 26	1145	3 10	...	6 15	9 30	1130	3 15	8 50	7
LONDONDERRY arr.	8	9 22	1040	1240	3 45	6 45	9 32	9 22	1040	1 28	6 5	...	7 30	1145	1 13	4 50	1030	8
BELFAST .... „	9	8 55	1045	1 30	3 55	6 20	9 15	8 55	1045	1 30	4 50	...	7 35	1045	1 35	4 40	1025	9

D—Calls on notice to Guard or Station Staff. Tho—Thursdays only. Thx—Thursdays excepted.

LMS (NCC) timetable Autumn 1945

left Ballycastle at 7.05am, 10.05am, 1.00pm, 3.45pm and 6.40pm, and Ballymoney at 8.50am, 11.30am, 2.30pm, 5.20pm and 7.45pm. In spite of this improved service, no trains had to cross en route, the Armoy loop was dispensed with, and the whole line worked as a single section. The most notable change, however was on Sundays, when in place of the solitary workings of BRC days, there were no less than three trains in each direction. First on the move was the 10.25am up, which returned at 11.25am ex-Ballymoney with its load of Sabbath-breakers. The next Sunday up train was at 1.20pm, which made no main line connection and came back from Ballymoney at 2.30pm. Finally, out of Ballycastle was the 7.25pm, which connected with the 8.00pm express from Portrush, due in Belfast at 9.50pm. These catered for summer demands and there were no Sunday trains during the winter. Virtually the same service was being operated in 1932, apart from the omission of the early afternoon run on summer Sundays, which must have always been light loaded.

The 1933 strike had the effect of cancelling the 6.40pm up and the 7.45pm down. On the main line, the effect was more drastic: there were in February only two more trains a day between Belfast and Coleraine, and no through trains to Derry. The afternoon train left Belfast at 3.20pm and reached Ballymoney at 5.37pm. In consequence, the 5.20pm down to Ballycastle was held back until 5.40pm. In March 1933, three trains ran north from Belfast, and one of them worked through to Derry; this was the 3.30pm ex-Belfast, and it was timed to leave Ballymoney at 5.47pm. Because of this, the down 5.20pm narrow gauge train was detained until 5.50pm.

The summer of 1935 saw something of a revival of the old 'Portrush Flyer' of prewar days, when an express train was run from Ballymoney at 2.20pm in connection with the 1.15pm ex-Belfast. The latter train, named 'The Golfers' Express', was already an established institution on the Northern Counties line, but up to 1935 passengers leaving it at Ballymoney did not reach Ballycastle until 3.20pm by the 2.30pm all-stations train. The 1935 acceleration involved a faster change of trains at Ballymoney, the narrow gauge train left at 2.20pm and, after a non-stop run, was into Ballycastle at 3pm. On the return journey, passengers could leave Ballycastle at 9.00pm, reach Ballymoney at 9.40pm, and leave again at 9.57pm on the 9.30pm ex-Portrush for a 63-minute non-stop run to Belfast. The broad gauge train crossed at Ballymoney with the 8.45pm Belfast–Portrush, and passengers off the latter were able to reach Ballycastle by a late express train, leaving Ballymoney at 10.00pm and running down to the sea in forty minutes.

The opening weeks of the Second World War saw up trains leave Ballycastle at 7.15am, 11.40am and 3.35pm, and down trains leave Ballymoney at 8.30am, 1.25pm and 5.00pm. No trains ran on Sundays, which was, of course, normal NCC practice on the narrow gauge. After a month of war, a revised working timetable was issued. On the Ballycastle line a 9.45am up train replaced the 11.00am, and allowed passengers to reach Belfast at 12.40pm by a Portrush train, instead of at 2.03pm as formerly by a train which had come from Derry. Smart running by the 8.30am up was noteworthy and the 45-minute timing to Ballymoney allowed for stops at every halt except Gracehill.

Later in the war, the frequency of weekday services increased, and Sunday trains were again run during the winter. In the winter of 1942 there were four weekday trains each way. The first up train started at 6.35am, took fifty-two minutes, and made connection with the 7.10am, ex-Portrush, which was into Belfast at 8.55am. These early up trains were actually initiated by the 1941 air raids, after which wholesale evacuation took place from the city. The other up workings left Ballycastle at 10.15am, 4.00pm and 6.40pm. Down trains left Ballymoney at 8.30am, 2.00pm, 5.30pm and 8.15pm, with the last train held until 9pm on Saturday night to let merrymakers get back from Portrush. The up Sunday trains in the winter of 1942 left Ballycastle at 10.00am and 7.05pm and down workings left Ballymoney at mid-day and at 9.00pm, the latter taking passengers off the 7.10pm Belfast–Derry train.

By the summer of 1944, there were four workings in each direction from Monday–Friday, but on Saturdays there were five. These left Ballycastle at 6.35am, 9.40am, 1.45pm, 4.10pm and 7.40pm, and Ballymoney at 8.15am, 11.45am, 3.05pm, 5.35pm and 9.15pm. Although the 1.15pm Saturdays only ex-Belfast no longer had the timings of the old 'Golfers Express', the narrow gauge made an outstanding thirty-eight minute connecting run, leaving Ballymoney at 3.15pm, calling at Armoy, and arriving at Ballycastle at 3.43pm. Sunday trains were maintained at two in each direction.

Over the 1944–45 winter there were still four up and four down trains on Mondays to Fridays, five on Saturdays and two on Sundays. The 8.45am up train running on Mondays only was very smartly timed, being allowed forty minutes, with a stop at Armoy. The down express on Saturday afternoons now left Ballymoney at 2.45pm, arrived at Armoy at 3.08pm, left at 3.09pm, and was in Ballycastle at 3.23pm.

By the autumn of 1945 the service became still more frequent. From Mondays to Fridays there were five up and five down trains, on Saturdays six, and on Sundays three. From 18 February 1946, one of the Saturday trains was dropped from a timetable that contained a multitude of minor changes over the whole NCC system. The summer service in 1946 was practically unaltered on the Ballycastle line.

The continuance of petrol rationing into 1948–9 kept a travel-hungry public on the railways, and generally five Ballycastle trains ran on weekdays. The three Sunday trains ran through the spring and summer of 1948, but were stopped in the following winter.

The final timetable in which Ballycastle trains featured became current on 19 June 1950. Two weeks later, workings on the last of Antrim's narrow gauge lines came to an end. Compared to Ballycastle Railway days, an excellent train service was provided up to the closure. From Monday to Friday, up trains left Ballycastle at 6.10am, 8.35am, 1.05pm, 3.55pm and 6.20pm, while down workings left Ballymoney at 7.30am, 10.45am, 2.45pm, 5.10pm and 7.50pm. Different timings were observed on Saturdays, the up trains leaving at 7.35am, 10.55am, 2.10pm, 5.40pm and 8.10pm, and the down trains at 9.45am, 12.25pm, 4.15pm, 6.50pm and 9.20pm. Sunday trains ran from Ballycastle at 10.20am and 6.30pm, and from Ballymoney at 11.40am and 8.50pm.

Operating the line

Under the Ballycastle Company the single line had three sections, which were worked by train staff and ticket. The sections were:

Ballymoney–Dervock .... 4½ miles
Dervock–Armoy .... 5¾ miles
Armoy–Ballycastle .... 6 miles

Armoy had a passing loop, but not Dervock, and although the Dervock siding was occasionally used to shunt a goods or stock train, as on Fair days, its status as a block station was to enable heavy traffic to be worked more expeditiously. Consideration was given to the provision of a loop at Capecastle during 1905–6 but, although it was apparently desirable from the operating aspect, it was decided that the expenditure of around £250 could not be justified.

Tenders for the installation of the signals were opened in March 1880 from the Gloucester Wagon Co (£679 10s), Saxby & Farmer (£1,067), Stevens & Sons (£1,241) and McKenzie & Holland (£1,244). The contract was awarded to Saxby & Farmer. Signal cabins were provided at Dervock, Stranocum, Armoy and Ballycastle, while at Ballymoney the existing BNCR cabin controlled the Ballycastle yard.

Armoy and Dervock had the usual home and distant signals for each direction. Stranocum had a single post in the middle of the station, carrying home signal arms on each side; there were also two distants and they all were worked from a signal cabin. This probably contained six levers, two for the distants, two for the double-armed home, and two for the set of points, one being the lock.

When Ballycastle station was enlarged and rebuilt in 1898, a certain amount of new signalling lines and fittings were required, and these were supplied by Dutton & Co of Worcester for the sum of £40 7s 6d. The Ballycastle cabin is believed to have contained ten levers, two for the starters, one down distant, one down home, one for the metal soldier guarding the catch-points to the goods yard, two for points and lock leading to the platforms, and two for points and lock leading from the main line to the goods yard. Initially there was a spare lever, which was later used to control the sawmill siding, and to operate the catch-point. There were five hand-worked points, two of them at the cross-over road between the two platforms, and the other three in the yard.

The sidings at Balleny (opened 1881 and probably closed about 1895), Capecastle (added in 1891) and at the Ballast Pit (opened probably in 1897) were worked by Pinkerton Patent boxes, which were unlocked by the key on the train staff.

The normal train set in Ballycastle Railway days consisted of two six-wheelers and a brake van, and since mixed trains were run as required, probably the majority of trains had a quota of wagons attached. It was the practice to marshal the wagons between the engines and the carriages, and as none of the vehicles had any form of continuous brake, the passenger carriages had the benefit of any 'rug' when starting. Understandably, the passengers grumbled from time to time about the erratic motion, and on 31 May 1895 the Board requested:

> . . . the locomotive superintendent to have the cushions on first class carriages put in order immediately, and his attention drawn to the jerky manner in which some of the trains are run.

On busy days, the two-carriage set was added to by attaching either a third six-wheeler or a bogie carriage, or both.

Unfortunately, existing records do not tell us much about the working of goods trains, but judged by the three staff sections and the Armoy loop, for which there is little justification in the passenger timetable, there must have been a fair number of goods trains running, of whose movements we have no detailed knowledge. Confirmation of this is afforded by the annual reports which, in 1913, replaced the half-yearly reports. The half-yearly statements gave the total train mileage run, but in the more detailed statistics of the annual reports the passenger and goods workings were separated, except in the issues abbreviated for security reasons. Thus in 1922 and 1923 the returns of train miles were:

Train Miles (inc empty trains run for traffic purposes on either the forward or return journey)

1922			1923		
Coaching	Goods	Total	Coaching	Goods	Total
23,696	8,960	32,656	22,160	9,520	31,680

If we assume that in 1922–23 goods trains were run on five days of each week, the above annual mileages correspond to about 30 miles a day, equivalent to one double journey a day along the line. The total tonnages of goods of all classes conveyed in these years were 11,079, and 12,305, of which a little over half originated on the Company's system. The totals of livestock were 5028 and 5130 head. If all the goods and livestock had been moved by the two daily goods trains (and none by the mixed trains), the goods trains would, on average, have carried 19 tons of goods and between eight and nine head of stock, certainly lightly loaded, and more so when one considers that the bulk of livestock movement would have been by Fair day specials.

The busiest days of the year on the line were during the Ballycastle Lammas Fair. Something of the details of the workings in the prosperous days at the end of last century are afforded by an advertisement in the *Coleraine Chronicle*:

BALLYCASTLE RAILWAY

Ballycastle 'Big' Fair

On Tuesday and Wednesday, 30th and 31st August 1898

On Tuesday, 30th August

A Special Train will leave Ballymoney at 8.20 a.m. and Dervock at 8.35 a.m.

The 10 a.m. from Ballymoney will run 40 minutes later.

A Cattle Train will leave Ballycastle at 3.20 p.m. and a Special Passenger Train at 7 p.m. stopping at all stations.

The 6.15 pm from Ballycastle will not stop at Capecastle, Armoy or Stranocum.

On Wednesday, 31st August

A Special Train will leave Ballymoney at 11.15am stopping at all stations.

After 3 pm the Trains will leave Ballycastle at 6.15pm (for Ballymoney only), 7.30 pm and 8.30 pm for all stations.

Third Class Cheap Tickets will only be issued to Ballycastle on both days by the morning trains (except by 8.50 am from Ballymoney and Dervock on Tuesday) at the following fares:

From Ballymoney 1/6; Dervock 1/3; Stranocum 1/-; Armoy 8d; Capecastle 4d.

No excursion tickets or half Cheap Tickets on either of the above days.

EJ Cotton, General Manager

And again, a description from the *Chronicle* two years later:

Lammas Fair at Ballycastle. 28-8-1900

Excursion tickets were issued on the Ballycastle Railway both days (28th and 29th August) and these were largely taken advantage of, several special trains having to be run to convey the passengers, but the arrangements on this as on all the other occasions were perfect. A number of extra police were drafted in, but their services were not much required.

The drastic simplification which was effected by the LMS (NCC) in the interests of economy have been referred to in the proceeding chapter. The three sections were made one, worked by staff and ticket, and in the busy times there was inevitably a wait of around fifty minutes after the dispatch of a train from either end, before another could move.

The trains were made up of vacuum-braked carriages which, unlike Ballycastle Railway practice, were marshalled next to the engine. They were followed by unbraked wagons, and the brake van made up the rear of the train. Two carriages was the usual load, with three during the busier days of summer. For certain heavy cattle trains, banking from Ballycastle to Capecastle was necessary, if stalling on the Ballylig curves was to be avoided. On these occasions the banking engine pushed, uncoupled, as far as Sharp's house at Capecastle, then cast off and returned immediately to Ballycastle. The sight and sound of two engines attacking the Capecastle bank was indeed stirring, and much is missing from the silent Tow valley of today.

Lammas Fair traffic in NCC days was worked at first by a train of six carriages, but after stalling on a bad rail on the Capecastle bank, followed by an ignominious return to Ballycastle, it became the practice to work two trains, each of three carriages and several wagons. The first train carried the ticket, and after a wait of fifty minutes or so, the second one set off with the staff after the first was past the Ballymoney home signal.

Double-heading was done with the last train of the day on these occasions, the two trains taking up all the six carriages which had formed the two train sets during the day. From Ballymoney, the two engines returned to Ballycastle, taking with them two carriages to make up the first up train of the following morning. A rather similar procedure was followed when the last trains ran on Sunday 2 July 1950, when the up train was hauled by No 41 piloting No 44 with four bogie carriages and two break vans, and on the last down working No 44, piloting No 41, both bunker-first, taking back two coaches and two vans.

A visiting photographer records the preparations for the departure of the last train on 2 July 1950, as Guard Jimmy Irons adds Christmas decorations to the front of No 41. The replacement buses are waiting ready in the yard. CP Friel collection

Accidents

The lines seems to have been remarkably free from serious accidents under independent ownership, though there were a number of near misses. There is a tradition that a train killed a man somewhere near Armoy in the 1880s, but the writer has not been able to substantiate it.

The Minute Book records an incident which was nearly an accident, in October 1887, when a ballast train was allowed to pass Armoy contrary to block regulations, and was fortunately prevented from running into the 1.15pm down passenger train, the engine of which had become disabled through the breaking of a spring hook. Some two years later, in August 1889, there is a record of an injury to the leg of "a woman named Mabin" who fell between the carriage and the platform edge at Ballycastle when the 5.55pm passenger train was being brought in.

Occasional collisions with straying cattle were inevitable, but seem to have been no more frequent than on other lines. In 1889, John Kelly of Stracam claimed £4 for a heifer which had been killed near a set of accommodation gates on 10 October. The gates were known to be faulty, and the Company admitted their responsibility. Ganger Magee was fined five shillings, deducted at a shilling a month from his wages, for neglect of an order he had been given to repair the gates. A bullock was killed near Chatham in February 1920, and the last such incident recorded in the BRC archives occurred in August 1921, when the 10.45am up train ran into several beasts near Mullaghduff, killing one and derailing a wagon.

Prior to 1924, the permanent way was never in the best of condition and derailments occasionally took place. One such was on Christmas Eve 1896, when a wagon on the 5.25pm up came off the rails between Stranocum and Dervock and, ". . . after running close on a mile regained the rail . . ." , doubtless leaving a trail of destructive evidence in the darkness. Somewhere about the same place there was a serious derailment on 16 March 1898, when the whole train of engine, three empty wagons, two carriages and the guard's van went off the road. It was the 8.55am down, and the entire engineering resources of the little Company were concentrated on getting the vehicles back on the track, a task that took the whole of that day. There is also a mention of a wagon derailment on 26 May 1903 when a special goods was being run.

What might have been two fatal accidents had reasonably happy endings. The first occurred in 1905, and at the Board Meeting of 12 August, Hamilton McAllen mentioned:

> . . . that a young lady, Miss Sara Sharpe, a passenger from Capecastle to Ballycastle, fell out of the train on 11 April last. She did not sustain much injury and was able to proceed on foot into Ballycastle – three miles – and transact her business there. It now appeared that she had been laid up and under medical care for some time. Miss Sharpe intimated that she did not intend to make any claim, but considered that she should have a free pass for a time. This was granted by the Board to the end of the year.

Taken almost exactly one hundred years later, this is the spot where Sara Sharpe fell from a Ballycastle-bound train on 11 April 1905. The details of the accident were recorded in the minutes of the Board Meeting held on 12 August 1905. (See also pages 129–32.)
Norman Johnston

The other accident was in June 1910, when a child of the Rev RJ McIlmoyle of Dervock fell out of a carriage between Stranocum and Dervock, yet according to the Minute Book ". . . did not appear to be anything the worse".

Towards the closing of the line under the NCC and UTA, the upkeep of the permanent way was curtailed, and over the difficult stretches a 5 mph limit was enforced. Derailments of a minor nature became commonplace, but one of them was memorable. It was on a Sunday in 1947; Limerick and McDuff were on No 41, hauling two carriages and a brake van of the first up train. At the top of the rise, between the Garry Bog and Ballymoney, Barry Limerick looked back and saw that Jimmy Irons had out his red flag. So they halted, and Jack McDuff went back to see what was the matter. He found the guard sorely rattled, and no wonder, for the leading wheels of the van had derailed nearly two miles back, and they had pulled it all that way, swinging on two wheels. To get the passengers on their way, they uncoupled, took the carriages on to Ballymoney and reported the line blocked. They then took the engine back, and tried to get the van back on the rails by jacks, only to find that the axle boxes were smashed and it was not fit to move. So it was back to Ballymoney again, where they got a permanent way trolley and towed it to the blockage. They eventually got the van jacked up, and the trolley underneath it. Rather than risk another derailment during a towing operation, the wreck was pushed slowly back to Ballycastle* and the line cleared for traffic.

Reference has been made in Chapter 5 to the two runaways that occurred in 1943 and 1949, during the descent of the Capecastle bank towards Ballycastle, and little more need be said of them. That the earlier one was not attended by more serious consequences is a tribute to Driver James McKissick's efforts to check the speed during the hectic descent into the terminus.

* *Dr Patterson states that the van was pushed back to Ballymoney but, given the rest of the account, this would have been impossible as the engine could not have been run round the errant vehicle.*

Chapter 7

Motive Power & Rolling Stock

The Ballycastle engines

The first move towards the acquisition of motive power was made at the Board Meeting on 26 February 1879, when Silas Evans was instructed "... to communicate with locomotive engineers regarding suitable engines". For the remainder of that year, the records, written in Evans' hand, tell the reader little or nothing of what progress he was making. We know nothing of how many engines it was proposed to buy, of how many firms approached, or what specifications they were asked to price. Sometime in April 1879, Evans submitted the technical details to the scrutiny of Lanyon and McKinnon but, as they were civil engineers they can hardly have been the most competent of referees. For eight months after that the subject is not mentioned in the Minute Books.

No doubt Evans' thoughts would have been influenced by existing narrow gauge experience in County Antrim, if not by the fact that he was concurrently secretary of the Ballymena, Cushendall and Red Bay Railway Company. Thus on the Cushendall line, three Black, Hawthorn 0-4-2 saddle tank engines had been working for four years. Two while not far away on the Glenariff mineral railway, two Stephenson 2-4-0 tank engines had been working for six years. Two years earlier, the Ballymena and Larne Railway Company had taken delivery of their first engine, a Beyer, Peacock 2-4-0 tank of a design which had used by the Isle of Man Railway since 1873.

At a meeting of the Ballycastle Board on 23 December 1879, Evans tabled tenders received from three firms: Black, Hawthorn & Co at £1145, Sharp, Stewart & Co at £1210, and Beyer, Peacock at £1350. It is significant that Sharp, Stewart & Co had entered the narrow gauge market the previous year, with the building of two 2-4-0 tank engines for the Manx Northern Railway. Beyer, Peacock's offer was close to the price which the Ballymena and Larne Company had paid for their first 2-4-0T. Decision by the Ballycastle directors was not long delayed; Black, Hawthorn & Co, making the lowest offer, won the contract and two engines were at once ordered. These differed from the engines which they had made for the Cushendall Company in having 13in cylinders against 12in, and in being six coupled, 0-6-0 tanks.

During the building of the engines, Evans reported to the Board that he had persuaded the makers to increase the thickness of the frame plates from ¾" to ⅞", and the number of boiler tubes from 123 to 146. He had also managed to get delivery to be made to Belfast instead of Liverpool, and thus saved the Company some shipping charges. By mid-March 1880, the engines were ready for their first inspection, and at a Board Meeting on 14 April, Evans reported that "... James Donaghey had made an inspection of the engines at Gateshead and reported favourably on them".

Already, Messrs Butler & Fry had applied for the use of one of these engines as soon as it was received, to assist with the ballasting of the line. They offered to pay a guinea a day as hire "... providing fuel, wages and everything necessary", according to the Ballycastle Board's Minutes. The directors agreed to the hire, with the stipulation "... that the driver and stoker be engaged by the Company and have full charge of the engine".

It seems likely, for reasons mentioned in a previous chapter, that the engines did not arrive in Ballycastle until the beginning of June 1880. They were named *Dalriada* and *Countess of Antrim*, the former taking the ancient designation of the northeastern part of the district, and they carried their titles in raised, sans-serif characters on rectangular brass plates, mounted on the saddle-tanks. The numbers, respectively 1 and 2, were mounted on the side sheets of the cabs. Each engine weighed 24 tons.

It was *Dalriada* which was hired to Butler & Fry for ballasting, but she soon caused damage to the new permanent way, through being unsteady and 'tight' on the

No 1 Dalriada *at Ballymoney in 1903. Union Street is on the left and the spire of Trinity Church can be seen on the right.*
JB Chirnside

No 2 Countess of Antrim *arrives at Ballymoney on 6 May 1920 with the 3.20pm train from Ballycastle.* KA Nunn

No 2 Countess of Antrim *at Ballymoney on 4 May 1920 with the 5.30pm departure for Ballycastle.* LCGB

curves. *Countess of Antrim* must also have been steamed, for it was noticed that she was exhibiting the same defects. On 11 August 1880, McKinnon told the Board this news and a complaint was wired to Black, Hawthorn & Co. Rather late in the day, the builders admitted that there might be some defect which needed attention, and telegraphed their reply:

> Your telegram received. The locomotives are thoroughly first-class in every respect; the oscillation is due to insufficient balancing of wheels and can easily be put right. Our works manager is now at Ballymena and will remain until additional balance weights are fitted to wheels; these will no doubt remedy the unsteadiness complained of. Shall lose no time with the necessary work.

In addition to using *Dalriada*, Butler & Fry were also ballasting the line with their own engine, *Lady Boyd*, which they had ordered in October 1879. This was a smaller Black, Hawthorn six-coupled saddle tank, very similar to the other two, but with 12" cylinders, and weighing 22 tons. It has been stated elsewhere that this engine was originally No 5 of the Glenariff Iron Ore and Harbour Company's stock, but this was not so.

At the Board Meeting held only two days after the line had been opened for traffic, Evans put forward his opinion that three engines were needed to work the railway. As a result, he sounded Butler & Fry regarding the purchase of *Lady Boyd*, and also approached Black, Hawthorn & Co. about the possible supply of a new locomotive. The latter, however, asked him to remind his directors that the other two locomotives were still not paid for, and that a total of £2290 was outstanding. At the November Board Meeting, the directors resolved to pay £1145 for the *Countess of Antrim*, but to withhold settlement on *Dalriada* until ". . . it is put in a more satisfactory condition". It is hard to see why these two locomotives, apparently identical, should have behaved differently, and one is tempted to think that the Company were perhaps making an issue of the original bad balance of *Dalriada* in order to postpone prompt payment. They were overdrawn at the bank at that time to the extent of about £4000, so there was reason for such a course of action. The idea of a third engine was allowed to lapse, and there for seven months the matter rested.

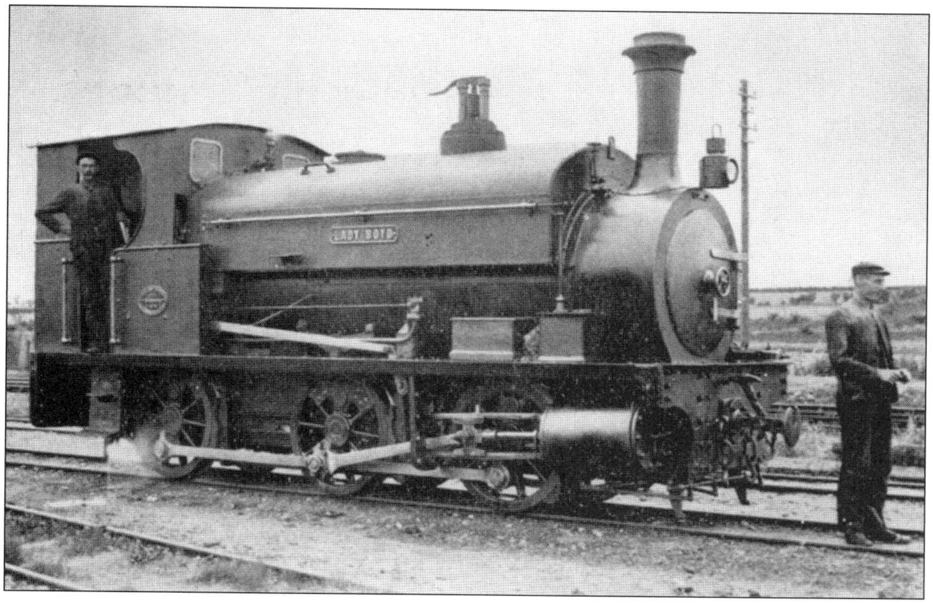

No 3 Lady Boyd *is seen at Ballymoney in 1905. This engine had been purchased in February 1882 from a Mr John Gault for the sum of £600.* Lady Boyd *had previously been used by the contractors, Butler & Fry, to ballast the line.*
H Fayle/IRRS

In May 1881, Butler & Fry offered to sell *Lady Boyd* for a rather odd sum of £807 0s 4d. The Company were, however, still short of ready cash and were not disposed to buy, so Evans was asked to try and hire it for the summer, and it was arranged for a guinea a day.

In November 1881, within thirteen months' experience of running the railway, Evans reiterated his need for a permanent stock of three engines. Butler & Fry were still disposed to sell, and the Company to buy, provided that they could get the engine for not more than £600. Three months went by, and then Evans reported to the Board on February 1882 that he had purchased *Lady Boyd* for £600 from Mr John Gault, a Ballymena gentleman associated with the firm of contractors. She was needing an overhaul, and was promptly shopped at Ballymoney. On 19 April it was reported that the outlay in making her serviceable had been £29 1s 6d in wages and £17 18s in materials. She emerged from the shops carrying the number '3', but from a 1905 photograph the brass digit appears to have been removed later, leaving the rivet holes.

The first repair of consequence to *Dalriada* was in June 1889, after the breakage of a piston head, cylinder and cylinder cover. She visited the repair shops again in the following November and was given a new set of tyres. Bowman Malcolm of the Belfast and Northern Counties Railway examined the boiler in December 1892 and after informing the directors that it was "in bad order", a fuller examination was made which gave a less serious verdict. Although the boiler needed attention, it was thought it was capable of several years' work. Eventually *Dalriada* was laid off for heavy repairs in the early part of 1895, and a new boiler and firebox was obtained from Messrs Kitson of Leeds at a cost of £315. The total overhaul cost the Company £397 15s.

Repairs to *Countess of Antrim* followed close upon those to *Dalriada.* In March 1895, her boiler was found to be worn out and not worth repairing. Tenders were immediately taken for a replacement, and came from six firms; Beyer, Peacock £420, Neilson £360, Black, Hawthorn £354, Sharp, Stewart £335, Stephenson £333, and Kitson £320. Not only did Kitson & Co submit the lowest tender, but they also offered delivery in the shortest time, two and a half months against three or four months, and, since rapid execution of the repair was important, they got the order.

It would seem that both *Dalriada* and *Countess of Antrim* were laid off for boiler repairs, if not actually together, then at nearly the same time, so that *Lady Boyd* would have to shoulder the entire traffic. Delivery of the new boiler for the *Countess* was expedited, the repair was completed in June, in time for the heavier summer trains, and at the end of June the old boiler was sold for scrap and fetched £30.

With the light repair that she received on purchase in 1882, *Lady Boyd* managed to run uneventfully until 1896, with only a set of new tyres in late 1892. On the day of the November Board Meeting in 1896, she broke a spring link near Armoy and held up the train for forty minutes. By that time her boiler was worn out and a quotation of £385 was accepted for a replacement from Messrs Kitson. At the Board Meeting on 9 November, Bradshaw told his directors that he hoped that the new boiler ". . . will make No 3 as near as possible to the other two engines, at a total cost of £600". He was a that time proposing to fit *Lady Boyd* with 13in cylinders, for at the next meeting a month later the secretary was asked to instruct Bradshaw not to make any alterations to the cylinders of locomotive No 3 but ". . . to take tenders for the new rods required". Just at that time Bradshaw was not entirely *persona grata* with his directors, for a motion was moved by Mr Gildowney censuring him for an inaccurate and false report of the November derailment. A fortnight later the motion was withdrawn, but Mr Cotton was asked to censure Bradshaw. Although re-boilered and generally overhauled, the 1896 shopping of *Lady Boyd* did not make her identical with Nos 1 and 2 as regards power.

At some date during October 1894, the engine hauling the 8.30am down train broke a drawbar. It was always the practice to run the engines with the cab leading on down trains, so that it would have been a front drawbar that failed. Bradshaw recommended that check chains should be fitted on the front of the engines (which suggests that they were already in use at the cab end), and this was agreed to.

At the end of 1894, Bradshaw reported to the directors on the general condition of the three engines. With heavy repairs imminent, it was clear that the small workshops at Ballymoney would be heavily taxed. So Bradshaw suggested that, when their time came, the engines might be sent to the Belfast and Northern Counties shops at York Road, Belfast, a proposal that no doubt had his general manager's approval. But the matter was not a simple one, since it called for the construction of some form of permanent transfer siding at Ballymoney so that the engines could be readily loaded and unloaded from the broad gauge vehicle that would convey them to Belfast. Bradshaw discussed the problem with the Northern Counties engineers, and estimated that the provision of the proper transfer facilities would cost £92 10s. The Ballycastle directors decided that this was more than could be justified, considering the few occasions on which it would be utilised. Reconsideration produced a lower cost estimate, but by then Bowman Malcolm had suggested that only the parts of the engines needing repair should be sent to York Road. This became standard practice; there were no transfer facilities in Ballycastle Company days.

The new boilers which were fitted to *Dalriada* and *Countess of Antrim* in 1895 had a life of fifteen to seventeen years. Bradshaw stated in December 1910 that the boiler of the Countess needed "immediate renewal", and that *Dalriada's* boiler would last a further eighteen months to two years. On 12 October 1912, Kitson & Co tendered for a new boiler and firebox for *Dalriada* at £321, and this was put in during the winter. These heavy repairs sufficed for the rest of the lives of these engines.

At the Board Meeting on 28 September 1907, it was decided to sell "one or two old locomotives" and to buy two new engines. The Minutes do not indicate how the latter decision progressed up to the actual placing of the order, but in September 1908, about the time the new engines arrived, the company decided to sell *Lady Boyd.* They hoped to get £350 for her, which was an optimistic amount for an engine that only cost them £600, and that twenty-seven years earlier. They were soon to learn the difference between buying and selling, for in March 1910 the old engine was still on their hands and an offer of £90 from Messrs Freidlander was declined. In December 1910 they were still unable to dispose of her, even at scrap prices. In April 1911 am offer of £80 was declined, and the matter of disposal dragged on. At the meeting of the Board on 20 July the secretary was told to sell the engine for not less than £100, and the object was finally achieved on 12 October 1912, when the Company obtained £120 for her from McCoy & Sons.

The new engines ordered in November 1907 were designed by George Bradshaw. According to the Minutes of the Board Meeting of 6 November, the design was approved by Bowman Malcolm of the BNCR, and it was hoped that they would be ". . . less injurious to the road than the present engines". The contract for their construction was entrusted to Kitson & Co and they were to cost £2375 each. In September 1908 there were delivered two massive

4-4-2 tank engines with 14½in cylinders. It is difficult to see why such engines were ever thought suitable for the Ballycastle road, with its light rails laid across miles of resilient peat bog, its three severe curves and, above all, the steep bank out of Ballycastle. The idea may perhaps have been based on Bowman Malcolm's well established 2-4-2 tank design for the Ballymena and Larne section, with a bogie in front for the Ballycastle curves, and simple rather than compound propulsion.

The total weight of a Kitson tank was 39½ tons, far above anything that had run previously on the line, while little more than half the total weight rested on the driving wheels and was available for adhesion. The fixed wheelbase was 6'6", and must have been what attracted the designers, with the memory of *Dalriada*'s 11'9" wheelbase spreading the curves at Ballylig and Dervock. With boiler pressure of 165 lb per square inch a tractive effort of 13,964 lb was developed, but was rendered ineffective since the low factor of adhesion produced chronic slipping, which steam sanding did little to alleviate.

As delivered, the Kitsons had steam brakes, and were fitted with vacuum pipes, which were ornamental rather than useful since none of the rolling stock, either coaching or goods, was braked. By November 1909, complaints were being made that they had insufficient brake power, a fault scarcely to be wondered at in view of the state of the rolling stock, and when a safe entry into Ballycastle off the Capecastle bank was a matter of co-operation between the engine crew and the guard, with the latter keeping his brake-blocks hot during the descent.

Neither of the Kitson engines received names. They were numbered 3 and 4 and carried the number circled with 'BALLYCASTLE RAILWAY' on an oval brass plate affixed to the side-tanks. The maker's plate was also oval, set on the side of the bunker.

Payment for the two Kitsons was a prolonged affair, with delays due to the besetting shortage of cash. The negotiations started well, with the prompt payment of £2375 for one of the engines, but then slowed to instalments of £500. In November 1909, when the matter was almost closed, Kitson claimed an additional £78 14s 3d as interest, for which the Ballycastle Board promptly disclaimed responsibility. The last one hears of the settlement was minuted on 11 December 1909, when Kitson had left the ". . . matter of interest in the Company's hands".

The two Kitson tank engines must have caused the Ballycastle Company considerable disappointment but, apart from the faults referred to, they seem to have been reliable enough, for nothing more is heard of them in the Board Minute Books until December 1923, when there was a request for a new tube plate for No 4 from JAQ Bradshaw, who had succeeded his father six months earlier. But at that date the end of the Company's independent existence was in sight, and there was no money available for a major overhaul. In fact, neither engine received any heavy repairs during its sixteen years of work under the Ballycastle Company.

The original livery of the three Black, Hawthorn saddle-tank engines is not known. In latter years, and certainly after about 1910, they were painted unlined black, relieved only with red buffer beams and a red background to the polished brass nameplate. The Kitson engines, so far as is known, were always painted dark green, with black smokeboxes and funnels. They were not lined out. The buffer beams were red, and red background colour was applied to the polished brass plate carrying the number.

The maker's official photograph shows elaborate lining, super-imposed on the 'works grey'. In the 1911 photograph, taken in Ballycastle only four years after delivery, there is no trace of lining to be seen, a fact which is confirmed by Mr HA Boyd of Ballycastle, who was familiar with the appearance of these engines from the start. As it is highly unlikely that they would have been repainted in such a short time, it is probable that Kitsons were asked to omit the lining in the final green livery as an economy measure.

A final glance at the engine stock under the Ballycastle Company is provided for us by two manuscript reports which JAQ Bradshaw wrote to McAllen on 16 October and 12 December 1923:

> ENGINE NO 1. The boiler in this engine has developed a crack in the firebox tube plate. This crack was first seen about four years ago and was repaired in the usual way by the insertion of bushings in the tube holes. These bushings only last about four or five months, when they require to be renewed. At present they require renewal and I intend to have the work done during the next month or six weeks. This will make the engine good enough as a spare engine, but not suitable for heavy traffic continually.
>
> ENGINE NO 2. The boiler and firebox in this engine are in good order and do not show any signs of failure at present.

Above: *Ballycastle Railway 4-4-2T No 3,* Maker's photo

Left: *Ballycastle Railway 4-4-2T No 4 at Ballycastle station in 1911.* SB Jackson

ENGINE NO 3. This boiler and firebox are also in good order and the engine has just had a complete overhaul and a new set of tyres put on.

ENGINE NO 4. The firebox in this engine is in a worse condition than any of the others. There is a very bad crack in the firebox tube plate and the laps are badly wasted at the rivet holes. We are unable to keep the tube plate or laps tight. At present there is a bad leak at both places. I would suggest that we get a new tube plate for this engine and have it put in this winter. This would leave us three engines in good order for the summer traffic next year and No 1 in fair order as a spare. No 1, of course, would have to be done next winter.

If we get a new tube plate from the makers the NCC would put it in for us.

I should say that No 4 will also require new tubes and stays and probably some repairs to the outside shell of the firebox which I cannot do at present until the boiler is taken out of the frame.

....

NO 4 BOILER, Re my report of 16th October last, I have to state that the cost of a new tube plate for this engine is as follows:

Ballycastle Railway No 4, as LMS (NCC) No 114 at Larne. Along with sister No 3, No 4 was rebuilt by the LMS (NCC) in 1926/7, re-appearing as Nos 113 and 114. As they were then intended for use between Ballymena and Larne, where the bridge clearances were less than on the Ballycastle road, the height of the boiler mountings was reduced and the cab roofs lowered. The circular cab side window was also removed. Ian Allan Library/Real Photographs 297

New plate	£47	15	0
Labour fixing same	£50	0	0
Rivets, bolts etc.	£20	0	0
	£117	15	0
12½%	£14	14	4
	£132	9	4

The cost of re-tubing the boiler would be £175 in addition to the above £132, but I do not intend doing this at present as I think we can use the greater number of the tubes at present in the boiler and make up the difference from what we have in stock.
The length of time required to complete the work would be about four months.

The Ballycastle carriages and wagons

The first reference in the Board Minutes to the rolling stock was on 9 October 1879, when the directors asked Mr Robert Collins to:

> examine the works of the line, proposed stations, uncompleted portions of railway, with the designs etc received for locomotives, carriages etc and report to the Board, provided his fee for this work does not exceed £25.

They had wanted VG Bell, their consultant of the previous year, to attend to these matters, but he was stated to be ". . . in Jamaica on business".

Three months later, at the Board Meeting on 7 January 1880, Silas Evans submitted a list of the required rolling stock:

6	passenger carriages that would carry 256 persons
15	covered goods wagons
40	open goods wagons
5	cattle trucks
2	guard's vans for goods trains
2	guard's vans for passenger trains with accommodation for goods.

It was then estimated that this stock would cost £5820. Somewhat surprisingly, there is no reference in the Minutes to the taking of tenders for the rolling stock, and the next thing we find is the placing of an order in March 1880 with the Railway Carriage Company of Oldbury. Apart from the omission of two brake vans, and the inclusion of more detail, the list was basically similar to that of January, though the estimated price was £1595 more:

4	thitds, 5 compts	@ £350 each	£1400
3	composites, 5 compts (2 First, 3 Third)	@ £440 each	£1320
1	passr guard's van	@ £225	£225
15	covered goods wagons	@ £90 each	£1350
40	open goods wagons (6 tons each)	@ £65 each	£2600
5	open cattle trucks	@ £80 each	£400
1	goods brake van	@ £120	£120
			£7415

In June 1880, the directors asked Evans to write to the builders and urge delivery of the carriages, and in the following month he went to Oldbury to inspect the stock. At the same time, he discussed the matter of deferred payments with the builders, a procedure which was unfortunately necessitated by the slow intake of share capital. The Railway Carriage Company agreed to allow the payments to stand over for a period; four months was optimistically mentioned, but they insisted on affixing their own plates to the vehicles, as owners, until they were paid for. Thus it was that the Company started to run their trains with seven carriages, 60 wagons and two brake vans.

To judge by the price of £225, the vehicle referred to as a 'passenger guard's van' in the second list was probably four-wheeled and photographs confirm this. They show that it was considerably shorter in length than the six-wheeled carriages, but built in passenger-body style with a single door at one end, a guard's ducket next to it, and a set of double doors in the middle of the remainder of the side, and vertical panelling. At the end remote from the ducket, the side panels were interrupted by two arrays of nine horizontal ventilation slats, set into low hinged doors, which gave access to a dog compartment. A footboard extended the full length of the vehicle.

The Board of Trade Returns show that in 1881 the coaching stock was increased by one vehicle, classed among the 'other vehicles attached to passenger trains'. Strangely enough, this purchase escaped mention in the Board Minutes, but one may infer that it was another 'passenger guard's van' similar to the 1880 vehicle. In the later half-yearly reports, additional to the other seven carriages, two 'third-class brakes' are listed, in the coaching stock. There can be no doubt that these are the same as the earlier 'passenger guard's vans'; the fact that they are assigned a passenger class indicates that they were being used on the mixed trains.

Before they had been long in use, it became clear that the requirement of forty open wagons had been greatly over-estimated Evans suggested to the Board on 23 August 1882 that 15 or 20 of them might be sold and, after a discussion, he and Mr Casement were authorised to try and dispose of them for £55 each. An easy sale might have been made to the Ballymena and Larne or the Cushendall lines, which had a considerable amount of goods traffic, but there were no moves in that direction, perhaps because the buffers on the Ballycastle wagons were 4½" higher than on the two neighbouring lines. Indeed, it was not until March 1884 that they had anything approaching a taker; the Letterkenny Railway had been completed nearly a year before on the 3'0" gauge, and was being worked by the Londonderry and Lough Swilly Railway Company, whose own line, still on the standard gauge of 5'3", was soon to be re-gauged. The Swilly indicated that they might then be interested and, in October 1884, Basil McCrea, a partner in the firm of McCrea & McFarland (and who was financially supporting the Swilly Company), was ". . . disposed to buy twenty open wagons", but nothing came of it. Then, in February 1885, a month before the Swilly did their re-gauging, their manager and secretary, Frederick Dawson, came to Ballymoney and examined the redundant rolling stock. He is stated to have expressed interest in 20 open wagons and in one of the third-class carriages but, once again, the arrangements did not develop. In fact, the Swilly had already ordered carriages and wagons from the Railway

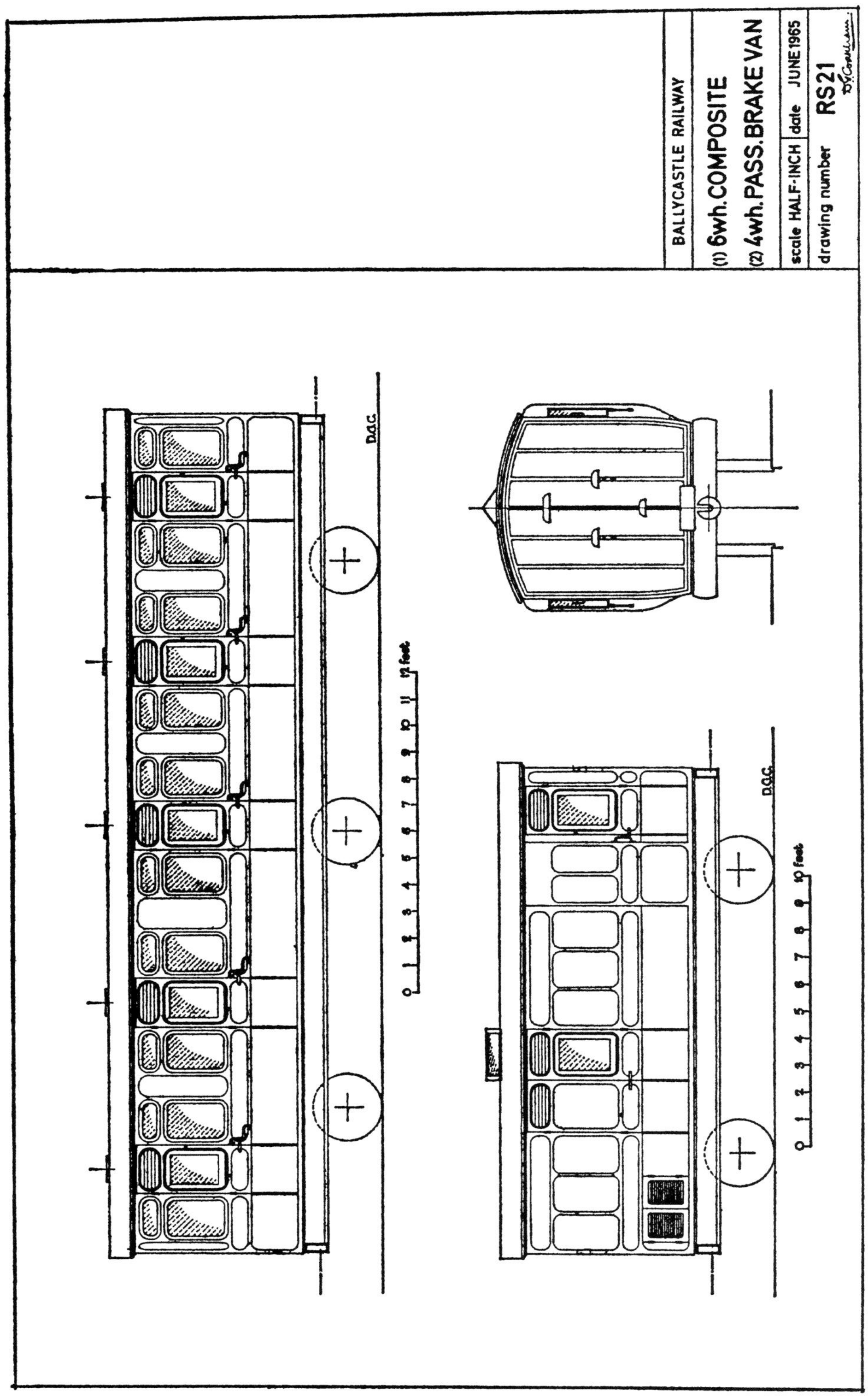

6-wheel composite carriage and 4-wheel passenger guard's van, built in 1880 by the Railway Carriage Comapny. Drawn by Mr DG Coakham, and reduced from the original.

Carriage Company, and it is possible that the difference in buffer heights between the two lines made purchase of the Ballycastle vehicles unacceptable.

No detailed specification is known to have survived of these Ballycastle carriages, but limited evidence can be obtained from photographs. Although bogie carriages had been in use for some years on other railways, the Ballycastle Company followed 1878 Ballymena and Larne practice in having six-wheelers built to the Cleminson patent. In this design the three pairs of wheels ran on axles and truck gear. The centre pair of wheels was capable of a degree of lateral movement, while the end pairs formed pivoted trucks, joined to the centre pair through radius links. By this means, the carriage was able to negotiate sharp curves with ease, and to avoid marked overhang at the ends. Although criticism can be made of the Ballycastle adoption of Cleminson-type six-wheelers, rather than of the more modern bogie carriages, it is noteworthy that later in the 1880s their example was followed by the West Donegal, Lough Swilly and West Clare Companies.

In the Ballycastle six-wheelers there were five compartments, separated by partitions reaching to the roof. In the composites, the compartments were arranged 3/1/1/3/3 and the exterior panelling shows that the first-class compartments were somewhat wider than the thirds. Originally, the seats in both classes were cushioned. A single footboards ran the full length of the vehicle on each side. The carriage sides were panelled, with raised mouldings around the windows, and they were curved inwards towards the frame. The fixed windows had radiused corners, with small, similarly radiused quarter-lights above them. Each door was surmounted by a horizontally slatted ventilator panel.

As we have seen, there was no second-class accommodation at first, but at the Board Meeting on 8 April 1881 the chairman proposed that this class should be provided by "... suitably altering some of the thirds". His motion won no support and was defeated. In a further effort to attract more custom, Mr McElderry suggested reducing first-class fares, and allowing second-class Northern Counties passengers to travel first-class on the Ballycastle line, and this suggestion was adopted. The decision to have second-class "on all trains" was taken on 22 April 1885, and was implemented by lettering two third-class compartments 'SECOND' in each of the three composites. The arrangement of these then became 2/1/1/2/3. The compartments were already cushioned, the status quo was maintained, but to differentiate then from the thirds, the seat cushions were taken out of the latter, leaving the passengers bare boards. The introduction of second-class was therefore nothing more than a down-grading of the third class. It is more than likely that the Company had decided that the cushioned comfort which it had bestowed on its more impecunious patrons could safely be dispensed with, without loss of custom.

The reasons for the disastrous runaway that occurred near Armagh on the Great Northern Railway of Ireland have often been described. The accident resulted in the urgent passage of Government legislation in the form of the Regulation of Railways Act 1889 which, among other things, required all trains carrying passengers to be provided with ". . . continuous brakes complying with the following requirements", namely:

- (i) the brake must be instantaneous in action, and capable of being applied by the engine driver and guard;
- (ii) the brake must be self-applying in the event of any failure in the continuity of a train;
- (iii) the brake must be capable of being applied to every vehicle of the train, whether carrying passengers or not;
- (iv) the brake must be in regular use in daily working;
- (v) the materials of the brake must be of a durable character and easily maintained and kept in order.

While the carriages of the ill-fated GNR(I) train were fitted with Smith's non-automatic vacuum brake, those of the Ballycastle Railway had no brakes of any sort, and the mixed trains being run depended solely upon the combined energies of the guard in the brake van and the screw handbrake on the engine.

With the passing of the 1889 Act on 30 August, there was tabled in due course at the Board Meeting on 9 November a circular memorandum from the Board of Trade, drawing the Company's attention to their obligations under the legislation. It was referred to a committee, and within a few weeks the following remarkable letter was sent to the Board of Trade from EJ Cotton:

> The directors of the Ballycastle Railway Company would request the Board of Trade to consider their exceptional position before insisting upon the requirements of the 'Regulation of Railways Act 1889' being carried out in this case.

> **First:** The Ballycastle Railway is constructed as a narrow gauge line of three feet and the traffic is very small and would not justify the directors running separate trains for their passenger traffic. The trains are all mixed, three each way per day for eight months and four for four months, and are run at low speeds, in no case exceeding twenty miles per hour. In the winter, only one engine is in steam, and in the summer there is only one train meeting on the line.
>
> **Second:** The Ballycastle Railway is at present worked on the staff and block system, and the points and signals are interlocked.
>
> **Third:** The cost of fitting all their engines, carriages and wagons would be about £2000.
>
> **Fourth:** The Company is at present barely able to pay three-fifths of their debenture interest, and a special arrangement has been made with the Board of Works to accept three-fifths of their interest for twelve years.
>
> **Fifth:** The Company, if compelled to raise £2000 in priority debentures, would be unable to carry out their obligation to pay three-fifths of the debenture interest. There would be a difficulty under any circumstances to raise the money.
>
> **Sixth:** The directors suggest that they be allowed to run their trains as at present, without the automatic vacuum brake; they would undertake to put steam brakes on their engines and run brake vans at the rear of all their trains: when trains are heavy they will run two vans. The engines are all tank engines; the steam brakes would act upon the six wheels and would on any part of the line stop an average train in a short distance.
>
> **Seventh:** The directors would wish particularly to draw the attention of the Board of Trade to the fact that their working expenses would be greatly increased if compelled to run their passenger trains from their goods trains, or else restrict the accommodation which they have hitherto given to the public.
>
> The last two half-yearly reports are enclosed herewith, also time-tables for summer months.

Considering the modern braking system then in use on the Belfast and Northern Counties line, this was a remarkable letter to be written by its general manager. It was not, however, in any sense defiance of a necessary regulation, but a sad admission of penury in a line only nine years old.

A year passed, and in December 1890 the Board of Trade made an Order under the 1889 Act. The Ballycastle directors met on 19 December to consider what to do, and requested Hamilton McAllen to say that the Company was unable to comply with it.

That the Company realised the potentially serious risk of an accident on Capecastle bank, can be seen by the decision in March 1891 to convert ". . . one of the flat wagons to a brake carriage at an estimated cost of £48". This complete rebuild was carried out in the Company's own workshops at Ballymoney and was completed by May 1892, yielding in the process a four-wheeled passenger brake van. According to Mr HA Boyd of Ballycastle, this vehicle had two doors and windows like an ordinary carriage and, having regard to its small size, substantial seating accommodation both along the sides and the ends. This informant is certain that the vehicle, after the start of the First World War, had no brake, so that if one was fitted at first it seems to have been subsequently removed. Between 1914 and 1924, it was not in constant use and sat, perhaps for days at a time, at the end of the departure platform at Ballycastle, where there was just enough clearance to allow the incoming engine to pass on its run-around.

In spite of its excuses, and the fabrication of a brake van at Ballymoney, the Board of Trade continued to be dissatisfied with the position, both in the running of mixed trains and in the lack of anything other than a guard's handbrake on the passenger vehicles. Correspondence between the two parties during 1892 and 1893 was inconclusive, but official pressure was renewed in the early part of 1894 when, in January and February, two letters came in from the Board of Trade. As a result, Cotton was asked to interview the Secretary of that Department. Apparently the meeting was without success from the Ballycastle's point of view, for in March, George Bradshaw was asked to prepare ". . . a statement as to the cost and number of vehicles to be fitted with continuous brakes for the next Board". There is, however, no mention of Bradshaw's submission in the Minutes of the meeting that followed. Then, in June 1894, the positive statement was minuted that "no further move" was ". . . to be made in the matter of continuous brakes at present."

The Board of Trade renewed its criticism in May 1896, but in reply the Company, continuing to drag its feet, referred them to its letter of December 1889 and stated that the position was unchanged. Shortly afterwards the

Company approached the Treasury to ask whether they would grant a suspension of payment on the Government loan for a period of two years, to enable them to meet the requirements of the Board of Trade. This playing-off of one department against another failed, and the Treasury pointed out that the Company should raise the money in the usual way, by the issue of debenture stock specifically for that purpose, as was provided for in Section 3 of the Act of 1889. The Company went to the Board of Trade in a further endeavour to get the necessary capital, and though eventually the Treasury did agree to a suspension of interest payment, the Company, in spite of this concession, took no steps to fit brakes to its rolling stock, nor were they ever fitted. It is a remarkable tribute to the Ballycastle train crews that, even with the lack of proper brakes, no runaway occurred on the dangerous Capecastle bank in forty-four years of working.

In their inimitable way, the Company had catered for the press of passengers on Lammas Fair day from as early as 1888 by placing seats in a number of the open wagons and fencing them around with netting wire. They were always a little uneasy about the practice, and no doubt took what care they could that the Board of Trade did not get to hear of it. The Minute Book states on 28 June 1895 that "... the position of open wagons seated for excursion traffic was considered, and it was resolved to continue to use them. No train to exceed 600 passengers."

The use of open wagons with seats continued until about 1907, by which time it would have been hallowed by tradition. The Board on 8 June 1907 discussed how they would cope with the demands of the public on the coming Twelfth of July, when the Orangemen were meeting both at Ballycastle and at Ballymoney. There was clearly insufficient carriage stock, and the normal train service was suspended for the day. 'Open wagons seated' were to be used, but the Company's solicitor was to be consulted as regards their liability in case of accident. Came 12 July and the Company manfully did its best with a succession of special trains to and fro. It got off lightly for its sins and only one accident was reported, ". . . to the thumb of the right hand of Samuel Shields Jr, a passenger from Stranocum to Ballymoney on the 10.15 am up special". The insurance company authorised settlement of the resulting claim "for a moderate amount" and £5 changed hands in November. That seems to have been the end of the open wagons.

By the summer of 1895, receipts were improving and the Company found that its market day and holiday traffic was taxing the capacity of the small carriage stock. Consequently Bradshaw was asked, in August 1896, to draw up the specification for a carriage ". . . to seat fifty passengers at a cost of £100–120". According to the Minutes, the specification was put out to tender in November, though only the name of the Metropolitan Railway Carriage & Wagon Co is mentioned. By this time, the directors were persuaded that something more modern than their £100 carriage was merited and the builders were asked to make ". . . a third-class carriage to seat eighty". The cost was to be £280, delivered in Belfast by 1 June 1896. The only other details of this carriage contained in the Minutes are a reference in March 1896 which states that " . . . it was not arranged to carry the partitions up to the roof".

The new carriage came in July 1896, an austere eight-compartment bogie, which was then the longest carriage anywhere on the Irish narrow gauge. In March 1898, the *Railway Magazine* contained an article on the Metropolitan Company, and the contributor had been amused by his sight of the Ballycastle bogie coach two years before. An illustration of it was captioned: 'The most antique style of bogie carriage constructed during the past twenty years'. The rather caustic remarks were enlarged upon in the accompanying text:

> It is like jumping back through several decades when the bogie third-class carriage for the Ballycastle Railway (Ireland) is come across. Lightness and cheapness were the objectives sought in the building of this class of stock. Both have been obtained. This curious coach is for a short narrow gauge line connecting Ballycastle with Ballymoney, where junction is made with the Belfast and Northern Counties Railway system. The car is open from end to end, and absolutely innocent of upholstery in the shapes of cushions and blinds. Riding in it on a bleak, cold day would not be a pleasant experience. However, at Saltley, orders have to be obeyed, and this vehicle is constructed to order from plans supplied. It may be assumed that the gentleman responsible for the plans has a carriage of a type best suited to the peculiar local requirements of the district in which it will be used.

In the May 1898 issue of the Railway Magazine an angry letter from a director of the Ballycastle Company was published under 'Pertinent Paragraphs':

> My attention has been called to an article in the *Railway Magazine* . . . in which your contributor, in an otherwise interesting article on the Metropolitan Railway Carriage and Wagon Works at Saltley, has seen fit to make some very disparaging remarks on a carriage built there for the Ballycastle Railway Company, Ireland; he calls it "the most antique style of bogie carriage constructed during the last twenty years". With regard to the word 'antique', the photo is its own denial, as any person conversant with railways knows that long bogie carriages, such as this one, are of comparatively recent introduction into these countries. If your correspondent seeks a study in the antique in railway stock, I would suggest his not journeying as far as Ballycastle (as I take it he is an Englishman, from his disparaging remarks about an Irish railway), but calling at ----- station and examining some of the four-wheel thirds (and even firsts) on the ------ local trains. With regard to the carriage in question, I defy your correspondent to find a more suitable one on any railway in England for its purpose, this being to carry the largest possible number of excursionists in summer weather, a distance of sixteen miles, at the least possible cost. Please insert the above letter in an early number of your Magazine.

The editor was, however, quite unrepentant and followed the letter with a final note:

> As the writer particularly asked for the letter to be inserted, we have done so. The peculiar part of the story, however, is that the writer of the article 'How the Nations Travel' happens to be a patriotic Irishman; so the director of the Ballycastle Railway is in error, in his surmise that Mr Wayman is an Englishman, his conclusion being arrived at merely because the latter stated an unpalatable fact concerning and Irish railway. Whilst as bogie carriages were in use on English and, for that matter, on Irish railways considerably over fifty years ago – although this director of the Ballycastle Railway apparently is not aware of the fact – the expression 'antique' is certainly allowable.

In the next half-year's accounts, capital was charged £284 8s 0d, so that the delivery charge from Belfast, levied by the Northern Counties Company, was £4 8s 0d.

Another eight-compartment bogie third was ordered from the Metropolitan Company in October 1897, and was to cost £330, delivered at Ballymoney. Although there is no record in the Minutes as to when it arrived, no doubt it was in time for the summer holiday traffic of 1898. The capital cost recorded in the report for the second half of that year is £331 19s 6d, suggesting that a charge of 39s 6d was incurred in getting it from a Northern Counties wagon at Ballymoney and safely on to the narrow gauge rails.

A third order was placed with the Metropolitan Company in November 1899, this time for two vehicles: another bogie third and a bogie third with brake and luggage compartment. The cost of these was £433 and £466 10s respectively. The third/van/brake had four passenger compartments, and the guard's compartment had side duckets.

In a general description of Irish narrow gauge rolling stock, written in 1912 by RM Livesey of the County Donegal Railways, a sketch is given of the bogie third/van/brake. The length over headstocks was 38', the overall height was 9'10" in diameter, the bogie wheelbase was 4'0" and the bogie centres were set at 26'8". It is likely that these dimensions applied also to the bogie thirds. Like their six-wheeled predecessors, they were supplied without any form of automatic brake, and depended upon the handbrake.

Surviving photographs show that these Metropolitan vehicles had flat sides, square-cornered windows, with plain rectangular quarter lights above. One of the thirds (No 14) had a partition of horizontal matchboarding reaching to the roof in the middle of the coach, thus dividing it into equal halves. The side panels are separated by raised mouldings, at the end of the coach were divided into six equal vertical strips by raised mouldings. The roof is elliptical, with eight openings for oil lamps. They have been described by those who used them as 'noisy' and 'rattly' and were apparently much less popular with the travelling public than the older six-wheelers.

From the start, carriage lighting had been by oil lamps, but after fifteen years' use some of the original fittings were becoming decrepit. EJ Cotton came to the rescue in characteristic style, and at the Board Meeting on 5 April 1895 it was minuted that he had ". . . arranged with his chairman to present the Company with forty of the Northern Counties Company's carriage lamps".

Repeated complaints from passengers eventually drove the Board on 26 October 1903 to ask George Bradshaw to report on improved methods of lighting. An acetylene lamp was obtained on trial for the winter of 1903–4, and in November 1904 it was decided to fit up one carriage with this type of light 'on trial'. Although a favourable report and a recommendation for general adoption was given in January 1905 by Bradshaw, the directors thought that fittings might 'be got on loan', but this apparently proved impracticable. The plunge was finally taken on 11 November 1905 when it was ordered that two composites and two thirds were to be fitted with acetylene gas lighting. The Company Minute Books never again mention the matter of acetylene lighting, and it is possible that only four or five carriages were ever so fitted, the others retaining colza oil as their illuminant. This would have given two normal train sets acetylene lighting, and left the occasionally-used stock with oil.

Upkeep of the carriage stock was not made any easier by the fact that most of it had to lie outside, owing to the limited shed accommodation. By 1893, the original six-wheelers were in need of painting and Bradshaw suggested in January that they ". . . be done up in a cheaper way than usual at a cost of £4 or £5 each". The Board ordered ". . . that one be painted in the way suggested and that Mr Bradshaw report further on the matter". It is unfortunate that the Minutes contain no details of the livery that was adopted. In April, Bradshaw told his directors that the work had cost £6 7s, and though this was above his original estimate he was told to have ". . . as many as possible repainted before the summer services". Attention to painting work was again given in February 1898 and the work was done by James Porter of Ballymoney, who was paid £5 15s per carriage, the Company supplying him with the paint.

Other minor improvements were dealt with in March 1896, when the Directors ordered that the covers of the lamp-holders, or what was termed "the plugs on top of the carriages", were ". . . to be fastened on the outside with chains or other simple means to prevent them being blown out". There had apparently been complaints about draughtiness, and it was decreed that ". . . doors of first-class carriages be made close at bottom". McAllen apparently minuted 'carriages' in error for 'compartments'.

Carriage heating was never done by engine steam, and was quite non-existent until 1891. In December of that year four footwarmers came – warming pans, in the vernacular – ". . . to be heated with hot water from the engines . . . for use in the first-class carriages". This concession to comfort

Ballycastle Railway Metropolitan bogie carriage No 14 at Ballymoney about 1900, with the locomotive workshop on the right. Beyond the carriage three men can be seen working at the First Presbyterian Church. EM Patterson collection

was deservedly popular with the travelling public, who were by then accustomed to better things beyond Ballymoney, and in January 1895 four new footwarmers were ordered, extending the facility to the second class.

In their 1919 annual report, the Company listed a total of fifteen coaching vehicles, made up as follows:

The detailed numbering of individual vehicles is not known, and

		Seats			
Passenger carriages	Number	1st	2nd	3rd	Total
Carriages of uniform class	7	–	–	440	440
Composite carriages	3	48	60	30	138
Miscellaneous	3	–	–	80	80
Total carriages	13	48	60	550	658
Other coaching vehicles					
Luggage, parcel and brake vans	2				
TOTAL COACHING VEHICLES	15				

only a limited knowledge can be gleaned from the few photographs that are known to exist. No 3 was one of the six-wheeler composites, and it is not unlikely that these three vehicles, which headed the 1880 list, were numbered 1, 2 and 3. While it is tempting to proceed to number the four six-wheeled thirds consecutively No 4 to No 7, there is at present no evidence to show that this was the case.

A photograph of No 14 proves it to be a bogie third, but with only one partition reaching to the roof. This might suggest that it is the bogie third which came in July 1886, since a published statement mentions "... the other bogie stock was on the accepted compartment principle". However, it is difficult to see how the 1886 carriage could carry a number as high as 14 in the coaching stock list at a time when the total is known to have been only twelve vehicles. It seems more likely that No 14 is the 1900 bogie third.

Of the three 'miscellaneous' passenger carriages in the 1919 stock list, one must be the 1900-built bogie third/van/brake, while the others are presumably the 1880 and 1881 four-wheeled 'passenger guard's vans'. The 1900 bogie is known to have had four passenger compartments; these would account for 40 out of the total of 80 seats allocated to these three vehicles. The remaining 40 seats must therefore be divided between the two four-wheelers.

The two 'luggage, parcel and brake vans', which bring the 1919 coaching stock up to 15 vehicles, are presumably the 1880 goods brake van (which is not listed in the 'mineral and merchandise' total of 59 vehicles) and the 1891 conversion, said then to have yielded a brake van from a flat wagon. This is not, however, in accordance with the knowledge that, by the end of the war, this

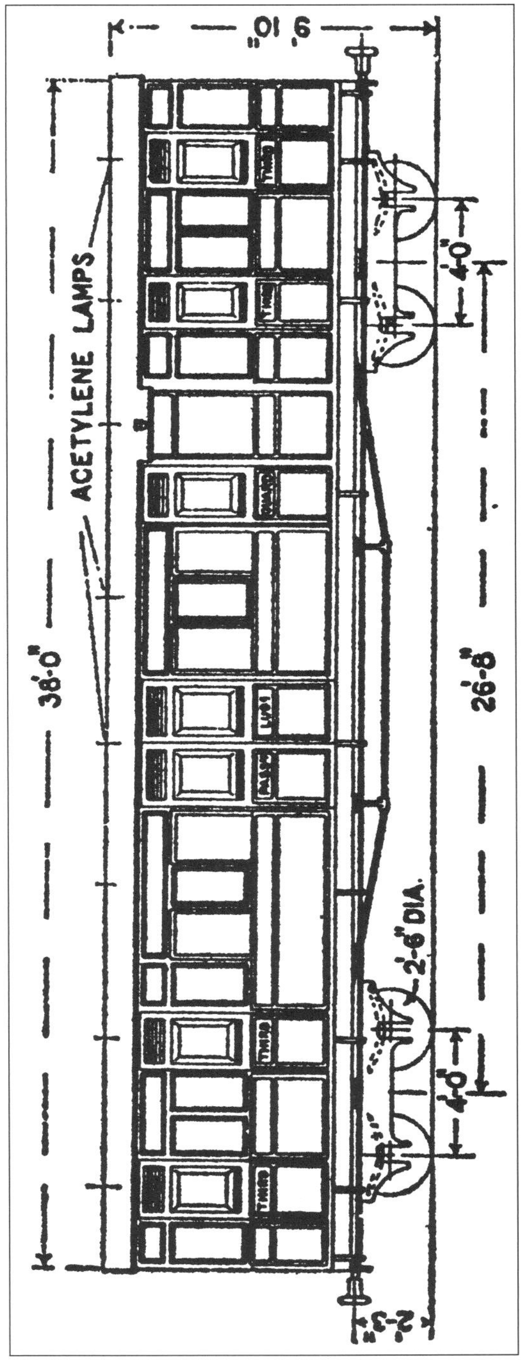

Ballycastle Railway bogie/third/van/brake, built in 1899 by the Metropolitan Railway Carriage and Wagon Co. From RM Livesey (1912). Proc Inst Mech Eng p599.

little vehicle was being used to convey passengers, and had then no brake. Perhaps it was placed for statistical purposes in the 'miscellaneous' section referred to in the previous paragraph, while one of the guard's vans was cited in the last section and regarded as having no seats.

The 1923 annual report shows that one vehicle in the coaching stock was scrapped during the year. Its disappearance from the list is accompanied by a diminution of 20 in the total of seats, which points to its being a two-compartment vehicle. There can be little doubt that it was one of the six-wheeled third/brakes, which was by then forty-three years old.

The entire carriage stock was withdrawn after the end of operation by the Ballycastle Railway Company in 1924, and was sold for seaside caravans or as scrap by the LMS (NCC). No attempt was made to modernise the BRC stock, and the process would probably have been uneconomical both because of its age and because of the difference in buffer heights from stock belonging to the Ballymena lines.

The carriage livery was two-coloured, the upper panels being cream and the lower panels and carriage ends dark brown. The roofs were white, or to judge by some photographs, also grey. The mouldings were lined in gold, though possibly yellow may have been substituted in the economical repaintings. Raised mouldings, coloured dark brown, separated the cream upper panels. Class designation was written in full in shaded block capitals on each door at handle level. 'B.R.C.' appeared at the same level, once on the six-wheelers and bogie/third/van/brake, and twice on the bogie third carriages. The number appeared as digits only, once on each side of the carriages. The Company's crest was not applied to the vehicles, to judge by photographs.

The original wagon stock was of 40 flats, 15 covered and five cattle wagons, totalling 60, which was reduced to 59 by the 1891–2 conversion of one of the flats, already referred to. They were numbered separately from the coaching stock. After 1892 the wagon stock remained unaltered. As far as it is known, all the wagons were 14'0" in length, on 8'0" wheelbases, and with 2'6" wheels. The cattle wagons had no roofs. Wagon capacity has been quoted at six tons. They were painted brick red, with 'B.R.C.' and the stock number in small white letters. The roofs of the covered wagons were painted grey.

Buffer centres of all the Ballycastle stock was 2'3" above rail level. This height compared with 1'10½" on the Ballymena and Larne, 1'11" on the Castlederg and Victoria Bridge Tramway, 2'2" on the Cavan & Leitrim, 2'3" on the West Clare, 2'7½" on the Londonderry and Lough Swilly, 2'9" on the Cork, Blackrock and Passage Railway, and 2'10½" on the County Donegal Railways Joint Committee, a gamut of levels which emphasises the difficulty of free interchange of vehicles.

The NCC engines

The engines used after 1924 came from Ballymena and Larne Railway, and of the Belfast and Northern Counties Railway which absorbed it in 1889. The BNCR was itself acquired by the Midland Railway of England in 1903, while the LMS took command twenty years after that. Under the aegis of the Midland and the LMS, their lines in Ireland were administered by the Northern Counties Committee.

The Ballymena and Larne Company owned six engines, which they got from Beyer, Peacock & Co at various dates between 1877 and 1883. These belonged to three different classes, and representatives of two of these classes went to the Ballycastle road.

Type	*B&L No*	*Built*	*Maker's No*
2-4-0T	1	1877	1687
	4	1878	1828
0-6-0T	2	1877	1700
	3	1877	1701
	6	1883	2304
2-6-0ST	5	1880	1947

The 2-4-0 tank engines were practically identical with the standard type used by the Isle of Man Railway, and it was the second of these, BLR No 4 which, many years later, spent a short time on the Ballycastle road. Like its classmate No 1, it had a leading pony truck with outside bearings, though the main frames were inside. The outside 11" x 18" cylinders were inclined at 1 in 9, and the side valves had Allan straight link motion. The smokebox and valve chests were integral, and the door to the smokebox sloped backwards. The original boiler was 2'10¾" x 7'8¼" with 103 tubes, but in 1898 it was replaced by one 2'10" x 7'11½" with 88 tubes. At the same time 12½" cylinders were fitted. The bell-mouthed dome contained the Salter safety valves. The driving cab was formed by a wrap-around plate which made the front, back and roof. The side sheets

This photograph of No 105 was taken around 1902. No 105 had previously carried the numbers 4 (Ballymena and Larne) and 64 (BNCR), becoming No 105 in 1897. It was transferred to Ballycastle shed in 1924, as spare engine, but did not stay long, being sold to the Castlederg and Victoria Bridge Tramway in November 1928. Ian Allan Library/Real Photographs 88702

LMS (NCC) No 106 at Ballycastle on 11 July 1931 with Driver McKissick carrying the 'long feeder'. No 106, along with No 108, was used to re-open the line in 1924. Ian Allan Library/Real Photographs X286

No 106 at Ballycastle on 10 August 1930. Note the very small NCC lettering compared to No 107 opposite. The engine has been fitted with Ross pop safety valves on the dome.
HC Casserley

No 106 being coaled at Ballymoney in 1931. This view shows the earlier timber-constructed coal stage. The houses in the left background are on Ozone Avenue.
Ian Allan Library/
LGRP 6772

No 107 was delivered to the Ballymena and Larne Railway, as its No 3, in 1877. It was renumbered 66 by the BNCR in 1889, becoming No 107 in 1897. This engine ran on the Ballycastle line for a period in 1927–8. This photograph is probably at Larne in 1929–31. It was withdrawn in 1931. CP Friel collection

This photograph of No 108 was taken at Larne Harbour on 3 August 1902. No 108 was one of the two engines used to re-open the Ballycastle line in 1924, and spent most, if not all, of its time there until 1932, when it was withdrawn. No 108 was scrapped around 1934. LCGB

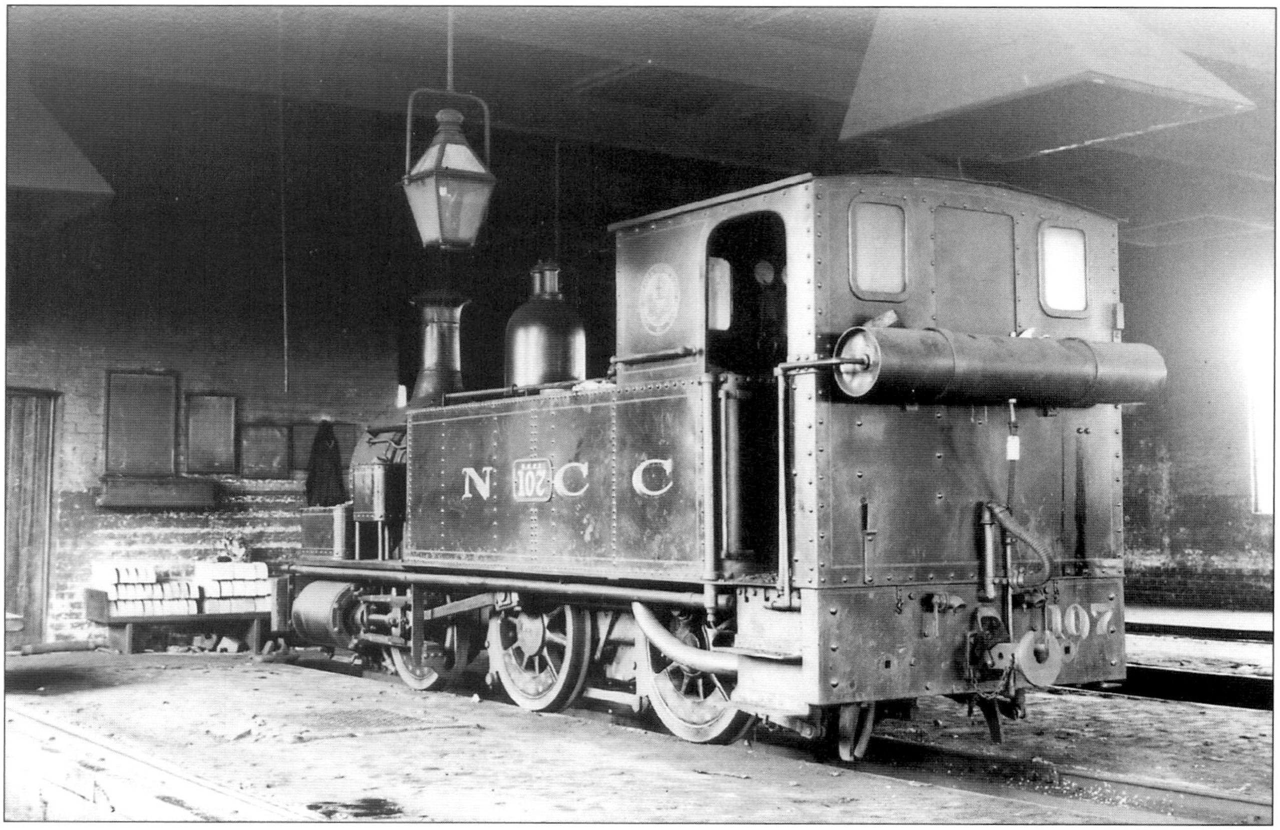

No 107 at Ballymena shed in 1931. The cylinder on the rear of the cab is the vacuum reservoir. JAGH Coltas

No 108 at Ballycastle on 11 July 1931 with small sans serif 'NCC' lettering. Ian Allan Library/ Real Photographs X289

No 101 is seen at Ballycastle on 1 August 1933, about five years after it was rebuilt to carry a rear bunker. This rebuilding entailed modifying the rear pony truck, thus extending the wheelbase by two feet. Along with similarly rebuilt No 102, they formed the S1 class of locomotive. The side tank carries the small 'NCC' lettering used about 1927–8.

Wm Robb, WT Scott collection

were short at first, but were later extended backwards. The spectacle glasses were rectangular.

BLR No 4 was renumbered 64 when it passed into BNCR stock, and retained this number from 1889 until 1897. It then became No 105 and was classified 'P'. Its days were spent on the Larne rather than the Parkmore road. By the time the NCC was stocking their Ballycastle section, No 105 was forty-four years old, and as there were then ten other narrow gauge engines in service, it was more or less in reserve. It was transferred to Ballycastle shed soon after the reopening and, according to Mr HM Rea of Bangor, it was there in the summer of 1926 as spare engine. In November 1928 it was sold to the Castlederg and Victoria Bridge Tramway Company, and allotted No 6 by its new owners though it never actually carried that number. When the tramway was closed in 1933, it was sold and scrapped.

The first two 0-6-0 tank engines were supplied with cabs open at the back, but BLR No 6 had a full cab when built. All three had inside frames, and horizontal 13" x 18" cylinders driving on the middle axle. The boilers of Nos 2 and 3 were 3'3" x 8ft , that of No 6 was 4½" longer, and at first they carried brass domes with salter valves. The smokebox doors were hinged vertically. These three locomotives became Nos 65, 66 and 67 in the BNCR stock list, and in the 1897 renumbering Nos 106, 107 and 108 of class 'Q' . All three found their way on to the Ballycastle section. Nos 106 and 108 opened the line in 1924 and spent much, if not all, of their time there after that, until they were scrapped in 1933 and 1934. No 107 was on the Ballycastle road in January 1927, when it hauled a special train carrying a profile frame to check bridge clearances, and at that time it had its original Salter safety valves. On all three engines the Salter valves were replaced by Ross pop valves, set in tandem on the dome casing.

During 1927, No 107 covered 36,940 miles, while No 108 is credited with 5438 miles, in the next year. This suggests that No 107 took the place of No 108 on the Ballycastle road during 1927–28, when the latter engine was away for overhaul. Mileage records also suggest that No 107 may have helped out in 1929 when No 106 was under repair.

Extant mileage records of Nos 106 and 108 covered the period from 1889 until 1933–34 when they were scrapped. They ran totals of 1,041,899 and 857,955 miles over this 43–44 year period, and averaged 23,100 and 19,400 miles per year. While on the Ballycastle line, the maximum annual mileage of No 106 was 22,770 miles in 1931. No 108's heaviest year was in 1930, when it ran 22,147 miles.

The unique 2-6-0 saddle-tank, BLR No 5, which formed the third of the original classes, and was the sole member

No 111 at Ballycastle with Jack McDuff.
CP Friel collection

No 44 at the water tank, Ballymoney on 28 June 1950 with Jack McDuff (on the footplate) and Barry Limerick. The water tanks at Ballymoney and Ballycastle were to a similar design. EM Patterson, courtesy CP Friel

of BNCR Class 'R' was never used between Ballymoney and Ballycastle. Affectionately termed 'The Bruiser' by the men, it was a tremendous puller, and would undoubtedly have performed well on the climb to Capecastle had it been given the chance, but it was retained for use up the stiff bank out of Larne, and the Ballyboley–Doagh branch.

In 1892, the BNCR ordered a pair of 2-4-2 tank engines from Beyer, Peacock. These two were the forerunners of an interesting and successful class of six engines (Class 'S') designed by Bowman Malcolm, locomotive engineer of the BNCR and MR (NCC) from 1876 until 1922. Malcolm was a pioneer in compounding locomotives, and during this term in office at York Road he built a large number of two-cylinder compounds on the Worsdell-von Borries principal. The narrow gauge examples had the high-pressure outside cylinder on the left, the low-pressure one on the right. Side-valves were operated by Walschaerts valve gear. Both cylinders received high-pressure steam during the first stroke, after which compound working began.

The first pair of 2-4-2 tanks were Nos 69 and 70 of the BNCR, and were renumbered 110 and 111 in 1897. No 110 is not known to have been used at Ballycastle, and was rebuilt as a 2-4-4T in 1931 (Class 'S2'). No 70/111 was not rebuilt and was renumbered 44 in December 1948. It was in service on the Ballycastle line for many years before the closure of the line and ran a total of 1,156,774 miles before scrapping.

No 44, of course, had her share of mishaps. One day the nut on the gudgeon-pin had no split-pin to retain it. The fitter tightened the nut before she left Ballycastle with a big cattle special, but on the run the nut worked loose, projecting until the side rod caught it. The two slide bars were knocked off successively, so that the released rod dropped. They had to stop, disconnect one side, and work the rest of the road as a simple. Another one-sided job was entailed with No 44 when the lubricator pipe to the low-pressure cylinder broke. Authority decreed that enough oil would get carried over from the high-pressure side to lubricate the low-pressure

No 102 on transporter wagon No 3045 at Ballymena in 1931. This engine spent its last years working from Larne to the paper mill at Ballyclare, although it did work on the Ballycastle line for a time in the mid-1930s. The paper mill closed in 1950 and, on 20 May, as No 42, she hauled the last train. The line was closed officially from Monday 3 July 1950. In this photograph the transporter wagon is clearly numbered 3045 but it is recorded in Dr Patterson's The Ballymena Lines *as being No 3094.*
JAGH Coltas

side as well. But experience proved this to be erroneous and, just before reaching Armoy, the low-pressure slide valve seized and the spindle broke.

After the acquisition of the first pair of 2-4-2 tanks a period of sixteen years elapsed before and addition was made to the class. The new construction was done at York Road, and the first engine, built in October 1908, emerged as No 112. It carried this number until February 1920, when it was renumbered 102, and then in November 1939 became No 42. As No 102 it worked for a time between Ballymoney and Ballycastle, and is known to have been there in 1936 (when a later engine, No 41, was away for a heavy repair), but its latter years were spent between Larne and Ballyclare on trains running to and from the paper mills.

York Road turned out No 113 in March 1909. Like No 112, it was renumbered in February 1920, becoming No 101. In June 1939 it went through a second renumbering and became No 41. It was in service on the Ballycastle line both as No 101 and as No 41, and probably replaced the 0-6-0T No 108 when that engine was scrapped in 1932. It went to Belfast for heavy repairs in May 1936, February 1945 and in January 1950. In its span of forty-one years it ran 469,761 miles.

No 41 was a most efficient engine and was popular with the men. In her later years of starved maintenance, she may not have been much to look at, but was nevertheless a vigorous performer. Barry Limerick was on the up-train out of Ballycastle one day when a number of senior officers of the NCC were on a tour of inspection. Their business had left them late, and they asked Barry to make a good run, to be certain of their Belfast connection at the other end. They had the usual two-coach train, and Barry, ably backed by big Jack McDuff, was through Capecastle in six minutes, leaving the Tow valley full of No 41's echoes. They were allowed twelve minutes on the working book for that. They went the rest of the road with the same *élan*, and were into Ballymoney in thirty minutes, which was ten less than the schedule for the express timings between the wars.

In July 1928, this engine, as No 101, was heavily rebuilt by modifying the rear pony truck so that the wheelbase was

No 101 coming off the Tow Viaduct with a Ballymoney train. Note the home signal towering above the train.
CP Friel collection

No 41 runs round its train at Ballycastle on 2 May 1946. Barry Limerick is on the footplate. The torpedo-shaped water tank on the platform can be seen above the carriage.
EM Patterson, courtesy CP Friel

No 41 in the platform road at Ballycastle, sometime after 1939. Note the number painted on the buffer beam. In 2006, the station building and platform are extant, though inaccessible to the general public. The building under construction in the background, also survives.
CP Friel collection

extended by two feet to carry a rear bunker. No 102 received the same surgical treatment in June 1930 and, as a result of these changes, these two engines were classified 'S1'.

The last pair of compound tanks were No 103, turned out from the Belfast shops in September 1919, and No 104, in March 1920. As far as is known, No 103 was never used at Ballycastle. After a short life, she was withdrawn at the end of 1938 and scrapped. The last of the series, No 104, spent many years working out of Ballymena. She became No 43 in October 1942 and in that state was transferred to the Ballycastle road, following heavy repairs and reboilering in 1946–47. During 1947, she ran 36,531 miles, and in 1948, 42,407 miles, both of which totals were in excess of any of her fellows. She survived until the closure of the line and, like Nos 41 and 44, was retained in stock until February 1954, when she was withdrawn and sold.

The livery of Nos 105/6/8, the first engines transferred by the LMS (NCC), was that of the old MR (NCC), and this was altered to the livery of their pre-grouping owners as the engines went through the shops, though there is now no record of the dates. The general colour was the so-called 'invisible green', a very dark colour which approached black. The initials 'MR', in shaded, sans-serif gold capitals, were on the side tanks, flanking the number plate. The Midland crest was on the cab side. The buffer beans were red, and smokebox black. The lining was in three colour, as follows:

Panel	invisible green	
1/8" line	vermillion	rounded corners
1" band	invisible green	rounded corners
3/8" line	light blue	rounded corners
3/8" line	yellow	rounded corners

No 43 on shed at Ballycastle on 2 July 1949. At the closure, No 43 was at Ballymoney where it remained until it was cut up.
Wm Robb, WT Scott collection

Maker's plate on No 43 showing its MR (NCC) parentage.
Wm Robb, WT Scott collection

No 43 crosses the Tow Viaduct at the head of the 5.40pm departure from Ballycastle on 2 July 1949. Just one year later the last trains would be running! Wm Robb, WT Scott collection

The numberplates were of cast brass, with the background colour invisible green.

The compound engines at Ballymena would have had a similar livery to the aforementioned until their shoppings in 1925–1930, but by the time they were transferred to Ballycastle they were painted in LMS crimson lake or maroon. The smokebox was black, an buffer beam red. The LMS (NCC) crest was carried on the cab side-sheet. The initials 'NCC' were sited on the side tanks, either as small block letters or as serif letters, either small or large. On the three six-coupled engines, the numberplate was in the middle of the tanks, and the 'NCC' transfers were applied behind the plate. The compound engines had their numberplates on the tanks, in line with the front of the cabs, and the letters 'NCC' were placed in front of the plates. The lining was as follows:

Panel	crimson lake or maroon	
1/8" line	yellow ochre	square corners
2½"–3" band	black	square corners
Edge		

The numberplate backgrounds were at first maroon, but later were red.

During the Second World War, all the narrow gauge engines were painted unlined black. Buffer beams remained red, as way the background to the numberplates. This sombre livery was followed in post-war years by the UTA's livery. Though some experimental colours were tried by the UTA, this was confined to the broad gauge engines. On the narrow gauge engines, for which there was no long-term future, the black colour of wartime continued, but was eventually enlivened on Nos 41 and 44 by vermilion and yellow lining:

Panel	black	
1/8" line	vermillion	square corners
1" band	black	square corners
1/4" line	yellow	square corners

The UTA's roundel, 14" in diameter, with 'ULSTER TRANSPORT' in orange block capitals, lined in red, surrounded a white shield bearing a red hand. The whole

4-4-2T No 113, the former Ballycatle Railway No 3, is seen in NCC days at Ballyboley Junction. After the 1924 takeover of the Ballycastle Company, No 113 spent most of her time on the Ballymena and Larne section. Withdrawn in September 1940, she was returned to stock in August 1942 and spent some time back at Ballycastle. She was withdrawn in July 1946.
CP Friel collection

had a mid-green background and was placed on the side tanks of Nos 41 and 44 (see page 66).

The style of the numberplates remained a characteristic from BNCR days. The plates were cast from brass, and were of rectangular, horizontal format, approximately 18" x 10". The corners were radiused and there was a raised ½" edge. The plates of the first BNCR number series (Nos 60–70), current to 1897, contained boldly serified numbers alone. The second series (Nos 101–111) had similar numbers, but had 'BNCR' lettering milled off when it was rebuilt, and in consequence the numbers were offset towards the bottom of the plate. The MR (NCC) renumbering of Nos 112/102 and Nos 113/101, and numbering of Nos 103 and 104, gave these engines plates with digits alone, but otherwise they were similar to the earlier series, and this principle was maintained in the last renumbering to Nos 41/44.

Mention must finally be made of the two Ballycastle Railway 4-4-2 tank engines which were rebuilt by the LMS (NCC) in 1926–7. Originally Nos 3 and 4, they emerged as Nos 113 and 114. They were intended for use on the Ballymena–Larne line but, as bridge clearances there were less that at Ballycastle, the height of the boiler mountings and cabs was reduced. New boilers were fitted to No 113 in December 1926, and to No 114 in November 1927, the original chimneys and domes being replaced by shorter versions. The cab roofs were lowered, and the round side porthole vanished. The front spectacle glasses, round in Ballycastle days, became radiused rectangular, though round windows remained at the back. Only No 113 ever returned to the Ballycastle road, and then only for a period of about a year during the Second World War. Back on its home ground, it repeated its slipping and became thoroughly unpopular with its crews. For its last six years its existence hung in the balance, for it was actually withdrawn on 30 September 1940. Its scrapping was deferred because of the war, and it lay unused through 1941, being put back into stock in August 1942. During the rest of that year it covered 13,739 miles. From then until it was withdrawn in July 1946, the miles run totalled 21,995, mostly from Larne shed.

NCC carriage stock

The carriages transferred to the Ballycastle section in 1924 had been built for the Belfast and Northern Counties Railway for use on their Ballymena–Parkmore line. The latter line had been built by the Ballymena, Cushendall and Red Bay Railway, and was used by them solely as a mineral railway. It was taken over in 1884 by the BNCR, who recognised its tourist potential, secured powers to work passenger traffic over it, and stocked it with verandah-ended carriages.

Passenger workings to Parkmore fell away after the First World War, and were terminated in 1930. By 1924 it had therefore become possible to release some of the 'Cushendall' carriages and transfer them to Ballycastle. There were ten of these and a brake van, built at various dates between 1886 and 1898. Since the BNCR generally numbered their narrow gauge carriage stock in chronological sequence, starting from No 301, vehicle numbers of a particular type are not necessarily concurrent. There was, however, an earlier, separate numbering series for the Cushendall stock, and it is known that Nos 4 and 5 of that series later became Nos 319 and 320. In that later series, the verandah-ended Cushendall carriages, officially termed 'tramcars', were:

Third Class	Nos 306/7	(built 1886),	
	Nos 316/7	(built 1891),	
	Nos 319/20	(built 1889),	
	Nos 331/2	(built 1898)	
			Total 8
Composite 1st/3rd	Nos 329/30		*Total* 2
Brake Van	No 333		*Total* 1

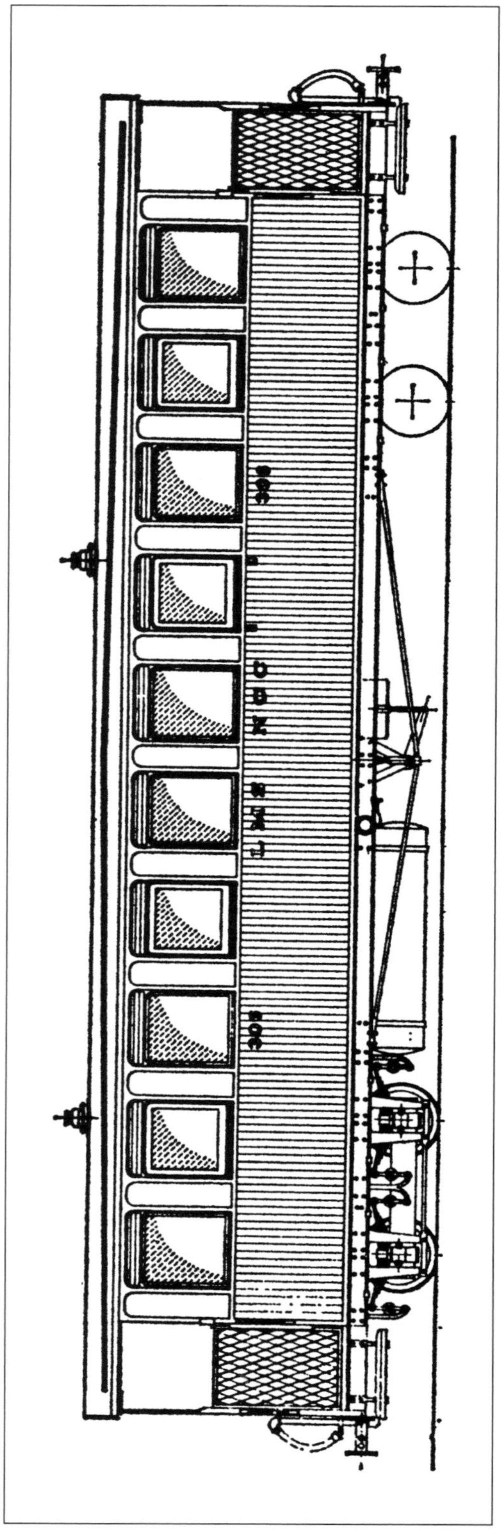

Ex-BNCR 1886-built 8-wheel carriage No 306 used by the LMS (NCC) on the Ballycastle section. Reduced from a drawing by Mr DG Coakham.

Three of these vehicles (Nos 306, 329 and 330) are known to have been on the Ballycastle section from the start, and would have been sufficient to form one train set. Probably two others were in use as well, enabling two trains to be worked on Lammas Fair days. All these vehicles possessed rather peculiar, semi-rigid suspension. The characteristics of No 306, the last survivor, are described by Mr DG Coakham:

> Its most peculiar feature lay in the suspension as the two four-wheeled trucks were not conventional bogies, having neither bolsters nor pivots . . . The axleboxes did not have any side-play in the trucks, which were merely two plates 8in x ½in connected laterally by one 5" by ½" member, and the only flexibility achieved was through a system of links between the leaf springs and brackets rigidly fixed to the main frames of the coach. Hornplates, set wide apart to allow for axlebox movement, were riveted to the solebars. As the clearance between horns and truck frames was only fractional, lateral truck movement must have been very restricted and a lot would have depended on the elasticity of the truck frame.

The general arrangement of the vehicles was of a flat-sided saloon divided into two unequally-sized parts by a partition with a communicating door. Longitudinal wooden seats were placed along each side, and entrances were from the end platforms, There were ten windows along each side, three of which belonged to the smaller saloon compartment. Early photographs show roofs which had a much steeper contour than in later days, but the date of rebuilding is not known. Some of the class also seem to have had clerestory roofs, and 16 side windows.

Steel channel solebars, 6" x 2¾", ran the length of the saloon body to form the main frame, while the platforms were supported on narrower cantilever frames. In the case of the 1886 vehicles, the wheelbase of the trucks was 3'9" + 20'3½" + 3'9" = 27'9½". The saloon body measured 31'10½", while the length over headstocks was 37'. Similar dimensions are believed to have applied to the 1889 and 1891 vehicles, but the 1898 passenger carriages were all about 3'0" longer. The length of the brake van, No 333, was 33'0", and it was built with observation ends to match the other tramcars.

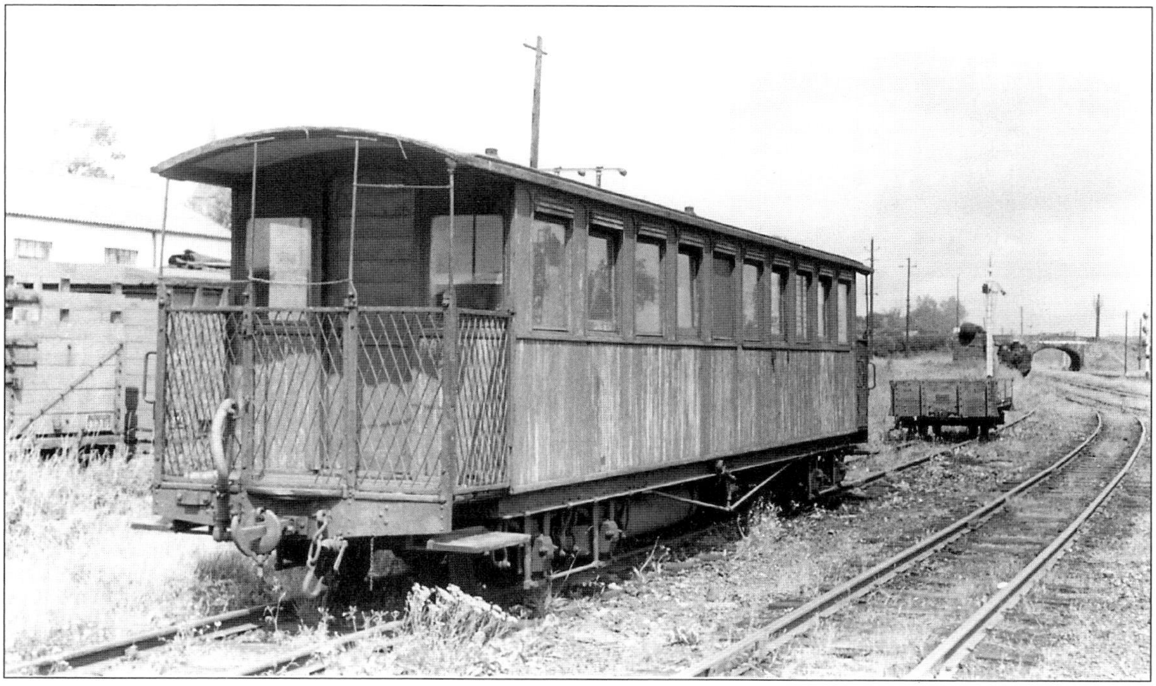

Ex-BNCR 8-wheel carriage No 306 at Ballymoney in June 1950. This 1886-built vehicle was a remarkable survivor, not being officially withdrawn until 1954. The water tank can be seen to the left of the signal and the engine taking water is No 44. The light-coloured building on the left was part of the creamery. EM Patterson, courtesy CP Friel

Roof ends were supported on ¾" diameter pillars, which were welded to 2" x 2" angle-iron verticals enclosing a framework covered with expanded metal. Side and end gates were similarly constructed, and pivoted fall-plates allowed passage between the vehicles. Lighting was by oil gas, stored in a cylinder below the frame.

Of the known Ballycastle vehicles, Nos 329 and 330 were scrapped in 1932. No 306 had a remarkable survival, and lasted as a spare carriage until the closure of the line, and was used on Lammas Fair days trains.

In 1928, the LMS (NCC) re-equipped their Ballymena–Larne narrow gauge line with new coaching stock. Five new vehicles were built at York Road, with corridor connections and lavatory accommodation.

They had a body width of 8'0", just over 1'9" more than the old Cushendall carriages that were working on the Ballycastle line, and in comfort they were far in advance of anything that had run on an Irish narrow gauge railway. They were, however, introduced at a time when passenger usage of the old BLR section was declining and, after the disastrous 1933 strike, it was decided to end passenger train working out of Larne. So the corridor coaches had only five years' service on the Larne boat trains before they were transferred to Ballymoney and unloaded on to the Ballycastle section, to replace the old BNCR carriages that had been there for nine years. The details of the 1928 corridor carriages were as follows:

			Compts		*Seats*	
No.	*Type*	*Length*	*1st*	*3rd*	*1st*	*3rd*
318	Third	41'3"	–	2	–	52
350	Compo	50'0"	2	2	12	31
351	Compo	50'0"	2	2	12	31
352	Bk/3rd	50'0"	–	2	–	24
353	Bk/Compo	50'0"	2	2	12	31

Note: No 318 – new body on 1879 BLR frame

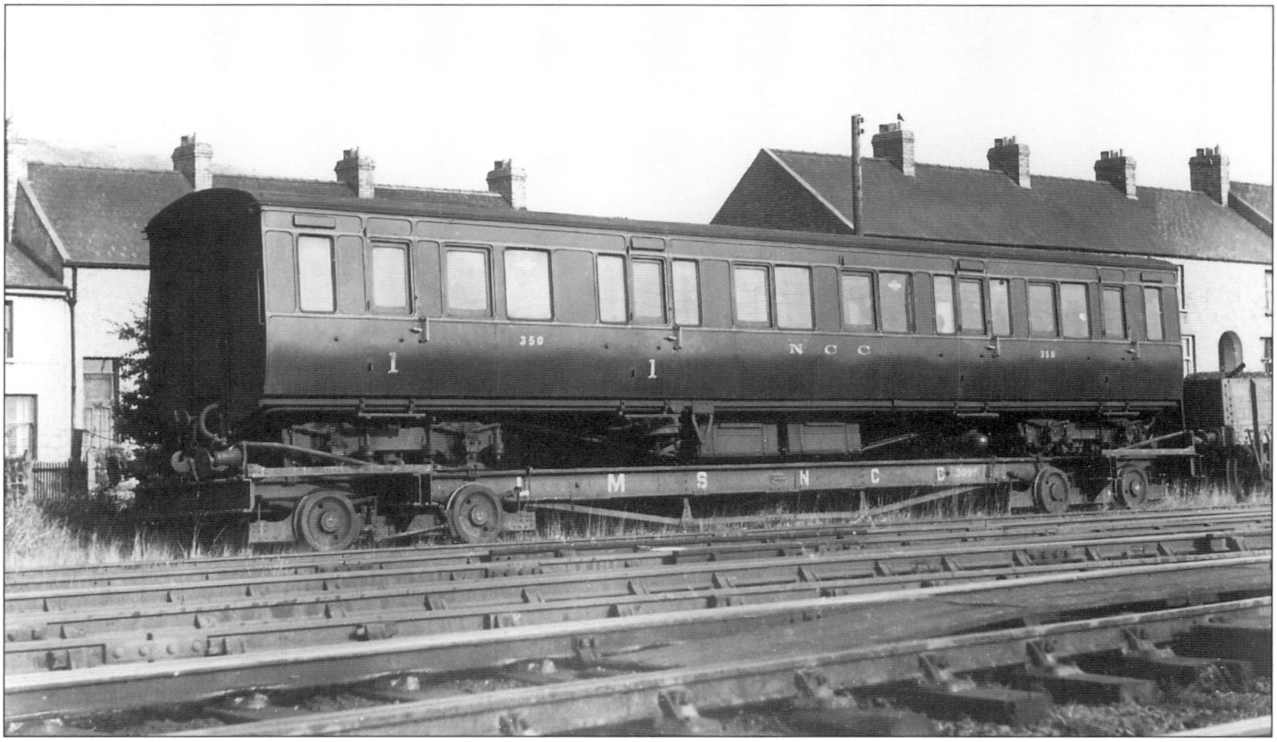

Coach No 350 on transporter wagon No 3095. The location is thought to be Ballymena Harryville. Transporter No 3095 was built in 1930 and was 54'4" in length. Ian Allan Library/Real Photographs X298

Coach No 352 was new in 1928 and is seen here at Ballycastle in 1936. When new it was a Brake/Third but the guard's compartment was converted to a 30-seat passenger compartment in 1936. Sold in August 1951, it became No 57 on the County Donegal Railway. Ian Allan Library/LGRP 7359

A second view of coach No 352 at Ballycastle in 1936. Note the corridor connection, later removed and boarded up.
Ian Allan Library/LGRP 7360

No 318, as rebuilt, had two compartments with communicating door, a non-smoker 17'3" in length and seating 22, and a smoker seating 30. Both compartments had a centre corridor and each had one door on each side. Bogie centres were set at 31'3½", bogie wheelbases were 4'9", and wheel diameters 2'1¾". The weight was 13¾ tons. The vehicle was retained after services ceased at Ballycastle, and in January 1952 it was sold to the County Donegal Railways Joint Committee. On that line it became No 58, and worked until the closure at the end of 1959.

Nos 350 and 351 were identical carriages, with end vestibules. The four compartments had connecting doors and a central corridor and were arranged as under:

Class	*Type*	*Length*	*Seats*	*Remarks*
Vestibule	(lavatory)	5'8¼"	–	door each side
1st	non-smoking	6'11"	6	no side doors
1st	smoking	6'11"	6	door each side
3rd	smoking	11'11"	15	no side doors
3rd	non-smoking	11'11"	16	door each side
Vestibule	(lavatory)	5'8¼"	–	door each side

The bogie wheelbases were 5'6", wheel diameters 2'1¾", and bogie centres at 38'. The weight was 16 tons. No 350 was withdrawn from stock in 1954. No 351 was sold to the CDRJC in January 1952, became No 59 and worked on that railway until its closure.

No 352 was built as a brake/third, but was altered in 1936 to a third, with a rather unusual compartment plan, inherited from the former guard's compartment in which thirty passengers were seated longitudinally. Positions and dimensions of the compartments were:

Class	*Type*	*Length*	*Seats*	*Remarks*
Vestibule	(lavatory)	5'8¼"	–	door each side
3rd	non-smoking	5'11"	8	no side doors
3rd	non-smoking	11'11"	16	door each side
3rd	non-smoking	25'7"	30	door each side

The wheelbase dimensions and weight were the same as No 350/1. This coach was sold to the CDRJC in August 1951, became No 57 there, and was in use until the railway's closure.

Coach No 353 was a Brake/Composite with seating for 43 passengers – 12 in First Class and 31 in Third. There were four passenger compartments. No 353 was withdrawn and sold in February 1954.
Ian Allan Library/Real Photographs 88710

Class 23 four-wheel goods brake van, either No 325 or 326 and ex-BLR, and Class 16 six-ton wagon No 4511 at Ballycastle in 1931. The cast number plate from No 4511 can be seen in Ballymoney Museum. Ian Allan Library/LGRP 6773

No 353 was again a unique vehicle, though its passenger accommodation had close affinities with that of Nos 350/1. Owing to the size of the guard's compartment, the single end vestibule had to be very small. The compartments were distributed as follows:

Class	*Type*	*Length*	*Seats*	*Remarks*
Vestibule	(lavatory)	4'1½"	–	door each side
1st	non-smoking	6'11"	6	no side doors
1st	smoking	6'11"	6	door each side
3rd	smoking	11'11"	15	no side doors
3rd	non-smoking	11'11"	16	door each side
Guard	–	7'2"	(2)	double side doors

The wheelbase, wheel sizes and weight were the same as Nos 350/1/2. This carriage was withdrawn and sold in February 1954.

All the 1928-built vehicles had electric lighting. On the Ballycastle section, corridor connections were unnecessary, and they were later removed and the openings boarded up, an arrangement retained on the vehicles which ended their days on the County Donegal line.

Although the above five coaches found their way on to the Ballycastle line, only two were used on the ordinary train. The others lay in the sidings at Ballymoney, and were brought into use on Fair days. Various combinations have been noted in photographs: 350/352, 352/353 and 318/351. It was likely that No 352 was transferred to the Ballycastle section for use during the summer of 1930, for a photograph taken on 10 August that year shows it in its original state, with brake compartment and end duckets, forming the last vehicle of a two-coach train, the front coach being one of the ex-Cushendalls.

Carriage livery was crimson lake, with a 3/8" yellow stripe and a 1/8" red line round all mouldings, except at the ends where only the 1/8" red line was used. The buffer planks were lined out in 1/8" red at the front and on the ends. The roofs were painted white at first, but were later repainted grey. The corridor coaches originally had double horizontal mouldings below the windows; between these mouldings was the lettering '353 LMS NCC 353' applied in gold, shaded red and black. The class designation was by large gold figures on the lower half of the door. In later years the horizontal mouldings below the doors were removed.

NCC wagon stock

As a result of the extensive damage which the station and offices at York Road, Belfast, suffered during the 1941 air raids, no records remains of the transfers of wagons to the Ballycastle section in 1924 and the year immediately following. In his search for details of the wagon stock the writer was fortunate in being granted access to unpublished information in the possession of Messrs DG Coakham and JH Houston.

It seems reasonable to assume that the majority of the wagons used on the Ballycastle line were taken there before the outbreak of the Second World War, and remained there until the line's closure, or at least until they became unserviceable. They were transferred as required from the Ballymena lines and, in consequence, they represent a part of the NCC's overall classification. The majority were numbered in a series, but in December 1934 some others were assigned numbers in a 53xx series and derived these by the addition of 5000 to an earlier 'other coaching vehicles' series of former Ballymena and Larne Railway stock.

The wagon stock on the Ballycastle line at the 1950 closure was as follows:

Type	*Numbers*	*Class*	*Total*
OPEN WAGONS			
End tipping	4360	1	1
End tipping	4216/47/61,4317/28/76/87, 4453	9	8
Centre door	4194/95/99, 4215/46/58/59, 4310/11/27/2/68/44		
	4350/65/70, 4414/15/21/30/31/78/88/91, 4540	10	25
Dropside or ballast	4354/94, 4493, 4541	14	4
Timber truck	4202, 4318	11	2
Travelling crane	4162	–	1
COVERED WAGONS			
Flat roof	4123/92, 4218, 4303/57	17	5
Flat roof	4124	18	1
Flat roof	5308/10/11/13	25	4
Cattle	4274/77, 4507	21	3
Open head or canvas centre	4458/59/76, 4510/11/13/20	16	7
BRAKE VANS	4252/53/55	24	3
	5325/26	23	2

Class 10 eight-ton open cattle wagon No 4311 and Class 16 six-ton wagon No 4513 are seen at Ballycastle in 1948. The three-plank extension to the bodysides of No 4311 was constructed at Ballymoney after the war, using parts machined at York Road and Ballymena. Ian Allan Library/LGRP 13981

Of these, the only vacuum-braked vehicles were the covered goods wagon (No 4124) and the five brake vans.

(Editor's note: The above information is contradicted by the detail of Class 25 vehicles given in the note to the table opposite. A further four vacuum-braked vehicles are listed therein.)

The brake vans were of two classes. Nos 4252, 4253 and 4255 were ex-BLR goods stock and were the lighter and had double side doors. Nos 5325 and 5326 were ex-BLR passenger stock, had single doors at one end, a sliding door in the middle of each side, and a side ducket between the two. Three centre-door open wagons, or flats, were fitted with sheep frames, and were Nos 4258, 4328 and 4478.

The twelve 'Classes' referred to in the above table belonged to a serial classification covering all the NCC's narrow gauge wagons. The main dimensions of those that ran on the Ballycastle line are given in the following table:

Class	*Length over headstocks*	*Overall height*	*Overall width*	*Wheel-base*	*Ave tare t.*	*c.*	*q.*	*Capacity c. ft*
1	12'6"	3'9¼"	6'6"	7'0"	2	8	0	100
9	14'0"	6'2¾"	7'0"	8'0"	3	7	0	280
10	14'0"	5'11¾"	7'0"	8'0"	3	7	0	280
11	12'6"	3'9¼"	6'6"	7'0"	2	11	0	–
14	12'6"	3'11¼"	6'6"	7'0"	2	7	0	99
16	14'0"	9'0¼"	6'6"	8'0"	3	14	0	466
17	14'5"	8'8½"	6'8"	8'0"	3	11	0	484
18	14'5"	9'0¼"	6'8"	8'0"	3	16	0	522
21	14'0"	9'6¾"	7'0"	8'0"	3	15	0	535
23	16'0"	9'3¾"	8'4"	9'0"	5	0	0	539
24	14'0"	8'9"	6'7½"	8'0"	5	3	0	483

Note: Class 25 (Nos 5308/10/11/13) were originally BLR four-wheel third class carriages. On rebuilding as wagons, their vacuum brakes were retained.

As a result of air raid damage suffered at York Road in 1941, no records exist of the transfer of wagons to the Ballycastle line, although it is accepted that most were moved prior to 1939. Class 25 van No 5310 was one of those transferred but in this view it is seen at Larne. CH Hewison

Chapter 8

Conclusion

The penalties of pioneering

From the point of view of its shareholders, the Ballycastle Railway began life several years too soon, and was unable to benefit to any extent from the Governmental benevolence of the 1880s and 1890s. Once begun, the Company had, perforce, to stand on a rather shaky pair of feet; its passengers mostly moved on Fair days, and its goods wagons were considerably under-employed. It was also a rather odd twist of fate that this line, which connected one of Ireland's few coalfields with the interior of the country, should have found that same coalfield largely exhausted and unable to contribute any significant traffic to the railway.

Although it was not the first Irish narrow-gauge railway line, the Ballycastle was one of the pioneers and, like many such, it paid a price for its enterprise. The whole conception of what a light railway might be, and how it might benefit from its 'lightness', was lost sight of, but this fault was common to most of the other narrow gauge railways in Ireland. Though with no firm expectation of heavy traffic, it cost £5723 per mile to construct, and its sponsors seem to have made it without any very clear idea of its potential earnings. Since the terminus was simply a small market town, and Armoy and Dervock mere villages, the ensuing disappointment at the small receipts was largely of the promoters' own making.

Inevitably, the line was not assisted by the inflexible Board of Trade regulations which called for, and insisted upon, the expense of full signalling, block working, massive stations and the rest. As built, the Ballycastle Railway was a far better copy of a main line than it could afford to be. The maintenance of the five stationmasters and ancillary staff cannot have been justified.

The situation was made none the easier for the directors by the slow intake of capital. Ordinary shares were never taken up completely and, to raise capital, recourse had to be made to the statutory loans, which channelled off most of the profits, and left little or none for the ordinary shareholders. Cheese-paring tactics were forced on the Board, and the permanent way, in particular, was chronically neglected.

In spite of able management and its close link with the Northern Counties line, the Company hovered on the brink of bankruptcy for much of its forty-five years as an independent concern. The inflation that followed the First World War completed its ruin, and the Company was forced to go into liquidation, even before the post-war breeze of competing road transport grew to a gale.

Liquidation brought no crumb of comfort to the ordinary shareholders, for the LMS (NCC) bought the line and buildings for one-eighth of what they had cost to put on the ground. It threw away engines, carriages and wagons as useless, and restocked the line with Ballymena and Larne cast-offs, proceeding then on a course of austere simplification that was forty-five years too late. The goodwill of the travelling public was maintained, and the line became an appendage which fed what we see today as the last surviving main-line railway in the north of Ireland. Profitable or not, the NCC carried the Ballycastle on its broad back, and gave it another quarter-century of useful existence. The line survived the Second World War and lasted to give a more intensive service that ever before.

Soon afterwards, nationalisation herded the railways of Ireland into two great groups, and in the northern of the two, the UTA fell heir to the Ballycastle. Under the new regime, such apparent anomalies as branch lines received short shrift; the public were offered buses with one hand and with the other the secondary railways were withdrawn. By 1950, the public were travel-hungry after eleven years of rationed fuel and food, preferred the mobility of the private car, and sealed the fate of the railways. Before five post-war years were gone, the Ballycastle section succumbed and County Antrim, which had cradled the Irish narrow gauge three-quarters of a century before, saw the last of its little lines close down and, in the middle of a busy summer, hand over to road transport.

Chapter 9

The Ballycastle Railway in 2006

This description of the remains of the Ballycastle Railway is based on a survey done in January 2006 and assumes the reader is starting at Ballymoney. You will find OSNI 1:50,000 map *Sheet 5 Ballycastle* very useful. At significant points on the route I will quote the OS grid reference. These references are based on GPS readings taken on the survey and if you follow the route equipped with a GPS device, it will help pinpoint certain locations.

Ballymoney

Our tour begins at Ballymoney railway station (IC95032539). You are reminded that all of the former station premises are private property and are requested to respect the current owners' privacy.

As you stand looking at the front of the station building, the Ballycastle line came in from the left/northeast to terminate in a bay platform where the station car park is now. The trackbed ran through the Ulsterbus depot where the buses are parked. The original goods store survives. Fyfe's building was the broad (standard) gauge goods shed while the Agrolon section, to the left, was the narrow gauge part.

The best view of the former narrow gauge section can be obtained from the footbridge in the NIR station (though seek permission if you are not travelling). The Ballycastle

Ballymoney goods sheds. Ballycastle trains ran into the section to the left of the picture, thus providing a cross-platform interchange with broad gauge services. Paul Savage

Opposite: *Ballymoney yard and narrow gauge platform. Passenger services from Ballycastle terminated in a bay platform just to the left of the photographer, who is standing on the station footbridge. The fence protecting the bus park is along the line of the platform edge. The coaling stage, where coal for the Ballycastle engines was loaded in hampers, was situated just beyond the end of the passenger platform. Compare this 2006 view with earlier ones on pages 9, 12 and 23.* Paul Savage

Railway ran parallel to the Belfast line for the first half mile and passed under the Ballymena Road by a smaller arch to the left of the present bridge visible in the distance. The ground beyond the Ulsterbus depot was occupied before 1950 by the narrow gauge engine shed and the goods yard, shared by both gauges (see diagrams on pages 14 and 15).

To look more closely at the area just described, leave the station and proceed to the traffic lights. Turn right on to Meeting House Street. By walking down a track/lane to the right you can find a short section of the goods yard boundary wall, close to the site of the cattle and sheep loading platforms (again see diagrams on pages 14 and 15).

Returning to Meeting House Street, continue to the roundabout and follow the signs for *Ballymena (A26)*. You will shortly cross the line on a bridge (IC95392582), the narrow gauge arch, now filled in, being on the town side. Although filled in, the top of the arch is visible from Belfast-bound trains. After passing under the bridge the line followed the Belfast line for a short distance on a slightly elevated alignment (visible from the road bridge) before diverging and curving northwards.

To see this section, continue on the Ballymena Road to the next roundabout and take the first exit into Kilraughts Road, signed *Armoy (B15) Kilraghts B16*. At the junction of Kilraughts Road and the A26 go left, signed *Coleraine A26*. This is Frosses Road. The line swinging out of Ballymoney hugged the edge of the high ground to the north of the town and crossed under this road (which didn't exist in narrow gauge days) at IC95962660, shortly after you cross the Belfast line and Breckagh Burn. Subject to finding a safe parking space, you can walk back towards Greengage Cottages where the embankment can be clearly seen in the back gardens of the houses. To get a better look at this section, continue on the A26 and take the next left into Kirk Road, the B147. At IC95532621, turn left into Greengage Lane and follow the signs for Greengage Cottages. You will be on or just below the line of the track.

Retrace your steps to the A26 and, having crossed it, take the B147 (Kirk Road) for Stranocum. In a short distance a dense line of trees on the right indicates the course of the line, which is now curving northwestwards. At the entrance to Drumart Farm Cottage (green sign) (IC95782712), the line crossed diagonally from the right, under the road. To the left, the line has been ploughed back into the field, although the hedge line still curves away to the right. At this point the line was crossing a ridge of high ground and having done

This is the view from the Ballymena Road (or Roddenfoot) bridge in the Ballycastle direction. The narrow gauge ran to the left of the picture, where the trees have grown. The NCC line towards Belfast runs in a northeasterly direction at this point.
Dr Patterson's view of this point, although taken in the opposite direction, appears on page 24. Norman Johnston

Opposite: *The trackbed at Greengage Cottages from the A26 road. The course of the line is to the right of the cottages and can be clearly seen running up towards the new cycle track in the foreground.* Paul Savage

This view is in the opposite direction to the previous picture. The two arches of the Ballymena Road bridge can be seen to the left. Anthony McKinnley is looking out of the engine. KA Benington

A short distance from the A26, along the B147 (Kirk Road) towards Stranocum, a line of trees on the right indicates the course of the railway. At the entrance to Drumart Farm Cottage, the line crossed from the right, under the road. To the left, the line has been ploughed back into the field, although the hedge line still follows the curve of the of the railway towards the Garry Bog.
Norman Johnston

so it then resumed a northerly course to the west of this high ground. The alignment and several overbridges are still visible from a number of private lanes that it crossed but, after about two miles, the formation is obliterated until it reaches Dervock.

Dervock

To reach Dervock, continue on the B147 to Kirkhills (IC98002952) and turn left on to Stroan Road, signed *Dervock 1½*. Approaching Dervock, the course of the line comes in on the left and parallels the road for a short distance. The station site is at IC97923154, just where the tarmaced paths are blocked by large stones. Locating the trackbed was difficult, as it is easy to be misled by the laneway you can see in front of you, between the two lines of trees near the modern houses. This is not the course of the line but is in fact the road access to the goods store. If you stand at IC97923154 you will see an old concrete path coming up from these houses and ending in rough ground. I believe this was the road from the village up to the station, the lower end of which is still Station Road. The rubble at the end of this path marks the site of the station building, which was on the down (village) side. The building was virtually identical to the one which still survives at Armoy. Leaving Dervock station the line continued ahead, by a bridge under Carncullagh Road, although this is not obvious from the present station site. The far parapet of this bridge is still extant.

After passing under the bridge the line curved sharply eastwards to follow the south side of the Stracam River to Stranocum. To follow this, proceed now to the T-junction and prepare to turn right. The parapet of the bridge is on the opposite side of the road, slightly to your left. Join the

Dervock station on 2 May 1946, looking towards Ballymoney. The locomotive on this occasion was No 41. The Stroan Road is visible to the left of the locomotive chimney. The goods store was out of sight beyond the station building.
EM Patterson, courtesy CP Friel

Carncullagh Road and follow signs for Stranocum. The course of the line is about 100 yards beyond the hedges on your left.

About two miles along this road is a sharp right hand bend with a minor road going straight on towards Moss-Side. The line passed under this road about 300 yards past the junction. However, we are continuing on the main road. At ID00293136, on the second right-hand bend, take the road on the left (Mostragee Road) to Mostragee (ID01053153) where you cross the line on a bridge. The trackbed is clearly visible on both sides.

Stranocum

A short distance beyond this, across the fields opposite the entrance to Mostragee House (200 yards from the T-junction ahead), Stranocum Station, now a private residence, can be glimpsed (ID01383163). Here the building was on the up side and there was a single siding and goods loading dock at the Ballycastle end of the platform. The house has been much modernised and an extension added across the former trackbed.

At the aforementioned T-junction turn right on to Ballinlea Road. (Stranocum station is the second house on the right, with the concrete block gate pillars.) Here the line crossed under the road to head northeast for Armoy. A short distance past the station turn left onto Ballykenver Road, towards Armoy. The railway line runs parallel on your left, about 100–200 yards from the road.

Gracehill

Continue to a crossroads at Chathamhall (ID03673277) and turn left into Bregagh Road. Park in the lay-by on

Opposite top: *No 44 on the 4.00pm ex-Ballycastle at Dervock station on Friday 16 June 1950. The bridge under the Carncullagh Road is in the distance and the far parapet is still visible today.* EM Patterson, courtesy CP Friel

Opposite bottom: *The site of Dervock station in January 2006 looking in the same direction. The remains of the concrete path are in the left foreground, just past the tarmac road. The line crossed under the road ahead, just by the small trees to the right of the bungalow.* Paul Savage

This is the bridge at Mostragee, looking back towards Dervock. Originally constructed with a steel deck and sides, these were later replaced with the concrete deck and stone parapets seen here. Paul Savage

The view from the bridge at Mostragee looking towards Stranocum. Most of the stonework visible in this picture is the original retaining wall, only the parapet in the bottom left being more recent. The dark area covered by trees is the trackbed.

Paul Savage

the left, a short distance along this road. Gracehill Halt (ID03503291) was at the bridge directly in front of you. It was on the left-hand side of the bridge and a concrete waiting shelter, built by the NCC in 1947 or 1948, still survives.

Return to the Ballykenver Road and turn left. The next road on your left is Chatham Road. A short distance along this road the abutments of a bridge, which carried the line across the road, still stand. Continuing on the Ballykenver Road, the line crossed at ID04823325 and ran down towards Armoy, although there is no sign of the bridge at this point. On the south side of the road the trackbed is clearly visible and is in use as a laneway to a building. At the next crossroads turn right onto the Carrowreagh Road. The line is now down to your right.

Armoy

Armoy station is passed before reaching the village. If you see a 30 mph restriction sign, you've passed it! It is on the left, on a site now occupied by John Laverty Tractors, at ID06203303, just past the crash barriers near No 39 Carrowreagh Road. The road opposite the station entrance, towards Peacock's Bridge, runs beside the trackbed. In railway days the Carrowreagh Road crossed the line on a bridge. This is the best preserved of the intermediate stations. The station building survives, along with part of the up platform. Farm buildings have obliterated the down platform and passing loop. The goods store was at the Ballycastle end, beyond the John Laverty buildings.

The view across the fields to Stranocum station (see page 25) from Mostragee Road, opposite the entrance to Mostragee House. The line ran to this side of the building. Paul Savage

Stranocum Station from the Ballinlea Road. The platform was where the car is parked in this view. After leaving the station, heading for Gracehill and Armoy, the line passed under the Ballinlea Road. Norman Johnston

Bregagh Road, above Gracehill Halt. The platform was in a cutting to the left, on the down side. The concrete waiting shelter built by the LMS (NCC) c1947 still stands. Norman Johnston (above), Paul Savage (below)

After leaving the station, continue to Armoy and join the A44 (Drones Road) towards Ballycastle. About half a mile beyond Armoy the line swings in from your left and runs alongside the road. Two overbridges can be seen at the end of the Ballykenver Road, which comes in from the left at Balleeny. Beyond Balleeny, on the left, an embankment can be clearly seen, running across the fields. At this point the line is on a very straight course for about a mile and a half and this is almost certainly the location of Dr Patterson's footplate shot looking towards Balleeny from the north on a southbound train (see page 131) . The route of the line crosses the A44 at ID07713508 and runs up across an open moss towards Capecastle and Glentaisie. The road passed over the line but there is no sign of the bridge.

Remain on the A44 and at a crossroads, just after a right-hand bend, turn right into Islandarragh Road, signed *National Cycle Route 93, Ballycastle 4.*

Capecastle

Just past Islandarragh House bed & breakfast, in the hollow, the stone parapet of Capecastle Tunnel can be seen on the right with the station in the cutting below (ID08693672). This is a delightful, tranquil location, now owned by William Glass, who remembers the trains operating and took me for a tour of the site in 2005. In the autumn/winter period, the trackbed tends to become flooded in the station area but the platform and the high-level loading bank can still be discerned. The tunnel ran off to your left but the portal at the far end cannot be seen. This was the only tunnel on the line.

Miss Sharpe's accident

Just beyond Capecastle the line meanders through a valley past a number of farms and this was the location of the accident referred to briefly in the text (page 76) and described to me in more detail by William Glass. Sara

No 41 pauses at Armoy with the morning Ballycastle to Ballymoney train on the last day of operation, Sunday 2 July 1950.
AD Hutchinson/Colour-Rail NG186

This is the platform side of Armoy station in 2006, looking in the Stranocum direction. The railway ancestry is very obvious. The farm building sits astride the platform edge and across the trackbed. Compare this view with those on pages 26 and 129.
Norman Johnston

Above: *This is the the embankment beyond Balleeny, looking roughly north. It is clearly visible from the A44 between the end of the Ballykenver Road and the turn for Capecastle. Jim Delargy's farmhouse, mentioned on page 56, was located to the right of this picture and beyond the embankment. The house is now a ruin.* Paul Savage

Right: *This is the same embankment viewed from the footplate of a Ballymoney-bound train back in June 1950. Balleeny bridge is in the distance. The engine is No 44, easily identifiable by the sleeve fitted over the chimney.*
EM Patterson, courtesy CP Friel

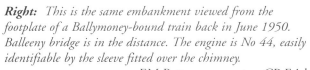

Opposite: *Armoy station, viewed from the entrance to John Laverty Tractors.* Norman Johnston

This is the view from the A44, at ID07713508, towards Capecastle, just over a mile distant. We believe that it was just on the other side of the bridge here (now removed) that No 41 got stuck in a snowdrift on 12 March 1947 (see Driver Barry Limerick's description of this incident on page 56 and the photographs on page 57). Paul Savage

Sharpe was a sister of Thomas Sharpe and his brother and their house is still extant. On 11 April 1905 the Sharpes were expecting delivery of a load of lime by rail. Miss Sharpe was taking the train into Ballycastle and would be able to ascertain if the lime had arrived. It was arranged that, as she passed the house, she would signal by a wave if the lime was in Capecastle and, if it was, the brothers were to take a cart to the station to load it. As she passed the house Miss Sharpe leaned out to wave that the lime had arrived, but the door was not properly secured and she fell out onto the track. Unaware of this, the train crew carried on to Ballycastle.

Although shaken, Sara Sharpe was not a woman to be put off her stroke and simply walked to Ballycastle along the trackbed. At first there was no ill effect from the mishap but some days later she took ill and remained in poor health until her death from asthma some time later. Blaming the ill health on her accident, she wrote to the directors and, in lieu of compensation, requested a free pass for a time from Capecastle to Ballycastle. This was granted.

Returning to our itinerary, on leaving Capecastle, proceed on to the T-junction and turn left on to Hillside Road. Carry on through Glentaisie. The line, initially, is down to your left, heading for the curves at Ballylig, but at Ballydurnian (ID09953863) the buttresses of a bridge, which carried the line across the road, still stand. This bridge was of steel construction. The course of the line can be glimpsed at various points on your right before we lose sight of it on the approaches to Ballycastle.

Ballycastle

Heading into the town we reach the Diamond (ID11434068). Turn right here, by the Antrim Arms Hotel and continue into Fairhill Street. At the end of this street is a patch of rough ground and a lane way. Park on the rough ground. You are now on the trackbed of the line coming in

This is the view over Capecastle station, taken from above the tunnel and looking in the Armoy direction, in January 2006. The flooded area is the trackbed, the platform still being discernible. The high level loading dock is in the centre distance. An earlier view of Capecastle station can be found on page 27. Paul Savage

from Capecastle. An overbridge should be visible to your right and this is the bridge that features in the photograph on page 28. (A 'then and now' comparison appears on page 136.) The route down to the Tow Viaduct disappears off to your left. Nowadays the viaduct is rather obscured by trees and vegetation which have grown up over the years but the four-arch structure survives in its entirety. Return now to the Diamond and call in at the Co-op (ID11564066). The remains of Ballycastle station, complete with water tank, can be seen from the car park, below and to the left.

Back to the Diamond again and turn right into Ann Street; this leads towards the sea front. At the next right follow the signs for Ann Street car park (Homestyle Interiors is on the corner). You are now at the end of the line (ID11584074). The station building is on private property beyond the Ulsterbus garage, which stands on the site of the Ballycastle Railway carriage shed. *Please note, there is no public access to either location.* At the time of writing, the station has an uncertain future, as it is in an area earmarked for redevelopment.

We haven't forgotten about the four-arch Tow Viaduct. A short walk from the car park, back up the station approach, brings you to a lane on the right. Walk down this lane towards the River Tow and you will be able to glimpse the viaduct across the fields to the right. This completes our tour of the Ballycastle Railway.

Mr William Glass, who took the photographer to visit various sites in the vicinity, is standing near the high level loading bank at Capecastle, with the tunnel portal beyond. Compare this view with that on page 27; the wooden hut, beside which the group of walkers is standing, would have been just to the bottom right in this picture. Norman Johnston

Opposite top: *The tunnel portal at the Armoy end of Capecastle. There are two refuges, believed to be about one-third and two-thirds of the way through. It was the narrow dimensions of this tunnel which prevented the line being converted to broad gauge, something which might have ensured its survival. The tunnel is now blocked at the Ballycastle end.* Norman Johnston

Opposite bottom: *On page 76, an incident is related where, on 11 April 1905, Miss Sara Sharpe fell from a Ballycastle-bound train, just beyond Capecastle station. This is roughly that spot. Perhaps surprisingly, Miss Sharpe picked herself up and walked the rest of the way into Ballycastle. Imagine the Health and Safety Enquiry that would be required if such an incident happened in 2006! Miss Sharpe didn't even claim compensation but the Company gave her a free pass for several months.*
Norman Johnston

With the Tow Viaduct behind and the climb towards Ballylig and Capecastle ahead, an up train, with No 44 in charge, passes under the first overbridge out of Ballycastle, above Fairhill Street, on the 4.00pm departure from the seaside town on 16 June 1950. EM Patterson, courtesy CP Friel

This is the same bridge seen in January 2006 and we are looking towards Capecastle and Ballymoney. The caption in Dr Patterson's original volume stated that this bridge was above the ballast pit but our survey shows that not to be so. At this point the trackbed forms part of The Moyle Way footpath. Paul Savage

The Tow Viaduct looking towards Ballycastle in 1948 (above) and towards Ballymoney in 2006 (below). Given that in March 1880 a split had appeared longitudinally along the entire length of this structure, it is perhaps surprising that it is still standing in the early years of the 21st century. KA Benington (above), Paul Savage (below)

A view of Ballycastle station in LMS days, taken, it is believed, on 2 May 1946. The wagons in the siding on the left have been hauled up the incline from the sawmill in the valley below while an unidentified engine, but thought to be No 41, awaits departure in the platform road. Moving right, the next two buildings are the locomotive shed and the goods store, beyond which three of the four caravan coaches can just be discerned.
EM Patterson

Ballycastle station building and platform still display their railway ancestry in 2006, but their future is very uncertain, the site having been sold for redevelopment.
Paul Savage

Right: *A busy scene at Ballycastle platform in the late 1940s. The water tank, on its stone supports, can be seen to the centre left of the picture, just at the end of the station building.*
KA Benington

Below: *Another view of the platform at Ballycastle in 2006. The cars are parked right on the platform, directly in front of the water tank, just about where the young boy with the fishing rod is standing in the picture above.*
Norman Johnston

Main entrance hall (top) and booking office (above). Paperwork found in the booking office gave the Ulster Transport Authority bus fleet at Ballycastle depot on 2 April 1963 as Austin No Q1, Leyland Tiger Cub single-deckers Nos 304, 305, 372 and 373, and Leyland PD3 double-deckers Nos 806, 807 and 808, with Tiger Cub No 454 on Hotels Tours duties. The following day Tiger Cub No 370 was replacing No 304 and Tiger Cub No 429 had joined No 454 on Hotels Tours.

Norman Johnston (top), Paul Savage (above)

Appendices

Appendix 1

List of Stations and Halts

	Miles Down	Up	Opened	Classification	Crane Power
Ballymoney	0	16¼	18 October 1880	GPLHC	2t 0c
Dervock	4½	11¾	18 October 1880	GPL	1t 10c
Stranocum	6¾	9½	18 October 1880	GP	
Gracehill	8¼	8	?? December 1890	P*	
Armoy	10¼	6	18 October 1880	GPL	
Capecastle	13	3¼	?? February 1882	GPL	
Ballycastle	16¼	0	18 October 1880	GPLHC	2t 0c

All stations and halts were closed on 3 July 1950. The classification and crane power is quoted from Official Handbook of Railway Stations, published 1812 by the Railway Clearing House. Abbreviations used are:

G = goods, P = passenger and parcels, P* = passengers but not parcel or miscellaneous traffic, L = live stock, H = horse traffic, C = carriages by passenger train.

Ballycastle station and water tank, as viewed from the car park of the Co-op store in March 2003. Paul Savage

Appendix 2

Ballycastle Railway – Traffic Returns
(Board of Trade Returns 1880–1921, Company Reports 1922–23)

		No of Passengers		
Year	**1st**	**2nd**	**3rd**	**Season Tickets**
1880	629	–	8664	5
1881	3685	–	50,870	71
1882	3682	–	55,857	96
1883	3537	–	49,577	106
1884	3959	–	52,901	103
1885	2368	2150	49,121	47
1886	2867	4863	77,631	45
1887	2846	5150	82,540	30
1888	2732	5324	83,530	35
1889	2431	6138	91,034	45
1890	2528	6071	92,277	51
1891	2980	5446	101,585	51
1892	2852	5106	97,359	27
1893	2662	4103	98,437	26
1894	2646	4111	99,348	51
1895	2990	4027	106,498	38
1896	3002	3347	101,327	33
1897	3287	3666	99,635	65
1898	3225	3593	105,589	65
1899	3857	3784	102,866	72
1900	3135	4050	99,685	55
1901	3248	4287	107,148	55
1902	3183	4494	104,053	15
1903	3577	4539	114,402	12
1904	2748	4641	105,912	6
1905	3086	5157	101,483	7
1906	3251	5669	107,100	6
1907	4109	5879	106,666	8
1908	3760	5718	105,593	7
1909	2458	5392	100,319	7
1910	2694	5267	102,845	12
1911	2652	5858	99,932	29
1912	2848	5702	99,889	25
1913	2588	5551	101,870	25
1914–1918	No records for war period			
1919	1182	3237	62,307	35
1920	908	3213	58,411	40
1921	517	2254	40,608	28
1922	894	2919	48,399	28
1923	1168	2728	50,911	28

Ballycastle Railway – Traffic Returns
(Board of Trade Returns 1880–1921, Company Reports 1922–23)

Year	Goods Traffic Mineral Tons	GM Tons	Livestock	Rolling Stock A	B	C	
1880	80	802		7	2	60	(Opened 18 Oct 1880)
1881	967	4879		7	3	60	
1882	2606	4942		7	3	60	
1883	3182	5926		7	3	60	
1884	2405	5405		7	3	60	
1885	1760	6028		7	3	60	
1886	1700	6172		7	3	60	
1887	1823	6317		7	3	60	
1888	1923	6101		8	2	60	
1889	1664	6269		8	2	60	
1890	1755	6855		8	2	60	
1891	2359	7191		8	2	60	
1892	2835	6501		9	2	59	
1893	2969	6561		9	2	59	
1894	4550	7475		9	2	59	
1895	4881	7530		7	4	59	
1896	3643	8470		8	4	59	
1897	4688	9652		10	2	59	
1898	5018	8853		11	2	59	
1899	5271	9300		11	2	59	
1900	3414	8868		13	2	59	
1901	5059	9241		13	2	59	
1902	5237	9423		13	2	59	
1903	7751	8169		13	2	59	
1904	9400	8298		13	2	59	
1905	10,035	8775		13	2	59	
1906	8610	9353		13	2	59	
1907	8442	9378		13	2	59	
1908	8035	8038		10	5	59	
1909	7247	8146		10	5	59	
1910	7658	8201		10	5	59	
1911	8344	8575		10	5	59	
1912	7970	9353		10	5	59	
1913	8828	9295	5205	13	2	59	
1914–1918	No records for war period						
1919	1620	7141	6003	13	2	59	Originating traffic only
1920	2221	6947	6670	13	2	59	Originating traffic only
1921	1642	4025	3512	13	2	59	Originating traffic only
1922	1391	6329	5028	13	2	59	Originating traffic only
1923	1257	4806	5130	12	2	59	Originating traffic only

Notes: A – Passenger Carriages, B – Other Vehicles attached to Passenger Trains, C – Goods and Livestock Wagons, GM – General Merchandise.

Appendix 3

List of Chairmen and Officers of the Ballycastle Railway Company

Chairmen

Sir Fredrick Boyd, Bart	August 1878–October 1878
John Casement	October 1878–January 1900
RM Douglas (deputy)	January 1900–January 1901
HM McGildowny	January 1901–June 1923
RP Woodside	June 1923–August 1925

Secretaries and Managers

Silas Evans	1878–November 1885	(Secretary and Manager from June 1880)
Edward J Cotton	November 1885–April 1886	(temporary General Manager)
	April 1886–June 1899	(General Manager)
TB Hamilton	November 1885–April 1886	(temporary Secretary)
Hamilton McAllen	April 1886–July 1899	(Secretary and Assistant General Manager)
	July 1899–July 1925	(Secretary and General Manager)
	July 1925–October 1926	(Liquidator)

Locomotive Engineers

George Bradshaw	August 1880–June 1923
James AQ Bradshaw	June 1923–August 1924

Civil Engineer

James F McKinnon	1877–December 1882	(continued as Engineer to his death in July 1905)

Audit Clerk

Hamilton McAllen	August 1880–April 1886

Medical Officers

Drs Boyd, Ewing, Gage, O'Connor and Woodside	(at various dates)

Appendix 4

Engine Dimensions – 1
Ballycastle Railway Company Engines

No.	**1 & 2**	**3**	**3 & 4**
Maker	B.H. & Co.	B.H. & Co.	Kitson
Maker's No.	554/5	513	4565/6
Type	0-6-0ST	0-6-0ST	4-4-2T
Cyls. (2 outside)	13"x19"	12"x19"	14¼"x21"
Boiler:			
Length	8'3"	7'10"	9'6"
Diam.	3'6"	3'6"	4'0"
Pressure	150psi	150psi	165/160psi
Tubes	145 x 1⅝"	145 x 1⅝"	170 x 1¾"
Heating surface:			
Firebox	43 sq ft*		83 sq ft
Tubes	530 sq ft*		769 sq ft
Total	573 sq ft*		852 sq ft
Grate area	7 sq ft	7 sq ft	12 sq ft
Wheel diameter:			
Coupled	3'3"	3'3"	3'7"
Bogie	–	–	2'6"
Trailing	–	–	2'6"
Wheelbase	5'6" + 6'3"	5'0" + 6'0"	5'0" + 4'5" + 6'0" + 6'0"
Weight, loaded	24 tons	22 tons	39 tons 11 cwt
Weight, adhesive	24 tons	22 tons	21 tons 8 cwt
Tank capacity	450 gall	400 gall	800 gall
Coal capacity	1¼ tons	1¼ tons	1¾ tons
Cost	£1145	£600 s/h	£2375

Heating surface areas marked thus * are given by Livesey (1912) as, respectively, 51, 531 and 582 sq ft.
0-6-0T No 3 originally had a boiler of 3'2" diameter

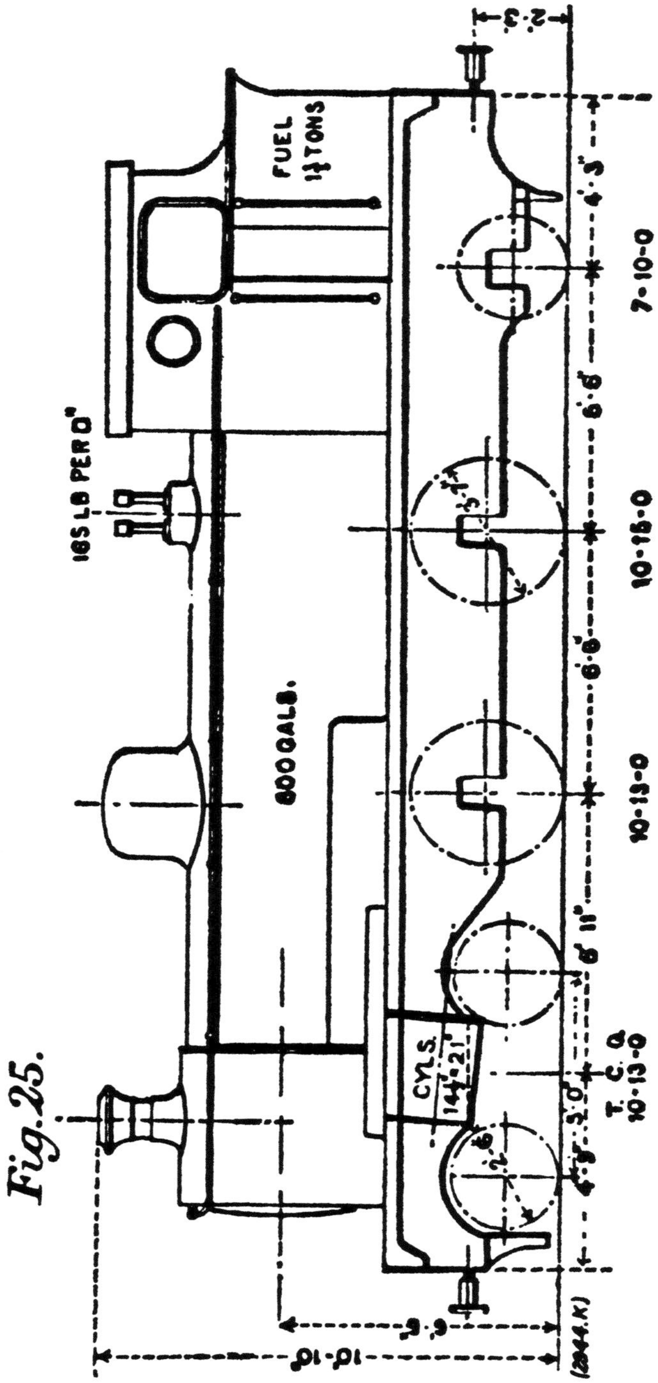

Elevation of Ballycastle Railway Company 4-4-2T loco. From RM Livesey (1912) Rolling Stock: the principal Irish narrow gauge railways. Proc Inst Mech Eng, p599

Engine Dimensions – 2
Engines transferred to Ballycastle Section by LMS (NCC)

Number (final)	105	106/7, 108	44/43	41/42
Class	P	Q	S	S^1
Maker	B.P. & Co.	B.P. & Co.	B.P. & Co./NCC	NCC
Maker's No.	1828	1700/1, 2304	3464/–	–
Building date	1878	1877, 1883	1892/1920	1909/1908
Type	2-4-0T	0-6-0T	2-4-2T	2-4-2T
Cylinders (2)	11"x18"	13½"x18"	14¾" & 21"x20"	14¾" & 21"x20"
Boiler:				
Length	7'8¼"	8'0"	9'4"	9'4"
Diam.	10¾"	3'3"	3'5¼"	3'5¼"
Tubes	103 x 1⅝"	132 x 1⅝"	150 x 1⅝"	150 x 1⅝"
Pressure (psi)	140	140	170/160	170/160
Height c. line	4'10"	4'10½"	5'5"	5'5"
Heating surface (sq ft):				
Firebox	43	43½	63	63
Tubes	349	464½	615	615
Total	392	508	678	678
Grate area (sq ft)	6.85	9	11	11
Wheel diameter:				
Leading	2'0"	–	2'0"	2'0"
Coupled	3'9"	3'3"	3'9"	3'9"
Trailing	–	–	2'0"	2'0"
Wheelbase	8'0" + 6'3"	5'0" + 5'6"	6'9" + 6'3" + 7'3"	6'9" + 6'3" + 9'3"
Weight in working order	19 tons 3 cwt	21 tons 1 cwt	31 tons 17 cwt	32 tons 17 cwt
		22 tons 9 cwt		
Adhesive weight	15 tons 6 cwt	do., do.	20 tons	20½ tons
Tank capacity (gall)	360 gall	450 gall	570 gall	570 gall
Coal capacity (tons)	1 (32 cu ft)	¾ (24 cu ft)	1	1½
Length over headstocks	20'1¾"	20'3¾"	25'6½"	27'6½"
Height from rail	9'6"	9'8"	9'8"	9'8"
Cost	£1431	£1560, £1610	£2060/–	–

Note: Class P loco – rebuilt in 1898 with 12½" cylinders, tubes 88 x 1⅝", heating surface 298 sq ft.

Appendix 5

First Report of Colonel FH Rich on the Ballycastle Railway

Donegal Hotel
Belfast
20th Sept. 1880

The Secretary,
Railway Department,
Board of Trade

Sir,

I have the honour to report for the information of the Board of Trade in compliance with the instructions contained in your letter of the 8th instant and that I have inspected the Ballycastle Railway.

The new line is single with sidings. It is constructed with a 3 ft gauge and is about 16 miles long. It commences at the up side of Ballymoney Station of the Belfast and Northern Counties Railway where there is an island platform, and extends to the town of Ballycastle.

There are intermediate stations at Dervock, Stranocum and Armoy. The ruling gradient is 1 in 50 and the sharpest curve has a radius of 9 chains.

The permanent way consists of a Vignoles Pattern steel rail which weighs about 45 lb. per lineal yard. It is fished and fixed with dog spikes and 6 fang bolts in each length of rail to sleepers laid transversely. The sleepers are 6 feet long, 7 in. x 4 in. and 6 in. x 4 in. There are nine sleepers to every 21 feet of rail. The ballast consists of sand and gravel and the fences are bank and ditch, and occasionally wire fences.

There are 21 over, 11 under bridges, 3 viaducts, about 11 cattle creeps, some large culverts and a tunnel 66 yards long. The widest span is 30 feet.

These works are principally constructed with stone. Several bridges have wooden tops, some have wrought-iron girders, and in many cases wrought-iron corrugated plates about ¼ to 5/16 inches thick are used to carry the roadways and in one or two instances to carry the Railway. I tested these plates by loading two of them with rails. They proved to be of sufficient strength, and the rest of the works sufficiently strong for a narrow-gauge railway.

There are horizontal deviations outside the Parliamentary limits at 14 to 15½ miles, and at Ballycastle station, and vertical deviations outside the limits at:

25	chains	to	0 m. 35	chains
60	chains	to	1.25	chains
1.60	chains	to	2.45	chains
6.50	chains	to	7.0	chains
7.70	chains	to	8.20	chains
9.35	chains	to	10	chains
13.25	chains	to	15.65	chains
16	chains	to	16.10	chains

I am informed that no objections have been made to these deviations. The following works are required:

The Bank and ditch fences required to have 2 wires stretched along the top of the bank.

The posts that carry the wires should slope outwards and the wires and fences generally require to be carried up to the wing walls of the Gates and Bridges to prevent trespass upon the Railway.

The Railway should be brought closer to the station platforms in each case where the distance of the carriage steps from the edge of the platform exceeds 2½ inches.

The accommodation gates require to be provided with Padlocks and notices "that if left open the owners will subject themselves to a fine of 40s". In two cases these gates require to be brought closer to the Railway, or the approach from the Railway should be fenced.

The Rock Cutting at 11 miles requires to be cleaned of loose stones and the big stones in the cutting near to Ballycastle should be removed.

The guard rail at the entrance to Ballycastle Station and at 13¾ miles requires to be extended further round the curves.

The home signal at Ballycastle requires to be altered so that it can be seen better as the engine driver approaches the station.

The abutments of the underbridge at 2 miles and 42 chains and the south abutment and Pier of the Bridge at 3 miles and 9 chains are not perpendicular and will require careful watching.

Shelter is required on the Ballymoney platform and the connection at the east end of the yard should be removed.

There are no engine turntables and although I do not think it essential to the safe working to require turntables on these small narrow-gauge, it is very desirable that turnatbles should be provided as the working is facilitated and the Machinery of the engines wears better when the engines are turned. The two engines that have been supplied to the Company by Messrs Hawthorn & Co. of Newcastle on Tyne are very unsatisfactory at present, they oscillate and jump to such an extent when running as to be unfit for the safe working of the Railway.

The interval between the sidings and the passenger line is only 6 ft 2 inches in some cases. It is desirable that this should be increased to 7 ft or 7 ft 6 in.

I submit that the Ballycastle Railway cannot be opened for Passenger traffic without danger to the Public using the same in consequence of the unfinished state of the works.

I have &c.

F. H. RICH, Colonel R. E.

Second Report of Colonel FH Rich on the Ballycastle Railway

Railway Department
Board of Trade
22nd Sept 1880

The Secretary
Railway Department
Board of Trade

Sir,

I have the honour to report for the information of the Board of Trade that in compliance with the wish of the Belfast and Northern Counties Railway Company I have inspected the re-arrangement of Ballymoney station, together with the new signal and locking arrangement in connection with the new narrow-gauge Railway to Ballycastle. Shelter is required the up line platform and it is very desirable that a Bridge should be constructed over the Railway to enable Passengers to reach the up line platform and the Ballycastle Railway without walking across the Belfast and Northern Counties Railway.

Subject to these remarks and the signal and points alteration required at this station which are enumerated in my report of 20th instant on the Ballycastle Railway, I submit that the new works may be approved.

I have &c.

F. H. RICH, Colonel R. E.

Third Report of Colonel FH Rich on the Ballycastle Railway

Railway Department
Board of Trade
23rd Sept 1880

The Secretary
Railway Department
Board of Trade

Sir,

With reference to my inspection report on the Ballycastle Railway I beg to add that the couplings between the coaches are in my opinion insufficient and dangerous.

The safety of the coupling depends on an eccentric which tightens the hook about ¼ of an inch.

In a very short time this ¼ inch will be reduced by wear and nothing will remain to keep the draw bar hook from jumping out of the —— (word uncertain).

The same principle if not the same patent (Steward's) has proved a failure on other lines and has had to be changed.

I have &c.

F. H. RICH, Colonel R. E.

Fourth Report of Colonel FH Rich on the Ballycastle Railway

Larne
14th Oct 1880

The Secretary
Railway Department
Board of Trade

Sir,

I have the honour to report for the information of the Board of Trade in compliance with the instructions contained in your minute of 1st inst. that I have reinspected the Ballycastle Railway.

The fencing has been completed, except a small portion which is in hand. The signals and other works have been completed.

The locomotives have had balance weights fixed to the wheels, the one called *Countess of Antrim* which was the most unsteady now runs fairly well, but the second, which is called *Dalriada*, had got rid of much of the side motion but has a jumping motion which is very unpleasant. I consider both engines very trying on the road and although I cannot report them dangerous I have advised that the Balance Weights on the driving wheels be increased and that cast-iron weights be placed on the footplates. I believe this will make them run more steadily and I would suggest that the Company should not fully accept them from the makers until they are put in a thoroughly satisfactory state. The couplings of the carriages have been put to rights. I attach a note from the patentee.

It appears that the company have not got any well-qualified person to look after the engines and the rolling stock. The vice-chairman of the company (Mr Casement) was present at the inspection and I tried to impress upon him the responsibility the Directors would incur if they did not provide a proper person to look after and keep their rolling stock in proper order, and I hope from what he said that this deficiency will be remedied, as if

any incident should happen in consequence of improper or incapable supervision, as was the case on the West Cork Railway permanent way, it may be a serious matter for the Directors.

I submit that, subject to these remarks, the Ballycastle Railway may be opened for the Passenger Traffic.

The undertakings as to working and as to providing shelter at Ballymoney are satisfactory.

I have &c.

F. H. RICH, Colonel R. E.

Appendix 6

Some Verse

On The Passing Of An Old Friend

(From the *Coleraine Chronicle* of 19 April 1924)

Have yez ever bin till Stranocum?
Yez haven't! Well, now, I declare!
Yez ought to down to Stranocum
And see the fine thrain they have there!
'Faith, the thrain, that's away at Stranocum
Is the quarest ould thrain yez could see,
    It don't go, me bhoy,
    As far as Armoy,
Let along all the way till the sea!

The boss in the yard at Stranocum
Has a quare aisy time of it now!
They're usin' the thrain at Stranocum
To shelter his pigs and his cow!
'Faith, ye'd laugh if ye'd wint till Stranocum,
And saw his live stock in a thruck:
    The furnace, so good,
    For h'atin' hins food,
And the tinder for houldin' the muck.

Bedad, if yez go till Stranocum,
Ye'll have to use Greene's chestnut hack
Or Foster's old bus, for Stranocum,
And with luck, yez might aisy come back.
For tho' there's a thrain at Stranocum,
There's only wan thrain in the day;
    'Tis stuck there, I hear,
    'Till the fall o' the year,
When the LMS takes it away.

No more shall we thrain till Stranocum,
No longer pick flowers on the way.
While the guard on the thrain at Stranocum
Has a crack and a mouthful o' tay!
No more shall the thrain for Stranocum
Be oiled with young cabbages now!
    Good Luck, anyway!
    And here's till the hay,
And the pigs, and the hins, and the cow!

W.B.M.

Appendix 7

Notes on Tickets
*by CR Gordon Stuart**

Of the tickets issued by this Company, it is difficult to say much, as specimens are exceedingly rare. A first-class single from Armoy to Ballycastle, which was illustrated on page 32 of *The Narrow-Gauge Railways of Ireland*, is of the single numeral type and, having no fare printed upon it, can certainly be taken as being one of the original tickets supplied in October 1880. Later issues had the conditions printed under the title and were numbered at both ends. First-class tickets were white and third-class green in the case of singles, but as the writer has never seen a return ticket he will not venture to give any information concerning them.

* This Appendix is reproduced, with minor alterations, from the late H Fayle's *Narrow-Gauge Railways of Ireland*, to which it formed an Appendix. The author is indebted to Mr CR Gordon Stuart for permission to make use of it.

EM Patterson's Acknowledgements

Even after thirty years' acquaintance with the north of Antrim, I soon became aware, on undertaking the writing of this book, how much its completion was going to depend upon the help and encouragement which many people gave me.

I am especially grateful to Mr Hugh A Boyd of Ballycastle. His personal recollections of the railway extend back for over half a century, and are the more valuable in that they combine detail with accuracy. Not only did he make available his detailed knowledge of the history of the district, but he devoted much time and trouble to reading and criticising the text.

Of the former NCC staff, there must be mentioned Mr JH Houston, Mr H Herron, Mr T Hutchinson, ex-Inspector W Hanley, ex-Driver B Limerick and ex-Guard WJ Waterman. The companionship of engine crews in the crowded cabs of Nos 41 and 44 will long be remembered. My consultation of documents relating to the original Company was greatly facilitated by help I received from Mr Newton Compton of the Secretary's Department of the UTA.

Information on engines and rolling stock was supplied by the Chief Draughtsman of Beyer, Peacock, Gorton Ltd, Metropolitan-Cammell Ltd and Hunslet Engine Co Ltd. Mr DG Coakham of Bangor also helped in that aspect of the history and his detailed surveys of station layouts have formed the basis for the sketches in this book.

My thanks are also due to the staffs of the Public Record Offices in Belfast and London, and of the British Railways Board Historical Records Offices in Edinburgh and London.

Mr CE Troy of the *Coleraine Chronicle* assisted in the abstracting of references in the files of that paper, and unearthed the verses about Stranocum.

Space allows merely the listing of others who have helped me in various ways, and I am very grateful to all of the following:
EN Carruthers (Belfast), RN Clements (Celbridge), T Cott (Kilcock), JH Court (London), the late H Fayle (Bournemouth), JD FitzGerald (Armagh), PJ Flanagan (Dublin), RH Inness (Darlington), GR Mahon (Dublin), IK McCollam (Ballycastle), TL McElderry (Ballymoney), JH McGuigan (Belfast), D MacLaughlin (Coleraine), DB McNeill (Southampton), HM Rea (Bangor), DL Smith (Ayr).

Publisher's Acknowledgements

Colourpoint Books is extremely grateful for the assistance given by the following individuals in the preparation of this book:

Keith Beattie (Ballymoney Museum), Kenneth Benington, Desmond Coakham, Charles Friel, William Glass, Jonathan Miller, Wallace McNaul and Anna Singer.

Bibliography

Boyd, H, An account of the progress of Ballycastle Harbour, together with a representation of the present state of the works, 1743, (Reprinted in *Londonderry Sentinel*, November 1929)
Dubordieu, J, *Statistical Survey of the County of Antrim*, 1812
Lewis, W, Narrow-gauge Railways, Ireland, *Transactions of the Institution of Civil Engineers of Ireland*, Vol 13, p 122, 1881
Fitzmaurice, *Life of Sir William Petty*, 1895
Timmins, DJ, The Belfast and Northern Counties Railway, *Railway Magazine*, Vol 1, p 560, 1897
The Ballycastle Railway, *Locomotive Magazine*, Vol 8, p 64, 1903
Shrubsole, ES, *Shrubsole's Guide, Ballycastle, Co Antrim*, 1911
Livesey, RM, Rolling stock on the principal Irish narrow-gauge railways, *Proceedings of the Institute of Mechanical Engineers*, p 599, 1912
Tatlow, J, *Fifty Years of Railway Life*, 1920
Gairns, JF, Northern Counties Section (Ireland) LM & SR, *Railway Magazine*, Vol 54, p 121, 1924
Wright, WB, Geology of the Ballycastle Coalfield, Memoir, *Geological Survey Ireland*, 1924
McCahan, R, *Geology & History of the Ballycastle and Murlough Coalfields*, c1925
The Locomotives of the Northern Counties Committee, LMSR, *Railway Magazine*, Vol 68, p 468, 1931
Rebuilt narrow-gauge compound tank locomotive, LMSR NCC, *The Locomotive*, p 382, 1932
Nock, OS, The NCC section of the LMSR, part III, *Railway Magazine*, Vol 78, p 413, 1936
Nock, OS, The locomotives of the LMSR, NCC section, *Railway Magazine*, Vol 81, p 119, 1937
Kidner, RW, *The Three-foot-gauge railways of Northern Ireland*, 1937
Bruce, RHW, The LM & SR in Northern Ireland, *Railway Magazine*, Vol 90, pp 145 & 203, 1914
Fayle, H, *Narrow-Gauge Railways of Ireland*, 1945
Marshall, WS, *LMS-NCC, The Operating Department in War Time 1939–1945*, 1946
NCC 1848–1948, 1948
The Two-Cylinder Compounds of the Northern Counties Railway, *Railway Magazine*, Vol 95, p 159, 1949
Houston, JH, The B&NCR and its Locomotives (Part III), *Journal of the Irish Railway Record Society*, Vol 1, p 88, 1949
Patterson, EM, County Antrim's Last Narrow-gauge Line, *Meccano Magazine*, Vol 36, p 310, 1951
Boyd, JIC, The Ballycastle Railway, *Railway Magazine*, Vol 98, 338, 1952
McNeill, DB, The Little Railway Mania in County Antrim, *Ulster Journal of Archaeology*, Vol 16, p 85, 1953
McNeill, DB, Ulster Tramways and Light Railways, *Transport Handbook No 1*, Ulster Museum & Art Gallery, 1956
Davies, GL, The town and coalfield of Ballycastle, Co Antrim, *Irish Geography*, Vol 3, p 206, 1957
Coakham, DG, LMS (NCC) Narrow-gauge Coaches, I, *Model Railway News*, Vol 40, p 608, 1964
McGuigan, JH, *The Giant's Causeway Tramway*, 1964

Directors' Minute Books of the Ballycastle Railway, Vols 1–6
Shareholders' Minute Books of the Ballycastle Railway, Vols 1 & 2
Half-yearly and Annual Reports of the Ballycastle Railway Company
Board of Trade Railway Returns
Board of Trade Railway Dept Inspectors' Reports on New Lines, etc
Various Working and Public Timetables of the BNCR, MR (NCC), LMS (NCC) and UTA
Various editions of *Bradshaw's Railway Shareholder's Guide and Directory*
Reports of the Vice-Regal Commission on Irish Railways, 1906–10
Minutes of Evidence and Report of the Commissioners; Railway Commission in Northern Ireland, 1922

Index

The End! Nos 41 and 44 meet their fate at the scrapman's torch, at Ballycastle, some time after the auction in February 1954. No 44 has already been well dismantled; the tubes in the boiler can be clearly seen. Note, too, the different diameters of the cylinders.
Courtesy Ballymoney Museum

If you have enjoyed this Colourpoint book, you may be interested in the following Colourpoint railway titles:

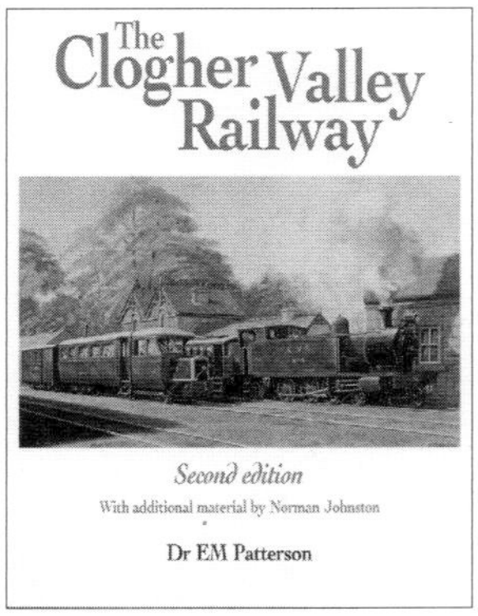

The Clogher Valley Railway
Second Edition
Dr EM Patterson
1 904242 15 4 £15
192pp, 232 x 180mm,
129 b/w photos

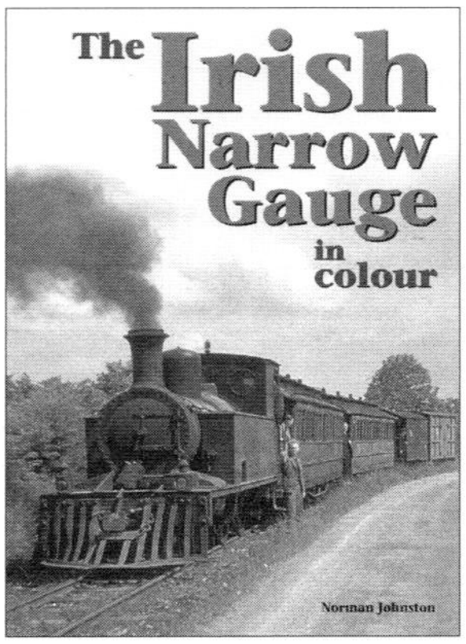

The Irish Narrow Gauge in colour
Norman Johnston
1 904242 13 8 £19.99
108pp, hbk, 298 x 205mm,
200 colour photos

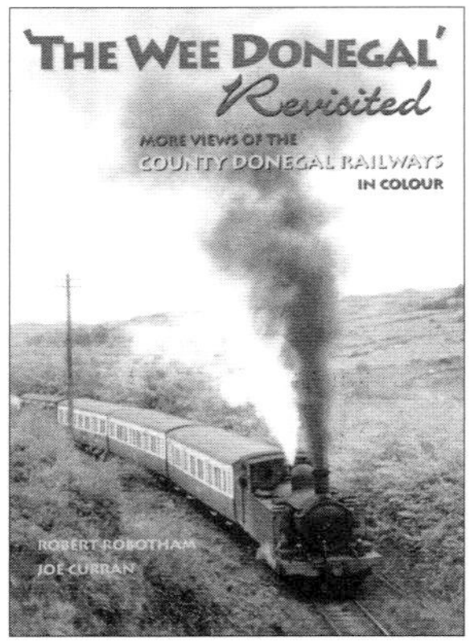

The Wee Donegal Revisited
Robert Robotham
& Joe Curran
1 904242 02 2 £19.99
108pp, hbk, 298 x 205mm,
155 colour photos

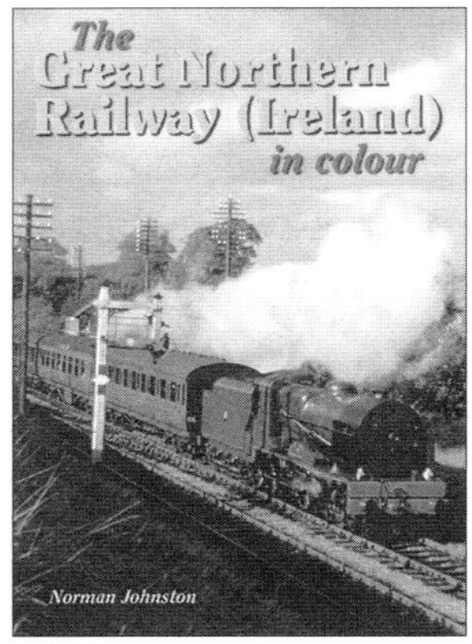

The Great Northern Railway (Ireland) in colour
Norman Johnston
1 904242 36 7 £20
112pp, hbk, 298 x 205mm,
235 colour photos

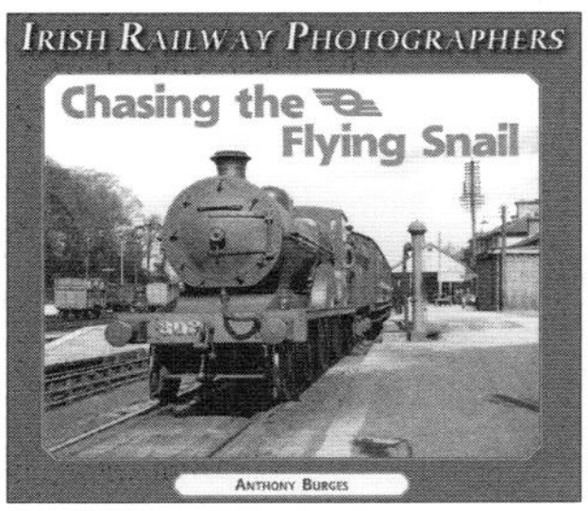

Irish Railway Photographers
Chasing the Flying Snail
Anthony Burges
1 904242 51 0 £8.99
64pp, 204 x 240mm,
54 b/w photos

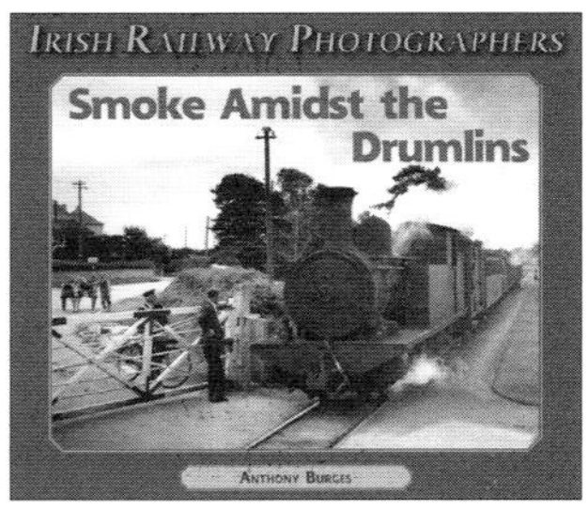

Irish Railway Photographers
Smoke Amidst the Drumlins -
The Cavan & Leitrim
Anthony Burges
1 904242 62 6 £8.99
64pp, 204 x 240mm,
61 b/w photos

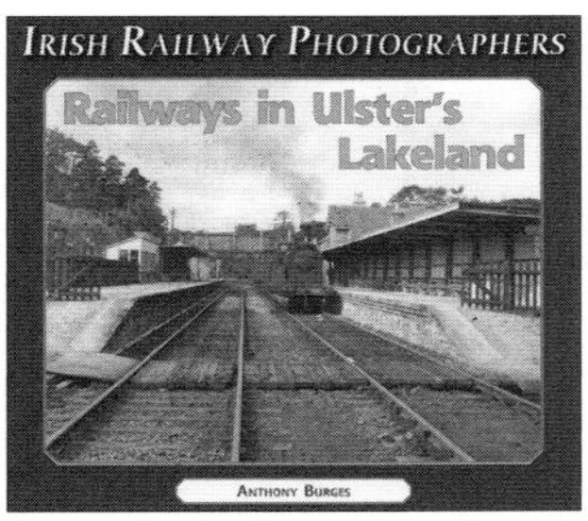

Irish Railway Photographers
Railways in Ulster's Lakeland
Anthony Burges
1 904242 52 9 £8.99
64pp, 204 x 240mm,
54 b/w photos

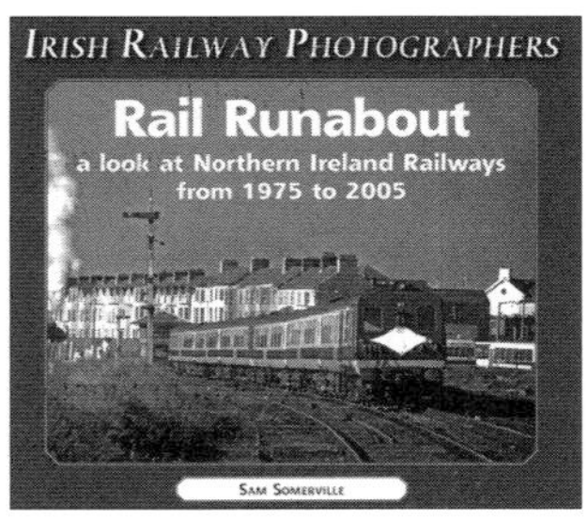

Irish Railway Photographers
Rail Runabout
NI Railways 1975–2005
Sam Somerville
1 904242 64 2 £8.99
64pp, 204 x 240mm,
64 b/w photos